"This book will be especially welcomed by busy pastors who can take time to look back toward the past as well as ahead to the future. What they will find is encouragement of the very best sort from historical exemplars who, though facing great challenges, embodied biblical insight, found Christian stability, and carried out unusually effective ministries. The book is a treasure that gives much-needed dignity and hope to the pastoral calling today."

Mark Noll, author of *The Rise of Evangelicalism*

"If pastors don't set the rule for their lives, everyone else is going to do it for them. This book invites the pastor back to the deep well of our tradition that offers profound insights for thriving in contemporary ministry. Ironically, it's the chosen rule that leads to freedom."

M. Craig Barnes, president, Princeton Theological Seminary

"Rather than lament the well-documented and much-discussed crisis of spirituality in western Christendom, especially among pastoral leaders, Burgess, Andrews, and Small provide a rich resource to bring about radical change. Their proposal is revolutionizing. They introduce six ecumenically diverse mentors of the holy life and build workable bridges to their spiritual legacies. We are led into the adventure of reclaiming these great traditions of spiritual discipline as resources and models for our own spiritual rule. The book is an invitation to pastoral leaders to engage, celebrate, and imitate these and other great exponents of spiritual discipline. The venture could bring about unexpected change, perhaps even the conversion of communities. It's a risk worth taking."

Darrell L. Guder, professor emeritus of missional and ecumenical theology at Princeton Theological Seminary, author of *The Continuing Conversion of the Church* and *Called to Witness*

"Pastors in North America today face enormous challenges that imperil faithful, joyful ministry. In this engaging and accessible work, John Burgess, Jerry Andrews, and Joseph Small open the wisdom of the Christian past, showing how pastors and the congregations they serve can flourish by disciplined attention to prayer, Scripture, theological reflection, and service with friends in ministry. All those who seek to follow Jesus will find this a rich and rewarding book."

Bradley J. Longfield, professor of church history, University of Dubuque Theological Seminary

"If you are a pastor who is feeling overwhelmed by responsibilities, intimidated by social challenges, or simply uncertain about your priorities for how to spend your time and energy, then please read this book. It will relieve you of false burdens, embolden your ministry of the Word, and energize you for your true pastoral vocation. And, for those contemplating a call to become ministers of the gospel, this book provides a rule of 'plumb'—namely, a practical plan for stewarding the mysteries of God and for making the potentially crooked pastoral path straight. Highly recommended."

Kevin J. Vanhoozer, research professor of systematic theology, Trinity Evangelical Divinity School

JOHN P. BURGESS, JERRY ANDREWS,
and JOSEPH D. SMALL

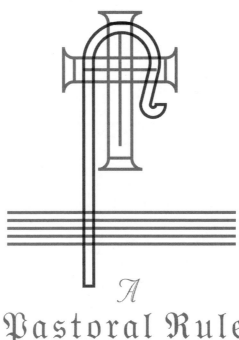

A Pastoral Rule
for TODAY

REVIVING *an* ANCIENT PRACTICE

IVP Academic

An imprint of InterVarsity Press
Downers Grove, Illinois

InterVarsity Press
P.O. Box 1400, Downers Grove, IL 60515-1426
ivpress.com
email@ivpress.com

InterVarsity Press® is the book-publishing division of InterVarsity Christian Fellowship/USA®, a movement of students and faculty active on campus at hundreds of universities, colleges, and schools of nursing in the United States of America, and a member movement of the International Fellowship of Evangelical Students. For information about local and regional activities, visit intervarsity.org.

Scripture quotations, unless otherwise noted, are from The Holy Bible, English Standard Version, copyright © 2001 by Crossway Bibles, a division of Good News Publishers. Used by permission. All rights reserved.

Cover design and graphics: David Fassett
Interior design: Jeanna Wiggins
ISBN 978-0-8308-5234-5 (print)
ISBN 978-0-8308-7302-9 (digital)

Printed in the United States of America ∞

InterVarsity Press is committed to ecological stewardship and to the conservation of natural resources in all our operations. This book was printed using sustainably sourced paper.

Library of Congress Cataloging-in-Publication Data
Names: Burgess, John P., 1954- author.
Title: A pastoral rule for today : reviving an ancient practice / John P.
  Burgess, Jerry Andrews, and Joseph D. Small.
Description: Downers Grove : InterVarsity Press, 2019. | Includes index.
Identifiers: LCCN 2019002862 (print) | LCCN 2019007434 (ebook) | ISBN
  9780830873029 (eBook) | ISBN 9780830852345 (pbk. : alk. paper)
Subjects: LCSH: Pastoral theology.
Classification: LCC BV4011.3 (ebook) | LCC BV4011.3 .B865 2019 (print) | DDC
  253—dc23
LC record available at https://lccn.loc.gov/2019002862

P 25 24 23 22 21 20 19 18 17 16 15 14 13 12 11 10 9 8 7 6 5 4 3 2 1

Y 38 37 36 35 34 33 32 31 30 29 28 27 26 25 24 23 22 21 20 19

To the members of the Core Cluster of Reforming Ministry,
with whom we experienced the grace of theological friends.

Jerry Andrews

Craig Barnes

John Burgess

Elward Ellis

Barry Ensign-George

Quinn Fox

Darrell Guder

Jill Hudson

Dedie Kelso

Michael Lindvall

Bradley Longfield

Kevin Park

Neal Presa

Melissa Ramos

Marianne Rhebergen

Joseph D. Small

Laura Smit

Leanne Van Dyk

Tom Walker

Rebecca Weaver

Charles Wiley

Steve Yamaguchi

Contents

Acknowledgments

T HE IDEA FOR THIS BOOK emerged out of an initiative of the Office
of Theology and Worship of the Presbyterian Church (USA) called Re-
Forming Ministry, which brought together pastors, seminary professors, and
denominational officials in an effort to analyze the current situation of the church
and to propose ways to strengthen the theological foundations of pastoral ministry. We are extremely grateful to our colleagues in the initiative, especially to
Barry Ensign-George, who headed it up. His wisdom and foresight made it possible for the authors of this book to gather and begin their work. We are also
thankful to the Religion Division of Lilly Endowment Inc., which provided gen-
erous financial support for the Re-Forming Ministry initiative.

While the three authors of this book reviewed and commented on one
another's work, Jerry Andrews had principal responsibility for the chapters on
Augustine and Gregory the Great. We are thankful for his rich background in
patristic thought and the Latin language. Joseph Small drafted the chapters on
Benedict and Calvin. As the former director of the Office of Theology and
Worship, Joe initiated two extraordinary programs—a Company of Pastors and
a Company of New Pastors—that drew from Calvin's insights in organizing a
Company of Pastors in Geneva. Joe's deep pastoral wisdom has helped guide our
entire project. John Burgess was the principal author for the chapters on Wesley,
Newman, and Bonhoeffer. We are grateful for his leadership in organizing our
work and editing the entire volume. John offers special thanks to the National
Institute for Newman Studies for awarding him a grant in the summer of 2016 to
do the research for the Newman chapter. John also wishes to thank several

pastors in Pittsburgh Theological Seminary's doctor of ministry program. We have learned from their experience in writing and practicing a pastoral rule in conjunction with a class that John taught. Insights from Rev. Andrew J. Florio and Rev. Andrew T. Kort have been especially valuable to us.

Several anonymous readers offered invaluable suggestions for improvement as did Dr. Roger Owens at Pittsburgh Seminary. Finally, we wish to express our deep appreciation to David McNutt, our editor at InterVarsity Press. David has been both patient and understanding as he waited for us to complete the manuscript, and he has guided it skillfully through the editorial process. Thanks to people such as David, IVP is truly an outstanding press.

Introduction
Why PASTORS NEED *a* RULE

THIS BOOK IS AN INVITATION to think about pastoral ministry and what lies at the core of the pastor's vocation. We, the authors, have many years of experience with pastoral ministry coming from several angles of service to the church, including seminary education, denominational resourcing of pastors, and pastoral work in particular congregations. We have become convinced that nothing today is more important for strengthening pastoral leadership than grounding it again in what Christians have regarded as the central spiritual practices of their faith: prayer, studying Scripture, theological reflection, and service to the world. We believe that when exercised in a disciplined way, these practices constitute a "rule" that helps pastors keep first things first amid the many possibilities and demands of their calling.

This book explores several classic rules from Christian history in order to stimulate our reflection on what a pastoral rule might look like today. We believe that the Christian past does not constrain our imagination but rather opens it to insights and possibilities for ministry that we have inherited but are not always aware of. This book does not call pastors back to some golden age of ministry that never existed, but it does assume that they do not have sufficient wisdom to sustain faithful ministry by themselves. Those great pastors who have gone before us cannot solve our problems, but, precisely because they are so different from us, they can help us think in fresh ways about our calling. This book is not an exercise in history for history's sake but rather a grateful acknowledgment of how Christ binds us together with the saints and wise elders of every time and place.

Let us begin by asking about the current context of pastoral ministry in North America. What particular opportunities and challenges do pastors face? How is the shifting landscape of religion in North America reshaping the character of Christian community and therefore of pastoral ministry? What theological skills, training, and preparation do pastors need in order to serve effectively? Only as we pay attention to these dynamics of church service will we be able to appreciate the difference a rule can make for strengthening pastoral leadership.

PASTORAL MINISTRY TODAY

This is how one should regard us, as servants of Christ and
stewards of the mysteries of God. (1 Cor 4:1)

Pastoral ministry has been and continues to be a wonderful, privileged calling. Pastors have the honor and joy of accompanying people through the most important moments of their lives, as when parents bring children into the world, or sickness or tragedy strikes a member of the congregation, or a young person seeks to know how God is at work in his or her life. Pastors find deep satisfaction in nurturing Christian community among those who gather week after week for worship and service, and pastors love to think deeply about how to proclaim the good news of Jesus Christ not only to those who call themselves Christian but also to a world in which Christian faith is no longer an obvious option for many. Those who are called to pastoral ministry ultimately cannot imagine doing anything else. That is not to say that they never experience doubt or frustration. But in the end nothing seems more important than daily proclaiming the love and truth of God's gracious presence to all humanity in Jesus Christ.

Pastoral ministry has always required a certain kind of nimbleness. Pastors must be good at quickly establishing trust with others. They must be good at judging other people's character—their gifts for ministry as well as their foibles and weaknesses. Pastors must be able to think on their feet and find the right words for the situation. They must be on-the-ground theologians who are able to interpret winsomely, in light of the gospel, every question and problem that people pose to them. Flexibility yet rootedness, compassion yet honesty—the pastoral calling requires unique skills, some of which may come naturally, while others may develop with time and experience.

In every era of the church's life, pastors have faced particular challenges to exercising their calling, and today is no different. In North America, the religious landscape is undergoing massive transformation. The so-called mainline Protestant denominations that have historically been dominant influences on American life have suffered deep declines in membership and significance, while evangelical Protestantism has grown rapidly. But the "nones"—those who claim no affiliation with a particular religious body—are now the fastest-growing portion of the American population. Historic congregations in parts of the country where dramatic demographic changes have taken place recently (racially, ethnically, or economically) often find that they can no longer afford a full-time pastor. At the same time, a wide variety of new worshiping communities has emerged—in storefronts, around restaurant tables, among new immigrant groups, and among young people committed, above all, to social justice and action. Christian communities will always need leadership, but whether they will need ordained pastors—and just what the functions of an ordained pastor will be—is not as clear as in the past.

New technologies raise further questions about the future of pastoral ministry. Church communities, both established and new, now rely on websites, email, texting, and social media in unprecedented ways. While Christians still gather in person for worship and fellowship, they also stay in touch with each other and learn about their faith by searching the internet and downloading various biblical and devotional apps. Pastors are increasingly seen not as honored authority figures but rather as facilitators and coaches who themselves are nimble with technology and use a variety of electronic platforms to reach out to people and invite them into Christian faith and fellowship. We do not know yet what all this will mean for how the Word will be proclaimed and how the sacraments will be celebrated in the future. But there is reason to believe that those who go into pastoral ministry will increasingly receive a theological education entirely or in part through distance learning—and will exercise their ministry in the same way.

Churches and pastors are responding to these new realities with bold and exciting experiments. Many seminaries and denominational church bodies have established initiatives in church planting and revitalization. Theological education is increasingly being integrated into students' pastoral service in particular contexts of ministry rather than asking them to move to a seminary campus to focus on academic work. Congregations and pastors are exploring new forms of worship as well as asking what it means for Christians to be a missionary presence in a culture whose public institutions are increasingly secular but whose public life is characterized by a wide array of religious and nonreligious options from which individuals choose what works best for them.

At the same time, these changes have thrown many of us as pastors off balance. As much as pastors love their work, they struggle to find the right language for communicating the central affirmations of the Scriptures and the church's great theological traditions. Even as new technologies enable them to stay in touch with the people they serve, pastors experience new forms of isolation and loneliness. In a time of rapid change and widespread experimentation in church and society, pastors suffer especially from constant distraction, interruption, and fragmentation. There are so many things to do—and many more things that they could do—that it is difficult for them to know where to begin, where to focus their energies. It is no wonder that many pastors look to management gurus and techniques to help them get a handle on all the business they are supposed to keep track of. Every cell phone text requires an immediate answer; every email should be acknowledged within a few hours; every preconceived plan for the day is subject to change and renegotiation, depending on who or what suddenly demands the pastor's attention. Pastoral ministry has always been busy and demanding; what is different today is the perpetual sense of what we sometimes call "the tyranny of the immediate."

A recent snapshot report of the state of ministry in the United States suggests that nearly half of all pastors report having experienced levels of depression or exhaustion that led them to seek a leave of absence. Seventy percent say that they have no close friends, and 80 percent worry that their work has negatively impacted their families.[1] So, again we ask, What lies at the core of pastoral ministry? What sustains pastors for the long haul and guards against burnout? How do pastors remain true to their calling to serve God and God's Word? How can pastoral service be appropriately "disciplined"—not in the sense of imposing more

---

[1] See Timothy Merrill, "Give It a Rest," Homiletics Online, June 5, 2018, https://blog.homileticsonline .com/the-back-page/give-it-a-rest/. For a more thorough analysis, see Rae Jean Proeschold-Bell and Jason Byassee, *Faithful and Fractured: Responding to the Clergy Health Crisis* (Grand Rapids: Baker Academic, 2018).

expectations on pastors to execute church or spiritual business (lest they be disciplined for failing) but rather in the sense of practicing spiritual disciplines that ground and strengthen pastors in their calling to be stewards of the mysteries of God for the sake of the salvation of the world?

CLARIFYING PASTORAL SERVICE

Therefore encourage one another and build one another up,
just as you are doing. (1 Thess 5:11)

In our many years of working with and serving as pastors, we have observed that the pastoral office today is increasingly held hostage to a multitude of competing demands. The pastor is supposed to be, among many other things, preacher, teacher, therapist, administrator, personnel director, organizational manager, business entrepreneur, and CEO—all at the same time. Each of these functions is critically important; moreover, they belong to the reality of pastoral ministry today. We cannot pretend that pastors are immune from the multiple pressures that increasingly define every kind of work in a digitalized, globalized world driven by values of efficiency and productivity. There is no going back to an era in which the pastor could imagine "himself" (as was the case in those days) to be nothing more than the congregation's resident theological scholar who would be honored for his educated sermons and wise pastoral counsel, while others took care of the church's "business."

But pastors also have a responsibility to shape our reality. We are not simply passive servants of the marketplace; we are called to live in the glorious freedom of the children of God. We can make choices about what is more or less important. We can strive for a measure of order that honors God even as we remain flexible in responding to the needs of the day as they come at us. We can seek to exercise our service with integrity, in the sense of wholeness, by reframing all that we do in light of what God has done and continues to do for the world in the resurrection of Jesus Christ. We will benefit by having a "rule," a disciplined way of life that keeps us grounded in the principal calling of a pastor: to be faithful to God and God's will for us and the people we serve.

What exactly is a pastoral rule? In English, the word *rule* implies something or someone with power and control over another. Sovereigns rule over their subjects. Parents make rules for their children. Employees are supposed to abide by the rules of their company. From an early age, we are taught that there are punishments for breaking the rules. *Rule* and *ruling* take us into the world of law and regulation. That kind of pastoral rule would hardly seem to correspond to the freedom of the gospel.

But there is a second sense to the word *rule*, as when a ruler refers to a measuring stick. A rule of life gives us a set of criteria for measuring our faithfulness to the gospel. A pastoral rule delineates basic rhythms and practices that define the life of a pastor. These kinds of rules are more than legal or bureaucratic obligations; they stimulate and encourage us to live out our calling in Jesus Christ more fully. They guide us, just as ruled paper (once upon a time) kept children's handwriting in a straight line and within the margins, or just as a rule of thumb gives us a general sense of what to do in a certain situation (how much tip to leave after a meal, or how much lemon juice to substitute for a squeezed lemon in a recipe).

Consider the following example of a rule: A pastor makes a commitment to begin each day at the office with twenty minutes of prayer. He reads aloud to himself the assigned daily Bible passages of the Revised Common Lectionary and prays the morning prayer of the day from his denomination's prayer book. He further commits to participating in a pastors' group whose members read a serious book of theology and meet once a month over lunch to discuss it. He takes his turn in leading the discussion. This pastor also adopts a pattern of visiting one homebound member of the congregation every Sunday afternoon, and before leaving the church in the afternoon he reads online the local news section of his city's newspaper to be aware of developments in his context of ministry. None of his rules is ironclad, and sometimes he has to make adjustments. But they come to define the rhythm of his ministry for the ten years that he serves in that congregation. They give him an anchor for remaining spiritually steady and upright as he attends to everything else that he has to do.

Another pastor's rule consists of beginning each workday with a half-hour walk in a nearby park. She uses the time not only to stay in shape physically but also to consciously meditate on the beauty of God's creation and the miracle of her own life. Once a week she gathers at noon with the church staff and any interested church members to pray aloud and spontaneously for the congregation as a whole and for any people who are in particular need. Over the course of a month, the group lifts up in prayer by name every person listed in the church directory. Further, this pastor commits to closing her office door and turning off her cell phone every afternoon at 3 p.m. and reading a great novel for an hour. One Saturday morning a month she gets together with another female colleague to process issues in ministry and to discern what she needs to be preaching about. And once a year she takes a weeklong retreat to a Catholic monastery on the other side of the state, where she meets each day with a spiritual director. Like the first pastor, she remains flexible in practicing her rule, and sometimes she finds it hard to keep it going. But eventually she comes to look forward to these basic rhythms of her day, week, month, and year. They give her a sense of rootedness in faith and service, no matter how hectic church business gets. And this rootedness feeds her preaching and pastoral care.

Rules of life have an ancient legacy in Christianity. Christians have identified certain spiritual practices and disciplines that guide their sanctification personally and with other Christians. To be sure, there is nothing mechanical or automatic about a rule of life; just because one follows the "rules," one does not necessarily become a better Christian. But Christians have been confident that the Holy Spirit, while free to blow where it will, blesses us with certain ordered activities that help us die more and more to our selfish, sinful selves in order to live more and more fully for Christ and by the guiding power of his Spirit. As an important book about practicing faith put it twenty years ago, "Christian practices are things Christian people do together over time in response to and in light of God's active presence for the life of the world. . . . All of them, woven together, suggest the pattern of a faithful Christian way of life."[2] It is such a pattern of practices and disciplines in the exercise of the pastoral office that we in this book are calling a pastoral rule.

A pastoral rule takes its bearings from the vows pastors make upon entering the ordained ministry.[3] While the exact wording of these vows differs from one Christian tradition or denomination to another, they generally have two dimensions: reaffirmation of one's baptismal vows of trusting in Jesus Christ as Lord and Savior, and additional vows of committing oneself as a leader to be guided by Christ, the Scriptures, and the church. A pastoral rule based on these vows both binds and frees. We can even say that it frees insofar as it binds, because a

---

[2]Craig Dykstra and Dorothy C. Bass, "Times of Yearning, Practices of Faith," in *Practicing Our Faith*, ed. Dorothy C. Bass (San Francisco: Jossey-Bass, 1997), 5.

[3]See "A Pastoral Rule: Re-forming Ministry" (Louisville, KY: Office of Theology and Worship, Presbyterian Church [USA], 2011), PDS #21165-11-001. Some of the material in the following paragraphs comes from this publication.

rule that binds pastors to their baptismal and ordination vows also frees them from the rules of technique, organization, management, and corporate effectiveness that too often distort the pastoral office.

Like St. Benedict's rule for the monastic life, a pastoral rule begs God "to finish the good work begun" in us.[4] Pastors have a special responsibility to practice spiritual disciplines that promote their personal growth in holiness, a dimension of pastoral service that has too often been obscured when ministry has been evaluated primarily in terms of numbers of members, programs, and dollars. At the same time, holiness is never simply a matter of personal spiritual achievements. Rather, the pastor's commitment to holy living is for the sake of the gospel and its proclamation. Only as the apostolic witness truly takes hold of pastors and rules their lives will their preaching, teaching, and way of life become credible to the church and before the world.

Further, growth in holiness depends on practicing "life together." Faithfulness to pastoral identity is best sustained not as an individualistic endeavor but rather among friends and colleagues in ministry. Pastors' confession of faith becomes concrete and convincing as it takes shape in a community of faith. They benefit spiritually by forging and participating in collegial communities whose members pray together, read the Scriptures together, think theologically together, and serve the world together. Pastors need one another in order to remain true to the gospel's guidance and correction. They depend on one another for strength and encouragement—and accountability—in those times in which, in Bonhoeffer's words, they are "scattered like seed . . . [among] unbelievers."[5]

We, the authors of this book, have learned to practice a rule of "life together" with one another and with other pastors and church leaders. Along the way, we have experienced for ourselves the blessings of basic spiritual practices, especially as they have shaped our way of life in Christian community. But we also recognize that something about the word *rule* may grate on pastors and provoke resistance. We understand because we, too, have sensed resistance within ourselves. We know that our culture awards personal choice and success, while a rule asks us to submit to a way of life together. We recognize that we and other pastors

---

[4]*The Rule of Saint Benedict*, trans. Anthony C. Meisel and M. L. del Mastro (New York: Doubleday, 1975), 43.

[5]Dietrich Bonhoeffer, *Life Together / Prayerbook of the Bible*, trans. Daniel W. Bloesch and James H. Burtness (Minneapolis: Fortress Press, 1996), 28.

prefer to make our own decisions, whereas a rule tells us what we should be doing. Nevertheless, we are convinced that a pastoral rule meets the needs of our time. We believe that a pastoral rule, by helping us focus on the core of our calling, can free us from the avalanche of demands that otherwise oppress us. A pastoral rule challenges us to grow in holiness for the sake of the gospel. A pastoral rule invites pastors once again to hear the voice of their living Savior: "Follow me, and I will make you fishers of men" (Mt 4:19).

HISTORIC AND CONTEMPORARY RULES

For neither circumcision counts for anything, nor uncircumcision,
but a new creation. And as for all who walk by this rule,
peace and mercy be upon them. (Gal 6:15-16)

Christian communities over the centuries have been guided by rules of life and service. This book explores the wisdom that seven major Christian thinkers from over the centuries offer for defining and sustaining Christian ministry today. Each figure played a key role in inspiring and organizing communal life in his time. Each either wrote a formal rule for the Christian life or left behind ideas that others used in composing a rule for Christians in general or pastors in particular. In no way is our list exhaustive, but it does represent a wide swath of the Christian faith: Catholic and Protestant (Reformed, Methodist, and Lutheran), ancient and modern, monastic and lay. Neither have we sought to explicate any of these rules in their entirety. Rather, each chapter lifts up a particular practice or discipline that pastors may consider incorporating into the patterns and rhythms of their ministry today.

Our survey begins at the end of the fourth century with the great church father Augustine (chapter one). Although he never wrote a formal rule of life for himself, he reflected on Christian community extensively in his correspondence and writings, which later inspired others to compose a so-called Augustinian rule for the monastic life. At every stage of his life, Augustine sought out and depended on friends with whom he could discuss the biggest questions of life and faith. His *Confessions*, as personal as they are, are really about the practice of *theological friendship*, which is also central to sustaining pastoral ministry today. To be sure, theological friendship has a fortuitous dimension in that it comes as an unexpected blessing. But it also requires commitment and practice. How can pastors today find and cultivate not only friendships in which they unload personal burdens and let down their hair but also friendships that give them space to think about God and their lives before God?

A century later, St. Benedict emphasized the importance of learning *obedience* in the context of a community whose members have mutual responsibilities (chapter two). He saw great danger in those monks of his time (the so-called sarabaites) who had no law other than "the pleasure of their desires. . . . Whatever they have thought or chosen . . . they call holy." He wrote a rule that would assist monks to "lay aside [their] own will" in order to "tread the path that [God] has cleared for us."[6] At the center of their lives was common prayer—seven times during the day and once at night. Today the word *obedience* is commonly associated with blind obedience, and many pastors would prefer to be free agents who determine their own path into the future than submit to a church hierarchy or bureaucracy. How does Benedict challenge us to learn obedience to God and each other and, especially, to a rule of prayer that we practice not only on our own but also with others?

Late in the sixth century, Gregory the Great, inspired by Benedict's life and example, wrote a rule to guide pastors (chapter three), arguing that pastors, like monks, need a life of disciplined prayer. Only so can they recognize and begin to overcome their personal temptations and foibles. But for Gregory pastors ultimately practice *holiness in order to serve.* As pastors grow in personal holiness, they demonstrate to the world how the gospel realizes itself in attitudes and deeds, not just words. As pastors grow in holiness, they acquire the wisdom and insight to guide others into the Christian life. How can pastors today find the right balance between personal spiritual growth and ministry to others? Where does spirituality become too inward looking and passive, and where does ministry become too outward and action oriented? Alternatively, how can each feed the other?

Reform of the pastoral office by means of a common rule once again became a driving concern at the time of Europe's sixteenth-century Reformation. As John Calvin headed up the reform of church and society in Geneva, Switzerland, he established the Venerable Company of Pastors, which met weekly for prayer and biblical and theological study (chapter four). Once a quarter, pastors could also take the opportunity "to speak in a brotherly way about the doctrine or conduct

---

[6]See Meisel and del Mastro, *Rule of Saint Benedict*, 43, 44.

of another. This *mutual supervision,* too, served the cause of unity in doctrine and life."[7] Calvin challenges pastors today to consider how they might reach out to encourage and strengthen one another's service. How can pastors meet together on a regular basis to discuss what they preach and how well it corresponds to the gospel? Such conversations make us vulnerable to criticism but can also save us from complacency and thoughtless conformity to the spirit of the age.

In the eighteenth century, John Wesley, working tirelessly to renew the English church, gathered believers into small groups (class meetings) in which they learned to practice mutual encouragement and accountability (chapter five). He also worked closely with the lay pastors who emerged out of these groups and committed themselves to riding on horseback across England to assist Wesley in calling even more people to a life of holiness. Wesley recognized that both the church's proclamation and the sustenance of trusting Christian community depend on the practice of *carefully choosing one's words.* Today, too, pastors need to be known as people who speak truthfully yet lovingly. In an era of "fake news" and endless social media exaggeration, how can pastors cultivate trustworthy words? What practices can discipline our tongues to proclaim the gospel rightly?

A century later, another Englishman, John Henry Newman, led another movement to reform the church and call people back to holy living (chapter six). Newman was no less active a preacher and organizer than Wesley. At least as much as Wesley, Newman found wisdom and guidance for his ministry in *serious and sustained study* of the Scriptures and the early church fathers, a practice that he made central to each day, to the very end of his life. Newman was convinced that pastors need to set aside protected time and space for reading deeply in the church's theology for the sake of cultivating and communicating a rich vision of God's presence to his people in Jesus Christ. How can pastors today make time and space for sustained study of, and reflection on, the Bible and the church's great theological traditions? How can biblical, theological grounding help pastors respond not only pastorally but also theologically to the questions and problems that people bring to them?

After Hitler rose to power in Germany in 1933, Dietrich Bonhoeffer organized a Confessing Church seminary whose members practiced key disciplines of faith to keep them firmly grounded in their identity in the living Christ (chapter seven).

---

[7]Willem van 't Spijker, *Calvin: A Brief Guide to His Life and Thought,* trans. Lyle D. Bierma (Louisville, KY: Westminster John Knox, 2009), 70 (emphasis added).

As later recorded in his book *Life Together*, the community's rule provided for morning, midday, and evening prayer; corporate singing; common meals, work, study, and play; and time for personal prayer and Scripture meditation. The members of the community pledged themselves to practice mutual forbearance but also to confess their sins to each other and to correct each other in love. They learned to practice *being physically present to each other* in lonely and difficult times. As we suggested above, today's new technologies for instant communication do not eliminate the isolation and loneliness that pastors often experience as they seek to live by the gospel rather than by the foreign expectations that church members and society as a whole gladly impose on them. How can pastors reach out to each other in support and encouragement, and what is the special role of physical presence in sustaining their capacity for ministry?

We, the authors of this book, are well aware that in investigating these particular rules we have not explicitly acknowledged the key role that women have played in organizing and guiding Christian communities and the Christian life. Although historically men have written rules of life and ministry, these rules have been equally important to women. St. Benedict's rule has guided thousands of monasteries, both male and female, over the centuries, and one of the most articulate contemporary commentators on his rule is Benedictine nun Joan Chittister.[8] John Wesley's rules were meant for small groups that included both men and women, and the holiness churches that arose out of his enthusiasm for gospel living were among the first Christian churches to recognize and affirm women's gifts for pastoral leadership. Similarly, Bonhoeffer's call for life together, while based on his experience with a group of male seminarians at a time when women were not yet ordained, was meant to stimulate the whole church and all its members, men and women alike, to shape more faithful forms of Christian community.

It is also clear that our historic rules do not include insights from global Christianity in its entirety or even from key movements and figures in more recent Western theology and church history, especially liberationist. Rather, our figures represent a seemingly "traditional" lineup of Western thinkers, beginning with Augustine. The global church, even as it teaches us new and necessary things, nevertheless draws on the rich legacy of each of these figures, sometimes in surprising ways. Augustine has never been strictly Western (he is also a saint to the

---

[8]See Joan Chittister, *The Rule of St. Benedict: Insights for the Ages* (New York: Crossroad, 1992).

Orthodox churches of the Christian East), and John Henry Newman's writings have recently inspired the founding of an Orthodox university in Moscow. Wesley's Methodism has become a worldwide phenomenon. Similarly, churches and theologians in various parts of the world have drawn on Bonhoeffer to insist that Christian "life together" includes a commitment to basic human rights for all.

Our task in this book has been to focus on key historical rules that still shape pastoral service, not to review every figure who can and should guide pastors in their ministry. Still, we hope that our list will inspire pastors to compose rules that draw on the rich spirituality of such figures as Martin Luther King Jr., Dorothy Day, Óscar Romero, and Gustavo Gutiérrez. These figures have been as concerned with shaping faithful Christian community and discipleship as Calvin or Bonhoeffer. And, like Gregory the Great, these more recent figures in Christian history have been deeply committed to integrating prayer and social action, theological reflection and church leadership. We need their wisdom to supplement what we in this book have distilled from the "classics."

None of these rules can by itself define the pastoral office today, but each does challenge us to delineate rhythms and patterns of the pastoral life for our time and place. Indeed, in 2011 several of these classic rules helped us as ministers in the Presbyterian Church (USA) to formulate a contemporary pastoral rule. We know of other Presbyterians who have found it suggestive and helpful, and we offer it again in this book as an impulse for developing and practicing a pastoral rule (chapter eight). While our suggested rule may reflect particular historical emphases of a traditional mainline Protestant understanding of the pastoral vocation, we believe that it demonstrates more broadly the value of a "ruled" life, whatever shape it may take, for pastors of all Christian traditions.

Finally, in a brief conclusion we review what we have learned from personal experience as well as from the experience of other pastors who have attempted to observe a rule. We note typical problems and pitfalls but also the real blessings that rules have brought and can bring to ministers. And we look forward to learning from you, our readers, as you engage these reflections. We are thankful for your ministries and pray that our book may be a further encouragement as you continue to grow in Christian faith personally and in service to our common Lord and Savior and his church.

1

𝒯𝒽𝑒 Grace 𝑜𝑓 Theological Friendships

AUGUSTINE

THOUGH HE IS BELOVED by many for his very personal and severely introspective autobiography—the *Confessions*—this project was addressed to God alone. And though it introduces a new literary form of individual psychological self-examination, containing thoughts throughout that are profoundly idiosyncratic, Augustine lived in chosen and constant community. He was never alone.

This chapter follows Augustine's life with friends and his thinking about his friendships, and it challenges us to think about who has accompanied us on our journey into the Christian life and ministry. What role have friends played in our thinking, speaking, and acting?

We may not agree with all that Augustine believed about friends and friendship. He and his friends in Hippo were celibate. Their community was gender exclusive. He defines friendship as agreement in things divine and human, accompanied by kindness and affection, in Christ Jesus our Lord, who is our true peace. He believes, in no uncertain terms, that friendship is true only between fellow believers.

Regardless of what we make of Augustine's own example, he pushes us to ask whether we as pastors are in mutually accountable friendships. What barriers are there to this in our lives and ministries? How will we remove these barriers, for the sake of God, for the sake of the other, and for our own sake?

The *Confessions* blesses us with an intimate account of the journey that God had been leading Augustine on since his boyhood and that now, as a man, he had consciously committed to walk. Every step along the way was taken with others. To trace Augustine's travels is to see a shared pilgrimage.

At first it was with family, dominated by his ever-present mother Monica and a gang of boys. Then it was fellow students who took their studies seriously and together sought the best in life. Here Augustine begins to distinguish himself within his circle of friends. Whatever they would decide, they would decide on it and live it out together. Their conversions to the Christian faith, though recorded as the work of God within individuals, were within a short space of time. Some of their baptismal dates were shared. Their calls to ordained ministry occurred one right after another as well, with Augustine leading the way. It is an overstatement, but nearly everyone who went to kindergarten with Augustine became a bishop.

Finally, what had begun in one of the most desolate places—Thagaste, a small village on the edge of the Sahara—and had ended in the bishoprics of the major cities of North Africa was, for the last part of the trail, characterized by intentional communal living and constant travel between the communities. In the violent days of the end of Roman rule, Augustine and his friends traveled dangerous roads to be with one another at the journey's end. The night before the barbarians entered the gates of Augustine's final home, the deathbed of the aged bishop was surrounded by leaders of the church in North Africa, many of whom had been his school friends. Augustine was never alone.

FRIENDSHIP AMONG THIEVES AND AS A PAGAN

Many of us vaguely remember the *Confessions* for a story told in painstaking detail—the childhood theft of a pear.[1] A gang of boys, out late at night as was their custom, plotted and executed a theft of pears from a neighboring orchard. With Augustine among them, they stole an immense load, took a bite of a few, and threw the majority into a nearby hog pit. The boys were neither hungry nor poor, Augustine reports. They did it for the hell of it—he did not even like pears, he confesses. The crime itself was the attraction. "In its commission, our pleasure

---

[1]Augustine, *Confessiones* 2.4.9–2.10.18. All translations of Augustine are from the Latin and are my own. For an excellent and new translation, see Sarah Ruden, *Confessions* (New York: Modern Library, 2017).

was purely that it was forbidden."[2] He did it for the love of evil alone, and truly loved it.

Augustine considers whether the company of that night influenced his deeds: Did my desire to be with and please them move me to do what I otherwise would not have done? No and yes, Augustine answers. He remained certain that he did this for the love of theft alone. That is what was in him all along, what came from within him that night. But, he says with equal candor, placing no blame on his teenaged companions, he knew for certain that he would not have done this if he had been alone. By rubbing against his late-night friends, the itch of his desires was inflamed. His accomplices did not put the distorted desire in him; they increased it and drew it out.

He reports that they laughed and laughed for having played a trick on the owners who knew nothing of it at the time and who, in time, they imagined, would become furious. And, he observes, people seldom laugh alone.

> This, O God, is the still vivid memory of my heart. I would not have stolen alone; my pleasure was not in what I stole but that I stole; yet, I would not have enjoyed it if done alone; I would not have done it alone. O unfriendly friendship, you inscrutable seducer of the soul, you avid appetite to do damage to the other out of sheer sport and silliness without gain or glory, you, with merely the word, "Hey, let's do it!" make us ashamed not to be shameful.

And with "I cannot bear to think of this any longer," Augustine quits the story.[3]

But the sober, sustained consideration of friendship will be seen in many passages to come. Augustine will attempt to penetrate the "inscrutable" nature of friendship so that he and his friends, all now adults, may receive friendship as a gift given them by God. Another story from his early years will help us see the wounds that Augustine bore when he reconsidered the friendships that God intended for blessing.[4]

His first teaching post was in his hometown. So too was that of an old playmate and school pal. They were the same age ("in the flower of our youth"[5]), their intellectual interests were alike, and their friendship became very dear. Their common studies further united them upon reunion, and they spent their days

---

[2]Augustine, *Confessiones* 2.4.9.
[3]Augustine, *Confessiones* 2.9.17-18.
[4]Augustine, *Confessiones* 4.7-4.12.
[5]Augustine, *Confessiones* 4.4.7.

together. Within a year, Augustine gladly recalls, this renewed friendship became sweeter to him than all other things in life.

They were both young and impressionable, but the friend was influenced more by Augustine than vice versa—all for the worst, Augustine remembers. He persuaded his friend to believe the same fairy tales he believed—those superstitions that caused his Christian mother to weep for him. They wandered in error together, and the togetherness was the dearest part of Augustine's life. "Until," he prays without complaint, "you, O God, who are at the same time both Lord of Revenge and Fount of Mercy took him from me."[6] All of this happened within a year's time.

While the friend lay on his sick bed, sweating in delirium and fevers, Christians came and, without the sick friend's consent or even knowledge, baptized him. Augustine paid little attention to this, knowing that when his friend's sanity was restored they would both have a good laugh. But when the friend partially recovered and Augustine told him what had happened and began to mock the event, the friend did not join in. Instead, with a severe look he warned Augustine that if he valued the friendship he would cease his mockery. "I'll wait until he fully recovers," Augustine reports thinking.[7] But his friend did not recover. The fever returned, and within a few days he died. "I was not there," Augustine says with grief.

> My heart was black with grief. Everything I saw looked like death; my hometown was a prison and my home an unfamiliar unhappiness; the things we had done together now became torture; my eyes searched for him, but he was not there; I loathed the spaces we had been because of his absence; and those spaces could not promise, "He will come soon again," as they once could do whenever he had been absent before. . . . Tears took the place in the love of my heart he had held. . . . I have no doubt I would have died, if given the opportunity to be with him. . . . I was weary of life and afraid of death . . . he was "the half of my soul" [quoting Horace]. . . . I thought of my soul and his as one soul in two bodies; and my life became a horror to me because I was unwilling to live life halved. . . . I raged and sighed and wept and was in torment, unable to rest, unable to think; I bore my soul, broken and bloodied and which I hated to carry, because I could not find a place to set it down. . . . I hated all things. So I left the town of Thagaste and came to Carthage.[8]

---

[6]Augustine, *Confessiones* 4.4.7.
[7]Augustine, *Confessiones* 4.4.8.
[8]Augustine, *Confessiones* 4.4.8–4.7.12.

There the narrative ends and Augustine's reflections on friendship begin. He never repents of this haunting (though at the end troubled) friendship, nor will he speak of another with such sustained passion or mourn a loss with such inconsolable grief. But he will learn to think and speak of it in different terms than he experienced it. God, he will say now after much reflection and his own baptism, spared the friendship by allowing the friend to die in the joy of his baptism rather than in a shared scorn, so that this friendship now awaits renewal when Augustine joins him in death. What Augustine only wondered about in the fables of the pagans—Pylades and Orestes, who would have gladly died at the same time to be together, as he remembers the ancient myth—he now is certain of in the promises of God. His grief is consolable because his friend can be found again in new and eternal places.

THINKING AND RE-THINKING FRIENDSHIP

A boyhood prank submitted to such a rigorous self-examination and considered so thoroughly in terms of friendship was unknown in the ancient world. Sin, its discovery in the heart, and the exacting, agonizing confession of it would be a distinctly Christian contribution to the literature of late antiquity.

Other ancients had written to express their grief at the untimely death of a friend. Though Augustine's rhetoric here was high, and few had risen to such heights in its telling, it was not unheard of. Death was universal, grief was common, and ancient authors had previously attempted to describe that grief, even in such powerful and personal terms.

Friendships too, of course, were known by the ancients and recorded in letters, journals, and speeches in both Greek and Latin literature. A few writers had written essays on the subject, Cicero chief among them. Augustine had very early on found his treatment of friendship persuasive, and he made reference to Cicero several times in his own essay on the subject and in passing in his letters.

Cicero's well-known work *On Friendship* states, "Friendship is nothing other than agreement on all things divine and human, along with good will and affection."[9] Augustine will quote this definition in essays and letters with uniform approval. While the referents for what is to be agreed on in "things divine and human" would become distinctly Christian for Augustine, the definition remained unchanged. The late-night raiders and the two school teacher pagans had

---

[9]Cicero, *Laelius de Amicitia* 6.20. Quoted by Augustine often, including in *Contra Academicos* 6.13 and *Epistulae* 258.1.

agreed on the wrong things, but the friendships were true nonetheless. One sees no variation in Augustine's thinking about friendship.

Until, that is, the writing of the *Confessions* in his mid-forties. When revisiting the friendships of his youth, he reconsiders the nature and then the definition of those friendships. Cicero will never again be cited on the subject of friendship without addition or correction.

This is a postconversion transformation of thought. Augustine's letters had cited Cicero approvingly without reserve after his baptism. But after the reflections necessary for writing the *Confessions*, friendship will come to have an altered definition, and Augustine will discuss friendships in more theological terms and with more spiritual urgency. He will repent of Cicero's definition.

In one of the first letters sent immediately after writing the *Confessions*, Augustine speaks at length of friendship to his "oldest friend" Marcianus.[10] With what can only be described as a sharp break with his earlier understandings, he declares that the two of them have only now become friends: "I really did not have you as a friend until we were bound in Christ."[11]

He quotes Tully (Cicero's nickname), "the greatest Roman author," as he had often done before, but now he insists on a revision. After offering to Marcianus the familiar quote, "Friendship is agreement on things divine and human with kindness and affection," he argues that the two of them never had that friendship before because neither had been a Christian. "We agreed on human things the way others (pagans) did, but our friendship was defective," he states, "because we did not agree on things divine, which is the more important part of the definition."[12]

Two things should be noted here. First, they were agreed, we would say, on things divine—both were pagans in their youth; they were both wrong about things divine, we would say, but in agreement. Yet Augustine has now defined agreement as not only shared thought but correct thought. Two "friends" equally wrong about things divine are no longer included in the definition of those who are "in agreement" or are "friends." Second, Augustine concedes gladly and with fond remembrance that their agreement was "with kindness and affection." Augustine is clearly enjoying the reconnection with his childhood friend, but he also takes the opportunity to announce his revised opinion on what makes a friendship.

---

[10]Augustine, *Epistulae* 258.

[11]Augustine, *Epistulae* 258.1.

[12]Augustine, *Epistulae* 258.2.

Later in the letter he denies that he and Marcianus were agreed even on things human, for one must be agreed first on things divine, which are the basis for things human. Then, stating the matter more severely, he says they had no friendship then, not even in part. In arguing this, Augustine continues to gladly admit his genuine delight in the friendship he had with Marcianus then and now. They were affectionate toward one another then, he will say, but it was impossible to be friends in the truest sense. "How could we be?" he reasons. "I could not even be a friend to myself, so sinful was I."[13] Christian theology was trumping a kind and affectionate memory but not denying it.

Augustine wrote this letter upon the recent conversion of Marcianus. It allows Augustine to clarify his new thinking about friendship and, at the same time, with the same words, celebrate a friendship that, in God's providence, had begun poorly in late-night pranks and that, just now, was begun again in the bright light of God's salvation. This, Augustine says, is the reason for the joy he had because of Marcianus, who had for so long been a friend "in some kind of way" and that now is a friend "in a true way": "You who formerly shared this passing life with me in the most charming kindness," he writes, "have now begun to be with me in the hope of life eternal. . . . Now we are agreed even on all things human because we consider them in the light of things divine."[14]

With that, Augustine returns to Cicero's definition and restates it: "We now have that 'agreement about things divine and human, with kindness and affection' in Christ Jesus our Lord, who is our truest peace."[15] Augustine will never again quote Cicero without that addition.

Further, Augustine will define, for the first time, what constitutes things divine and human. It is the keeping of the great commandment—you will love the Lord your God with all your heart and with all your soul and with all you mind, and you will love your neighbor as yourself. The first part is agreement on things divine, the second in agreement on things human. If, Augustine concludes, you tenaciously hold these two things with me, then our friendship will be true and for always. We will be joined not only to each other but to the Lord himself.

In the letter's last paragraph, Augustine quotes Terence and Virgil back and forth with Marcianus, announcing that Christ is the culmination of their hopes

---

[13]Augustine, *Epistulae* 258.2.
[14]Augustine, *Epistulae* 258.3.
[15]Augustine, *Epistulae* 258.4.

and prophecies. He urges him to be baptized as soon as possible and offers a benediction: "May the Lord God, in whom you now trust, both in this world and in the world to come, keep you—you, my rightly honored lord and brother in Christ, most loved and most longed for."[16]

DEFINING FRIENDSHIPS OF GRACE

Several new themes on friendship are sounded in the writings of Augustine. If a title is to be given to this score, it is best named *The Grace of Theological Friendships*. We have seen him redefine friendship as that which is *in Christ Jesus*. With that small phrase attached to Cicero's definition, Augustine has transferred human friendships from the created order to the redemptive. He will write about general human friendships only in passing and in relation to what he has left behind. Occasionally he will contrast these redeemed relationships with those of the pagans. Augustine, who will become known through the centuries as the church's "doctor of grace," has now placed friendship within the realm of grace. He is the first to do so, and later Christian writers will follow his lead.

Because there is no one complete treatment of friendship in Augustine, it is not possible to write systematically of the characteristics of friendship or to prioritize them. Yet some themes appear so frequently that we can safely assume their centrality to the whole.

Honesty, the attribute that Augustine found so necessary for writing such a revealing autobiography, must be ever present. This, in part, is honesty with oneself. He is humble (that is, honest) enough to say that he still does not know himself; that the friend he knows best, Alypius, does not know himself; and that the two are unknown to each other.[17] What he expects in the absence of full self-knowledge is frankness and openness—a willingness to speak the truth as best we know it and to live in full view of one another. The virtue beneath this honesty is truth: "A person must be a friend of truth before they can be a friend to any human being," Augustine says.[18] He seems to mean two things by this one announcement: there must be truthfulness between the two friends, and there must be a common pursuit of the truth. This honesty knows no subject too grand

---

[16]Augustine, *Epistulae* 258.5.
[17]Augustine, *Soliloquia* 1.3.8.
[18]Augustine, *Epistulae* 155.1.1.

(the ways of God in the world) nor too small (friends admit to each other what bothers and irritates them).[19]

Trust emerges, but only over time: "How confused it all is! The one who at first appears an enemy is revealed as a friend, and the one who is thought to be a friend later is known as our worst enemy."[20] Nonetheless, Augustine counsels, jump in and take chances. Friendship is too important to miss for fear, and isolation is a vice.[21] Do not be too cautious; it weakens a friendship in its inception, so be willing to be a friend with anyone. You cannot know friend from foe until you engage. "A man is known only through friendships."[22]

Equality is a theme less pronounced but seems to be assumed throughout. Mutuality is mandated and reciprocity recommended. Different needs and gifts at different times are inherent in all friendships and may suggest temporary comparative strengths and weaknesses: One person may need to correct, another to be corrected; one may need to speak recklessly, the other to listen intently; one may need to be brave for the other; one may need to suggest caution to the other. But there is no indication that these roles are not reversible and to be found in the friends alternately and equally.[23] "The eyes of friends look *at* each other, not *up or down* on each other."[24]

Care is a lovely theme heard perhaps most often. We want the best for our friends. Again, the doctor of grace defines that in distinctly Christian terms. The best for them is God, so we want their conversion and the life of holiness that follows.[25] We want to know God, we want our friends to know God, and we want to know and enjoy each other—in God.[26] This care is practical. We bear each other's burdens.[27] To illustrate this mutual help, Augustine paints the scene of a herd of deer fording a stream: one will go first to break the force of the water for the sake of the others, but when he becomes tired he will go to the rear of the herd so he can benefit from the protection of others.[28] True friendships, meant to be

---

[19] Augustine, *De Diversis Queastionibus Octaginta Tribus* 71.6; Augustine, *Epistulae* 82.36; Augustine, *Sermones* 87.12.15.

[20] Augustine, *Sermones* 49.4.4.

[21] Augustine, *De Civitate Dei* 19.12.

[22] Augustine, *De Diversis Queastionibus Octaginta Tribus* 71.5.

[23] Augustine, *De Trinitate* 9.4.6; Augustine, *De Fide Rerum Invisibilium* 1.2.4.

[24] Augustine, *Contra Duas Epistulae Pelagianorum* 1.1 (emphasis added).

[25] Augustine, *De Doctrina Christiana* 1.12.21; Augustine, *Epistulae* 258.1-2.

[26] Augustine, *De Doctrina Christiana* 1.27.28.

[27] Augustine, *De Fide Rerum Invisibilium* 1.1.3.

[28] Augustine, *De Diversis Quaestionibus Octaginta Tribus* 71.1.

enjoyed in good times, are forged in bad times. They are tested and found true and then valued all the more. Friendships make difficult times bearable and glad times all the more glad. Praying for each other, forgiving each other, acknowledging the need of each other, readily assisting each other, and sacrificing and sympathizing for each other define this Christian caring and bearing.

Love is the one strain that unites these themes. Love of God is the only right and true love. From this all good comes. Love of friend is a love of God for the sake of the friend, and a love of God is a love of the friend for the sake of God.[29] The two greatest commandments meet here. This love of God is an upward gravity, Augustine will argue in many places, and our love is made possible by it only. He seems to be imagining a triangle in which two otherwise separated people are drawn closer by both being drawn toward the apex. Friends spur each other on to love God more and, in doing so, make possible, even probable, their greater love for each other. Likewise, friends love each other most truly when they see more closely God in each other. When they do not see it, they are to encourage it and correct any waning of or error in that love. Friends do not fault the temptations and inclinations of each other. These things are to be revealed to each other in mutual tolerance and understanding. Thus, these friends become better positioned to help each other avoid sin and correct each other when one sins. This is the most important duty friends owe. It is hard work, for the temptations to sin are fewer than the temptations to avoid correcting the friend who sins. Friends are tempted to avoid both loving the other in this way and receiving this love from a friend because of shame, fear, danger of spiritual safety, flattery, or simple selfishness. We are not to be silent with a friend out of a bland kindness. The friend is more important than the friendship—do not risk the first for the sake of the latter. We have a preference, Augustine announces, that our friends should die rather than fall from faith and virtue. We are to resist in others what we resist in ourselves. This work of correction is to be done in such a way that it both protects the friend's good name and restores the friend. Only in this way does the friendship itself fulfill its purpose and thrive.

Christ-centeredness is the note most distinct from anything Augustine had heard in his pagan predecessors and was sounded first in Augustine's redefinition. Friendships are to be rooted in Christ the mediator,[30] who unites the friends,

---

[29] Augustine, *Sermones* 336.2.
[30] Augustine, *De Civitate Dei* 10.32.

purifies the whole person and cleanses both the friends and the friendship,[31] enables the friends to cleave to each other with a pure and holy love to God,[32] and sends the Holy Spirit, who accompanies the friends in their elevation and transformation as fellow pilgrims.[33] Christ gives the grace of friendship.

This friendship is perfected in the presence of Christ in heaven, not here, as Augustine was painfully aware.[34] Here there are slights and suspicions, quarrels and wars, unknown hearts, fickle friends, secret treachery.[35] Augustine will warn of this but report little of it in his letters.

What he will report repeatedly in his correspondence is anxiety for the well-being of his friends—those who were at a distance and exposed to the trials and temptations of life and death. Augustine will say more than once that fear for friends multiplies with the number of friends. As he ages, his fears are heard more often. Augustine will speak of disaster, disease, captivity, and slavery. His letters reveal the torments of a man whose friends suffered greatly.

Augustine will say that the joy of saints is the death of a friend—one no longer in danger of being broken or corrupted.[36] This is triumph, not defeat. Hear in this musical phrase how much the young, unconverted Augustine, now a mature Christian who has witnessed much suffering and lost many friends along the way, has changed since the long-lamented death of his beloved early companion. He will affirm that this change, all for the better, is grace—the grace of friends.

LIVING THEOLOGICAL FRIENDSHIPS

From these themes emerge not only a fuller sound but a vision of how Augustine lived in the grace of friendships. The vision is made more vivid by the scenes we glimpse in his own portraits of the life lived with his friends and in the scenes painted by his first biographer. The scenes are robust and tender, daily and lifelong, and both deeply emotive and highly spiritual.

They were also profoundly intellectual. Augustine and his dear friends were united in intellectual conversations and theological endeavors. These friendships

---

[31]Augustine, *De Civitate Dei* 10.12, 14; 11.1-2.
[32]Augustine, *De Civitate Dei* 10.26-27.
[33]Augustine, *De Civitate Dei* 13.24.
[34]Augustine, *De Civitate Dei* 15.3.
[35]Augustine, *De Civitate Dei* 19.5.
[36]Augustine, *De Civitate Dei* 19.8.

were theological friendships. Friendship was still agreement on matters divine and human, which demanded committed, sustained conversation.

While some of this agreement might have been easily present at the outset and quickly recognized in one another, resulting in friendships formed on a shared basis, it is far truer of Augustine in his youth that he and his friends were fellow seekers of the truth. The agreement was more a matter of method and common travel than content and arrival.

The cohort journeyed together through various philosophies and heresies. Augustine will talk of being converted to Cicero; his biographers will speak of his being converted to Mani. These conversions could be led by one and joined later by others, but often, in a short space of time, they would agree together that they were closer to finding the truth of matters divine and human, then just as quickly agree that they were not, and thus continue the journey in another direction. The young Augustine, we think, followed as much as led. His mother was so convinced of this that her prayers for his conversion to the Christian faith were accompanied by her appeals that he separate from his friends.

At times these friends also parted ways. Friendship was based on agreement, and to agree no longer on which direction the search should travel was to cease journeying together. From their youth into their thirties, the ship sailed constantly. It would stop briefly at port, but failure to board in the morning was to break company. Often, it appears, some would drop out for a while only to catch up later. But it also appears that they were willing to part company. The search was serious. Truth was the highest value, and leaving travel companions to search for it was dreaded but possible.

These journeys were intellectual and practical. These young men were seeking a way to live. One would arrive at the final destination by thinking it through fully—never being fully satisfied with anything other than being fully satisfied. And though they truly prized each other's companionship along the way, they were determined to seek truth until it was found. They expected to arrive and seem not to have celebrated the journey for the journeying's sake, however enjoyable sailing together had been. The prayer of these young pagans and heretics was to arrive together. And they did.

Augustine's conversion was accompanied by those of his friends. Here he seems to have led, but close readings of the *Confessions* suggest that some of his friends were waiting for him. Augustine signaled his readiness to be baptized soon after conversion, and his baptismal date was shared.

The journeys of the North African friends had been literal as well. From the remote villages to the neighboring towns to the big city of Carthage, they had moved together. They arrived at a particular place and philosophy together; they stayed in schools of thought and spaces with each other. Lately the journey had taken them to Italy and the highest and most robust academic culture of the empire. Augustine's appointment was as the Emperor's Chair of Rhetoric at the imperial city of Milan. He traveled and lived there with his friends.

Ambrose was bishop there. No living person—pagan, heretic, or Christian— would ever impress Augustine more. His descriptions and declarations of admiration for Ambrose in the *Confessions* are highly personal, but they were experiences, for the most part, shared with his friends. They attended his sermons together in the mornings and debated them together later in the day.

Augustine and his friends also moved together. Following the path of Ambrose, who had been brought to Milan by the emperor as governor and later had very publicly and dramatically resigned this post to become bishop, Augustine resigned his emperor-appointed academic position upon conversion. In a profound sense, when Augustine traveled to Milan he was never further from home, and when he came to Christ by the ministrations of the bishop of Milan he was never closer to where he had begun his journeys. All that remained was to go home.

And home he went, but after completing her life's work—the prayers that were answered with the conversion of her son—his mother died soon after his baptism. There was irony as well as resolution in this timing and place. Years before, to avoid either saying goodbye to her or taking her with him, Augustine had fled to Italy, lying to her about his intentions. He stole away across the Mediterranean on a sailing ship late in the night with his friends. Now they all returned home together, leaving Monica's body in an Italian churchyard.

Before leaving Italy, Augustine toured a monastery—a place that, in the centuries to come, historians would recognize as an intentional Christian community that would be a precursor to the monasteries of later ages. He and his friends were impressed with what they saw. The memory did not leave them, and it is easy to imagine that plans were formed and reformed until they had a chance to do something about them. Soon they did. Augustine was soon pressed into being ordained a priest back home and shortly thereafter after a bishop. *Pressed* is a fitting description, summoning images of civilians being kidnapped and forced into serving on sailing vessels for commercial or military purposes. Devout Christians avoided the press of ordination so that they could attend to their faith. Although a bishopric was prestigious, some reasoned that ordination would stunt faithfulness since the bishop was a slave to the demands of public life and, what was worse, the public. It was inescapable and largely undesirable.

Augustine and his friends invented a solution—the home of the bishop. As priest, not knowing he would become a bishop elsewhere (Augustine writes of carefully planning travel itineraries to avoid any diocese that lacked a bishop), he and his friends set up housekeeping with the permission of the bishop. The committed, sustained conversations continued. All matters of faith and faithful living were now open before them. And, just as important, they were committed to the rigorous demands that this new Christian life placed on each of them and between them. Augustine, and the priests gathered around him, attempted a variety of forms of common living. They made adjustments. But, being priests, under a bishop, however understanding and partial that bishop was to Augustine, did not permit them enough freedom to build the community they desired. When he was pressed into being a bishop, they knew what they wanted to do and they did it.

Possidius had been a friend and companion of Augustine from well before this time, and remained so until his death. He expresses gratitude for having known Augustine for "almost forty years."[37] Possidius was Augustine's appointed trustee of his library and literary corpus and was also his first biographer. His account of this season in the theologian's life picks up where the *Confessions* left off.

It is the report of a household. Augustine and his friends gave up possessions and lands for "fasting, prayers, and good works, meditating day and night in the Law of the Lord."[38] Augustine had sold all he had to buy a large home with a garden. It was the bishop's residence and home to the parish priests under him. More and more of these priests were his friends. The home would have many additions through the years to accommodate the growing number of these friends and to provide hospitality for the many pilgrims who came to consult the great bishop.

It was also a seminary of sorts. Lay people became priests, and the priests bishops. The towns and cities of North Africa were asking Augustine for priests and bishops like himself. He was now providing the North African church with

---

[37]Possidius, *Sancti Augustini Vita Scripta a Possidio Episcopo* 31.11.
[38]Possidius, *Sancti Augustini Vita Scripta a Possidio Episcopo* 45.3.

its clergy, who in turn used their residences as places of theological training and pastoral duty. Eventually, more than ten of his childhood friends became bishops. The bishops and theologians in the North African ecclesiastical debates against the Donatists, Pelagians, and others resembled the roll call an earlier generation of Augustine and his schoolmates.[39]

Augustine traveled for primarily two reasons in this last season of his life—first, for theological consultations, to and from which he traveled with his friends, and second, simply for visiting friends. Matters of faith and the friends of faith were all that mattered in the end.

The intentional Christian community Augustine and his cohort set up in Hippo was modeled after the early church in Acts. Possidius reports that their intention was "to live with the servants of God according to the manner and rule instituted by the holy apostles."[40]

This garden house is best described as being moderately ascetic. The priests all wore simple but well-made black robes, ate their meals together at the same table, and held possessions in common, having given all previous possessions to the community.

The church fund for the clergy was the same fund for the poor. When the congregation murmured about this, Augustine offered to let them be the trustees and live as he did. They declined. Augustine appears to have administered this fund so as not to put anyone else in the unenviable position of deciding whether to provide medical care for a companion versus the daily bread of the poor. But this managerial role seems to be an exceptional one for Augustine to play within the community. He never had the key to the property or wore the bishop's ring, says Possidius. Everything, even his own expenses, was paid by voucher and open for all in the home to inspect.[41]

Possessions united the residents and once nearly divided them. Augustine's handling of this matter says much about his community and his leadership within it. All the priests who served with Augustine gave all their possessions to and lived in the community. Yet one priest, Januarius, who had some measure of wealth, gave much to the community upon ordination and entrance. At his death, his will revealed he had not given all. He bequeathed a large sum to his daughter,

[39]Possidius, *Sancti Augustini Vita Scripta a Possidio Episcopo* 63.11.
[40]Possidius, *Sancti Augustini Vita Scripta a Possidio Episcopo* 49.5.
[41]Possidius, *Sancti Augustini Vita Scripta a Possidio Episcopo* 95.23.

excluding his son, and bequeathed a still sizable remainder to the community. Augustine declined the gift. He argued that if Januarius were alive, he would persuade him to reconcile with his son. The revelation of withheld funds produced much ill will in the community. A priest had entered the community but not given all to be held in common. This was deception. To prevent this from happening again, Augustine reluctantly changed the terms of entrance into the community. There would no longer be an absolute condition of poverty for the priests under his care, but, and here was the sting, if the priest did not take the vow of poverty, he could not live with Augustine and the others in the bishop's residence.[42]

Another story, told by Possidius, shows another side of Augustine's community and leadership. It was at the dinner table that Augustine welcomed guests, participated in conversation, and read with others. He loved this more than the eating and drinking that took place. Augustine had inscribed in the table this poem in Latin, "Who injures the name of an absent friend, May not at this table as guest attend." In this he warned against gossip, coarse speech about others, and bearing false witness against a neighbor. At one meal with mostly fellow bishops in attendance, Augustine became so exasperated with their conversation that violated this warning that he rebuked them in the midst of the meal, asking which was to be done: should they remove the inscription or should he remove himself? "Both I and others at the table," Possidius reports, "experienced this."[43]

This community probably had some rules, but, contrary to claims from the Middle Ages, no written record of them remains. Perhaps they were never written. How many written rules do friends need? The closest we can come to reading an "Augustinian Rule" is from a letter he wrote to the leader of the women's community under his care. The women's residence had been established by Augustine's widowed sister and apparently was of some size and at some distance from the bishop's residence. His sister died, highly beloved by the sisters of the community, and was replaced by her chosen successor, less beloved. The sisters complained to Augustine, noting how wonderful his sister was and how her assistant and now successor was less so. They asked him to come and replace her, but he declined to come, stating that he would delay coming until harmony was restored and that he supported the new leader, asking the women to honor the memory of his sister by honoring her beloved successor.

---

[42]Possidius, *Sermones* 355.
[43]Possidius, *Sancti Augustini Vita Scripta a Possidio Episcopo* 95.12.

Apparently more than personalities were at issue, for Augustine takes the occasion to write some ground rules for the community:

+ Unity was of the first importance.

+ All of each person's possessions were to be given to the community upon entrance.

+ The sister who led was solely responsible for redistributing goods.

+ Pride in giving was to be avoided. (In this he acknowledges that sometimes fathers who placed young daughters in the community gave large amounts of monies, and also that sometimes women came with nothing, needing someone to care for them.)

+ Prayer was emphasized—the oratory was to be used for prayers only, and prayers were defined as psalms and hymns.

+ When fasting and eating, one was to sit in silence, listening to readings.

+ Differences in accommodations were to be tolerated among the sisters if prompted by age, health, and the family gift given at entrance.

+ Attire was to be simple and the hair covered, encouraging chaste minds and appearances.

+ Discipline, defined as obedience to the lead sister, was to be observed, and cross looks were to be confronted one on one, then by two or three if unheeded, then by expulsion if no repentance.

+ Do not wash clothes too often; bathe once a month.

+ Serve in the storeroom, wardrobe, or library without grumbling.

+ Check books out of the library only during stated hours.

+ Do not quarrel, make up quickly, forgive without reserve—better to be quick to anger and quick to ask forgiveness than slow at both.[44]

This letter, though it may reflect more of a response to specific complaints than a general rule, must give us some insight into the men's residence. Compared to what was happening in the Egyptian desert east of Hippo with Anthony and those who followed him, this was a mild asceticism. What happens at the table is central, relationships are core, and libraries and reading are an unquestioned part of the home.

---

[44]Augustine, *Epistulae* 211.

The communities built by Augustine, by contemporary friends (including his sister), and by those imitating his community soon after were bodies of theological friends. In them the leadership of the church lived and loved, talked and thought, served and sheltered others. In the community of theological friends, matters of the formation and reformation of the soul and the church were discussed, deliberated, debated, and determined. From there came the ideas and practices that would shape not only the community and those within but the whole church. From there, a millennium later, an Augustinian monk would start the great Reformation.

DYING IN THE GRACE OF THEOLOGICAL FRIENDSHIPS

The final sounds and sights of Augustine's living and dying are heard and seen in the biography composed by Possidius, bishop of Calama. He had returned to the garden residence of his friend and would be present during his dying. So too were other bishops and priests—all friends of Augustine. Some had come because their hometowns had been burned down by the Vandals, who were sweeping across North Africa, setting up rule in Carthage, and imposing Arian alternatives in the parishes and bishoprics of the cities and desert. The last letter Possidius carried for Augustine, delivered after Augustine's death, encourages the remaining bishops to stay at their posts until all is lost. Calama already had been lost, and the old friend had come home to the residence of the bishop of Hippo—his own residence when he became a priest nearly forty years ago.

Some had come because Augustine was dying. He had a fever, and his strength was waning. Their memories of the intimate and theological conversations around the table drew them back one more time. It would be their last. The Vandals would soon burn down much of Hippo and all the bishop's beloved residence. Augustine's friends gathered at his bed and reportedly spoke together as before, agreeing on things human and divine, with kindness and love, in Christ Jesus.

Augustine had told them all earlier that he had been taught how to die by another friend and bishop whom he regularly had traveled to visit during a prolonged illness. Augustine had begged him to live longer because of his great benefit to the church and their friendship. The friend, Possidius noted, was from a small town and barely literate, but he had taught the great bishop this last grace:

"If I were never to die," said the ailing friend of Augustine, "that would be well; but if I am to die, why not now?"[45]

The time had come for Augustine. Possidius writes, "As I, by the grace of God, have lived with this man, who now is dead, on terms of intimate and delightful friendship, with no bitter disagreement, for almost forty years, may I also continue to emulate him in this world, and may I enjoy with him the promises of God Almighty in the world to come. Amen."[46] Augustine died as he had lived—in the grace of theological friends. He was never alone.

THEOLOGICAL FRIENDSHIP TODAY

Augustine was the most personally reflective writer in the early centuries of the church, revealing his most intimate thoughts on the most public of stages. Matters of life for him were always matters of the soul and thus always matters for introspection and wonder. We have followed Augustine's life in the context of his thinking about friends and friendships. We too would do well to think about our lives in light of the grace of theological friends.

I (Jerry) knew Augustine's theological friends before I knew my own. Somewhat disappointed in my early exposure to contemporary theologians and theology, I set a path after seminary graduation of reading the church fathers to keep me company. I studied the ancient languages to read authors like Augustine more closely. My first church was a rural congregation and a solo pastorate, which added to my theological isolation. I do not recall a single theological conversation during these years except with my congregation, who lovingly tolerated my academic interests. I did not know until nearly halfway through my years of ministry what I lacked so thoroughly and what I hungered for so greatly. An invitation from the two other authors of this volume to join in a theological colloquium whetted my appetite for more. I have been fed and continue to feast.

Though I am perhaps introverted in temperament, my sheer joy in shared company and sustained conversation is experienced as a great grace of God in my life. I discovered that I am not alone in this need for the grace of theological friends. God gave me a calling to accompany this grace, a way of showing my gratitude—offering an invitation and affording a hospitality to others seeking

---

[45]Possidius, *Sancti Augustini Vita Scripta a Possidius Episcopo* 109.27.

[46]Possidius, *Sancti Augustini Vita Scripta a Possidius Episcopo* 145.31.

such a community. The takers are many, the conversations widening and deepening. Grace abounds.

The time I spend alone, the quiet times—just me and Jesus, just me and the psalmist, or just me and Augustine—the times I have always cherished, have been enriched profoundly by the times spent with others in mutual study and deliberation. When I pray and read and think and write alone, I am not really alone.

I wrote this chapter with the prayer that you too may come to know this grace of God. If you are like me, you may need to seek out others and be ready to accept invitations for distinctly theological engagement and have a strong bias for those relationships that have the promise of being sustained through the years. Make the glad sacrifices to sustain them. If your temperament is more extroverted, you may need to consider if the multiple interactions of your ministry and the many friendships of your life are truly theological and whether they foster thinking, if not agreeing, on things human and divine—whether they challenge you, even hold you accountable, to consider the things of God with more discipline and rigor.

Childhood friendships sustained in our adult years are precious and rare. Do you have them still? Can they be revived? Are they suitable for theological engagement? The fellow students of your college and seminary years may still be in place and can now become a continuing theological fellowship. Do not let distance or difference dissuade you. In my experience, pastors and others (writers, teachers) that have the same unspoken or acknowledged needs for theological friendships as you are nearby and waiting to be befriended. Make the contact, extend the invitation, offer hospitality. Some environments may already be in place but require a renewed refocus. Local ecumenical clergy gatherings typically do almost everything but reflect and engage theologically. Dare you suggest theological study and conversation? Denominationally based associations, also not known for theological reflection, may nonetheless be the cohort of pastors with whom lifelong theological friendships can be formed. Lead. Ask. Invite.

Gift this chapter and this book to someone whose trust and affection you share or would like to gain. Ask them to consider forming a circle of friends for the purpose of shared study and sustained conversation. Set the table. Offer barely eaten pears.

Grace is grace and thus of God. Augustine would be glad to tell us that the only work which God has promised to bless is the work of prayer. So pray. Pray for the grace of theological friends.

QUESTIONS FOR DISCUSSION

+ Review the itinerary of your early paths. Have they been journeys with friends? What role did your earliest friends play in your thinking, speaking, and acting? Now that you are an adult, have the roles changed? Have the friends changed?

+ Augustine will say, in no uncertain terms, that friendship is true only between fellow believers. Do you agree? Augustine further defines friendship as agreement in things divine and human, accompanied by kindness and affection, in Christ Jesus our Lord, who is our true peace. Do you agree? If not, what other definition would you substitute?

+ Augustine and his friends in Hippo were celibate. What parts of that intentional community are attractive and available for us who are married (and with children)? The community was gender exclusive. What values would be gained and lost if our communities/friendships were gender inclusive or exclusive?

+ Are you in mutually accountable friendships? What barriers are there to this in your life and ministry? How will you remove these barriers—for the sake of God, for the sake of the other, and for your sake?

+ What rules, if any, could help you experience at its fullest the grace of theological friends?

FOR FURTHER READING

Brown, Peter. *Augustine of Hippo: A Biography.* Berkeley: University of California Press, 2000.

Griffin, Em. *Making Friends and Making Them Count.* Downers Grove, IL: InterVarsity Press, 1987.

Meilander, Gilbert. *Friendship: A Study in Theological Ethics.* Notre Dame, IN: University of Notre Dame Press, 1985.

Nystrom, Carolyn. *Friendship: Growing Side by Side.* LifeGuide Bible Studies. Downers Grove, IL: InterVarsity Press, 1996.

Welty, Eudora, and Ronald A. Sharp. *The Norton Book of Friendship.* New York: W. W. Norton, 1991.

2

"*The* Work *of* Obedience"

BENEDICT

ENEDICT OF NURSIA, a sixth-century monk, later canonized a saint, has attracted renewed twenty-first-century notice. Philosopher Alasdair MacIntyre concludes his influential *After Virtue* with the observation that "what matters at this stage is the construction of local forms of community within which civility and the intellectual and moral life can be sustained through the new dark ages which are already upon us. . . . We are waiting not for Godot, but for another—doubtless very different—St. Benedict."[1] In a more popular vein, Rod Dreher's *The Benedict Option* uses St. Benedict to call for "a radical new way of doing politics" and a church that "must stop being normal."[2]

What accounts for St. Benedict's newfound fame? Although the Rule of St. Benedict has shaped Catholic monastic life for centuries, he seems an unlikely inspiration for philosophical conjecture and evangelical political-ecclesial proposals. He also seems to be a doubtful guide for pastors seeking a path to faithful ministry. The Rule of St. Benedict is designed to govern life in a monastery, which makes it problematic on two counts. First, Protestant pastors, heirs of an anti-monastic Reformation tradition, do not live in monasteries. Second, Benedict's rule stresses the need for multiple forms of obedience, a need unrecognized and

---

[1] Alasdair MacIntyre, *After Virtue: A Study in Moral Theory*, 2nd ed. (Notre Dame, IN: University of Notre Dame Press, 1984), 263.
[2] Rod Dreher, *The Benedict Option: A Strategy for Christians in a Post-Christian Nation* (New York: Sentinel, 2017), 78, 102.

a discipline generally resisted by contemporary pastors and their congregations. On both counts, the relevance of a monastic rule for the life of contemporary pastors is not immediately apparent.

The sixteenth-century Reformation was marked by harsh criticism and pervasive condemnation of monastic life. Martin Luther, himself a former Augustinian monk, wrote a scathing 150-page judgment on monastic vows "because we see them multiplied and spread abroad to the utter ruination of Christendom and the wholesale destruction of souls."[3] In Luther's view, monastic vows conflicted with Scripture, faith, Christian freedom, the commandments, and reason. He was particularly adamant in condemning vows and the obedience they demanded as inimical to the freedom of a Christian. "It does not help the soul if the body is adorned with the sacred robes of priests or dwells in sacred places or is occupied with sacred duties," he wrote. "Such works produce nothing but hypocrites."[4]

Luther's critique of obedience to vows was encompassed within an attack on the entire monastic system. He disapproved of forsaking the world and denying self within a system of poverty, chastity, and obedience, but he reserved his harshest judgment for monastic piety. In his view, monasteries "adapt the divine oracles of Christ to fit in with this childish, ridiculous, and foolish performance, in which they actually stand in rows to worship God like rows of tubes, pipes, and trumpets, mute and insensate."[5]

John Calvin was also unsparing in his critique of monasticism, although, like Luther, he distinguished between the pure monastic life of Anthony and the desert fathers, and the corrupt monastic system that followed. Calvin added to Luther's condemnation the charge that "all those who enter into the monastic community break with the church. Why? Do they not separate themselves from the lawful society of believers, in adopting a peculiar ministry and a private administration of the sacraments? If this is not to break the communion of the church, what is? . . . For every monastery existing today, I say, is a conventicle of schismatics, disturbing the order of the church and cut off from the lawful society of believers."[6] Luther's "priesthood of all believers" and Calvin's dismantling of

---

[3]Martin Luther, "On Monastic Vows," in *Luther's Works*, vol. 44 (Philadelphia: Fortress Press, 1966), 251.

[4]Martin Luther, "The Freedom of a Christian," in *Martin Luther's Basic Theological Writings*, 2nd ed., ed. Timothy F. Lull (Minneapolis: Fortress Press, 2005), 393.

[5]Luther, "Freedom of a Christian," 325.

[6]John Calvin, *Institutes of the Christian Religion* (Philadelphia: Westminster Press, 1960), 4.13.14.

the division between clergy and laity were expressions of their refusal to sanction a special class of "super Christians."

Given the Reformation heritage of disparaging the monastic life and resisting patterns of imposed obedience, it may help to explore the impulses that led to the monastic life and thus to understand the need for monastic patterns of obedience. Only then will we fully appreciate the potential of Benedict's rule for contemporary pastoral life.

A SCHOOL FOR THE LORD'S SERVICE

Jesus sent his followers *into* the world, knowing that they did not *belong to* the world. "I am not asking you to take them out of the world," he prayed to the Father, "but I ask you to protect them from evil" (Jn 17:15, NRSV alt.). Jesus' prayer for his disciples, and his continuing prayer for us, is generally summed up by saying that Christians are to be "in but not of the world." This is, of course, easier said than done. It is often difficult to determine the difference between *in* and *of*, not only for individuals but for congregations and denominations. The more the church attempts to become relevant to society, the more it is drawn into a crisis of its Christian identity and integrity. Yet the more the church fails to relate to society, the less relevant it becomes. Where is the line between conformity to the world and mission in the world? "In but not of the world" is not a simple, clear-cut standard.

The quandary is real. There have always been Christians (and pastors) who blend into their milieu so completely that they are indistinguishable from the cultural norm. Their values, convictions, and actions are reflexively aligned with their surroundings; they not only participate in the culture's values but also become captive to its hidden grip. Conversely, there have always been Christians for whom the world seems far too worldly, so they determine to be "not in" in order to be "not of" the world. The Amish are a conspicuous contemporary instance of this impulse. In an earlier time, the most common form of this determination was the cloistered life of the monastery.

From "in but not of" to "in and of." From the apostolic era onward, Christian faith spread slowly but steadily, even in the face of social marginalization and intermittent persecution. Throughout the early centuries of the church's existence, the necessarily cohesive life of an outsider community strengthened Christianity in its refusal to compromise with social customs and moral practices of the day. Becoming a Christian took far more than a sudden decision to believe; it took a radical change in the way one lived. Belief was not simply mental assent to God's truth but a radical departure from prevailing social norms in order to live in God's new Way. Protracted catechetical instruction was required to induct converts into the demanding habitus of Christian life. They not only had to learn a new narrative of God and humankind but also had to adopt the new ways the narrative required them to live. It is not going too far to say that people found it more difficult to live as Christians lived than to believe as Christians believed.

The accelerating expansion of the church from the mid-third century on was accompanied by a gradual relaxation of the church's discipline and moral requirements. The transformation of the church from a disdained yet fervent sect to a favored religion led to lowered expectations and relaxed discipline in order to accommodate an influx of new adherents. Requirements for admission to the catechumenate were lessened and norms of Christian living were tempered. The difference between the church's first two and a half centuries and its subsequent expansion and Constantinian establishment may be characterized by Alan Kreider's formulation: "Conversion, which had made Christians into distinctive people—resident aliens—now was something that made people ordinary, not resident aliens but simply residents."[7]

From "in and of" to "not in and not of." The relaxation of requirements for becoming a Christian, and the consequent blurring of the lines between the Christian community and Roman society, led first a few, then some, then many Christians to withdraw from the immorality and temptations of the world and the ambiguity of the church in order to live in unhindered communion with God. They became known as monks, from the Greek *monos*—alone, solitary. First applied to hermits, who lived in solitude, the term soon designated all who "left the world," whether they lived alone or in community.

Monasticism originated in Egypt and became widely known and appreciated through Athanasius's biography of St. Anthony, one of the first hermit monks. According to Athanasius, Anthony heard a priest read the words of Jesus: "If you wish to be perfect, go, sell your possessions and give the money to the poor . . . then come, follow me" (Mt 19:21 NRSV). That is exactly what Anthony did, living alone and dedicating himself to God in prayer and manual labor. His

---

[7]Alan Kreider, *The Change of Conversion and the Origin of Christendom* (Harrisburg, PA: Trinity Press International, 1999), 91.

example was followed by others (now known as "the desert fathers") who lived alone—praying, working, reading, and memorizing Scripture. Although hermits, they did not isolate themselves totally, for monks usually met in small groups weekly to celebrate the Eucharist and to encourage and advise one another.

One of the early monks, Pachomius, after living for years as a hermit, felt called to provide the benefits of monastic life for the many. He established a monastic *community*, providing a set of shared rules that regulated life together. Recruits came by the hundreds, and soon monastic communities sprang up throughout the Christian world. The proliferation of monasteries was spontaneous, without official planning and without standardized organization. Monastic rules, developed from Pachomius's originating rule, varied in length and rigor, but most elaborated on Pachomius's already extensive rule, ordering the most minute affairs of the monastery and each of its monks.

Monasticism became the way of life for Christians who wished to devote themselves fully to God. Monasteries were established throughout both Eastern and Western Christianity as places of common prayer, shared labor, and service. One of these monastic communities was established in early sixth-century Italy by Benedict of Nursia. The course of Benedict's life is known primarily from a brief account in Pope Gregory the Great's *Dialogues*. Gregory relates that while Benedict was a student in Rome he became appalled by the vices of the city and his fellow students, fearing that he would be drawn into spiritual ruin. He renounced his inheritance and all worldly goods, devoting himself wholly to God as a hermit monk. He was later drawn out of seclusion to be the abbot of a nearby monastery, but his first experience of communal religious life did not go well. Benedict was not able to bring about the common discipline that he believed was necessary to the cloistered life, so he returned to a life of solitude.

But his seclusion was brief. Benedict's spreading reputation for holiness attracted visitors who wished to emulate his devotion. Gregory states that Benedict accommodated his growing number of followers by establishing twelve monasteries, each with twelve monks and an abbot. He later founded a larger monastery at Monte Casino, where he presided as abbot for the rest of his life. It was for Monte Casino that he wrote the rule by which he is now known.

Benedict was familiar with previous rules but found them overly long and complex, focusing on minutia rather than the central purposes of communal prayer and labor. His originality lies in distilling and centering the monastic rule tradition. Benedict's Rule is characterized by its brevity, psychological awareness, pastoral sensitivity, and deep appreciation of the core of Christian faith. The rule's simple yet evocative language made it accessible and inspirational, commending itself to other monasteries as it became known. Today it is the standard for monastic rules throughout the Catholic Church and beyond.

Aversion to monasticism endures in Protestant understandings of Christian faith and life. Monasteries appear to represent such "un-Protestant" practices as withdrawal from the world, celibacy, routine, and ritual, all of which are at odds with contemporary Protestant understandings of the life of pastors. Problems with monastic life go even deeper, however, for the monastic staples of common life, obedience, and accountability—all accompanied by directives for observance—make Benedict's Rule difficult for pastors to appreciate, and even more difficult to heed. Although some elements in Benedict's monastic rule are not suitable for congregational ministers and priests, the real problem lies in its emphasis on collegiality, obedience, mutuality, and required conduct. All are conspicuously problematic issues in modern pastoral life.

MONKS AND PASTORS

At the outset of his rule, Benedict identifies four kinds of monks: cenobites (monks living in a monastery with a rule and an abbot), anchorites (hermits), gyrovagues (travelling monks), and sarabaites (independent monks).[8] Benedict's Rule is intended for cenobites, considered to be the strongest, best kind of monk because they live in community with a rule to shape common life. He also approves of anchorites, assuming they have been tested in a monastery before undertaking the rigors of solitude. Perhaps Benedict's own experience of beginning as a hermit and then living in the common life of the monastery led him to reverse the pattern for others.

Benedict holds gyrovagues in contempt, for they wander from region to region, village to village, and monastery to monastery, serving their own desires and abusing the hospitality of others. It is Benedict's description of sarabaites that suggests an unsettling resemblance to contemporary pastors. His judgment is not complimentary. Why? Because they are

---

[8] All citations and allusions refer to Bruce L. Venarde, ed. and trans., *The Rule of Saint Benedict* (Cambridge, MA: Harvard University Press, 2011).

tested by no rule nor instructed by experience . . . they go around in pairs or threes or, of course, singly, with no shepherd, shut in their own sheepfolds, not the Lord's, and the pleasures of their desires is their law, since they call holy whatever they have thought or chosen and they deem forbidden what they have not wished to do.[9]

Benedict is critical of monks who live independently rather than in community, who are not accountable to a director, and who have free reign over the shape of their ministry. Too many contemporary pastors—particularly Protestant and Pentecostal pastors—follow that pattern. Pastors are essentially "free agents" whose solo ministry is congregationally focused and independently determined. While most pastors are officially responsible to a bishop or a council—diocese, presbytery, association—they are seldom held to account for the shape and quality of their preaching, teaching, pastoral care, and missional leadership. They conduct their pastorate as leaders whose own vision and initiatives shape their ministry and their congregation. Benedict established a rule for cenobites; can we imagine the relevance of his rule for sarabaites?

Most contemporary pastors are the solo pastor of a particular congregation. Even churches with two or more ordained ministers preserve the solo pastor model by means of clear hierarchy and compartmentalized responsibilities. Senior pastors determine the responsibilities of associate or assistant pastors, whose position descriptions focus their ministry on education, or pastoral care, or outreach, or youth, and so on. Multiple-staff churches are rarely characterized by deep spiritual and pastoral community, instead following a business model of patterned authority and designated responsibilities.

Solo pastors may have other pastors as friends, and they may engage in occasional cooperative ventures, yet their independence remains intact. Ministerial associations, lectionary reading groups, and annual small group retreats draw some pastors together for occasional fellowship or study, but these do not diminish pastoral autonomy. National and denominational surveys indicate that pastors lament the loneliness of their profession, yet pastoral independence is assumed and jealously guarded.[10] Loneliness is a consequence of atomized self-determination.

Pastoral self-rule cuts against the very concept of a pastoral rule. Rules necessarily imply obedience. The rules of grammar, golf, driving, algebra, and baking

---

[9]Venarde, *Rule of Saint Benedict*, chap. 1.

[10]National and denominational surveys include several in both the Lilly Endowment's "Pulpit and Pew" initiative and the Research Office of the Presbyterian Church (USA).

are meant to be observed, followed, obeyed. But obedience to pastoral rules is not a natural or comfortable concept. This is nothing new, however. Obedience to monastic rules was no more natural or comfortable in the sixth century than in our time. That is why the prologue to Benedict's Rule accentuates the character and shape of obedience. Benedict addresses each monk: "Listen carefully, my son, to the teachings of a master and incline the ear of your heart. Gladly accept and effectively fulfill the admonition of a loving father so that through the work of obedience you may return to him from whom you had withdrawn through the sloth of disobedience."[11] Benedict's Rule has nothing to do with *blind* obedience, for its purpose is to "return to God" by way of communal disciplines. The prologue enumerates elements of the obedient life:

♦ You should ask with most urgent prayer that whatever good work you begin be completed by [God].

♦ Let us at last arise, scripture rousing us. . . . And with our eyes open to the divine light, let us hear with thunder struck ears what the divine voice, calling out daily, reminds us.

♦ But let us ask the Lord, along with the prophet, saying to him, "Lord, who will live in your dwelling place and who rests on your holy mountain?" After this question, brothers, let us hear the Lord in reply, showing us the way to his dwelling place.[12]

Benedict's way to God's dwelling place begins with earnest prayer and immersion in Scripture. It continues through such markers as working for justice, speaking the truth, doing no harm to neighbors, and avoiding rumors and gossip. Yet all these markers lead to a central point, that those who live in God's dwelling place are to take no pride in their good observance but instead glorify the Lord who works in and through them. In our present age of statistics, organizational expectations, outcomes, metrics, performance reviews, and résumés, all buttressed by best practices, coaching, management literature, and church growth seminars, it is unsettling to hear that performance is not something to be proud of and that accomplishment is the Lord's doing, not ours. For Benedict, all forms and occasions of obedience derive from foundational *communal* obedience to God.

---

[11]Venarde, *Rule of Saint Benedict*, prologue.
[12]Venarde, *Rule of Saint Benedict*, prologue.

Benedict's Rule stipulates the daily practice of reading Scripture and praying as the primary means to "hear the Lord." Prayer is offered in community seven times a day—matins/lauds (dawn), prime (early morning), terce (mid-morning), sext (mid-day), none (mid-afternoon), vespers (evening), and compline (night)—as well as vigils in the middle of the night! Each of these times is shaped by three or four psalms, Scripture readings, canticles, hymns, and prayers. The rule recommends an order of psalms, but not rigidly, for Benedict notes that if monks prefer a different arrangement they are free to alter the order as long as the entire psalter is sung every week. Praying the entire psalter each week undoubtedly strikes contemporary pastors as excessive and impossible. Benedict responds with a wry observation: "What our Holy [Desert] Fathers energetically completed in a single day, we, more lukewarm as we are, ought to manage in an entire week."[13]

The rule's seven times of community prayer shape each day, but prayer and Scripture reading are not confined to the daily office. At each meal, Scripture is to be read by a lector while monks eat in silence.[14] Each day is divided between manual labor and private Scripture reading. Even private reading takes place in the context of the community, for the rule recommends that two senior monks should go around the monastery during the hours monks are free for reading to ensure that no one spends his time in idleness or gossip, neglecting his reading. Benedict observes that "such a one is not only harmful to himself but also a distraction to others."[15]

Today's pastoral life is far different from monastic life. A daily rhythm of seven extended times for prayer, twenty-one psalms, hours of reading Scripture, and so on is unrealistic. The range of pastoral responsibilities and family life exceeds the ordered responsibilities of monks. But the wider range also creates disorder accompanied by the constant temptation to respond to the immediate. The pastoral life of indiscriminate claims on time and energy makes it *more* necessary to follow a rule that sets times for prayer each day, incorporating ordered psalms and Scripture. Morning, midday, and evening prayer is not beyond the capacity of pastors. Ruled prayer and Scripture reading are not only possible but necessary to pastors' spiritual fidelity and ability to lead a congregation.

One reason that the Rule of St. Benedict has been loved and observed for centuries is its sensitivity to the limits of human capacity. It recognizes that the

---

[13]Venarde, *Rule of Saint Benedict*, chap. 18.
[14]Venarde, *Rule of Saint Benedict*, chap. 38.
[15]Venarde, *Rule of Saint Benedict*, chap. 48.

rule was made for people, not people for the rule. Its clear expectation of obedience to the rule is played out briefly and sensitively, not exhaustively and harshly. It recognizes the need for adaptability to circumstances, for the *purpose* of the rule shapes the elements of the rule. The prologue concludes with Benedict's intention and the rule's purpose:

> To found a school for the Lord's service. In its design we hope we will establish nothing harsh, nothing oppressive. . . . Instead, by progress in monastic life and faith, with hearts expanded in love's indescribable sweetness, we run along the path of God's commands, never turning away from his instruction and persevering in his doctrine.[16]

The rule's concentration on shaping service to the Lord, avoiding minutia and severity, is apparent throughout. Regarding prayer, for example, the rule counsels, "Let us know that we will be heard not in loquacity but in purity of heart. Therefore, prayer should be brief and pure. In community, however, prayer should absolutely be short."[17] Regarding manual labor, Benedict says that "all tasks should be done in moderation out of consideration for the weak."[18]

The rule's sensitivity to both the needs of individual monks and the needs for ordered community is evident in the chapter "If a Brother Is Assigned the Impossible":

> If it happens that difficult or impossible tasks are assigned to a brother, let him receive the command with all mildness and obedience. But if he sees that the weight of the burden utterly exceeds the measure of his strength, he should patiently and opportunely bring up the reasons why it is impossible with his superior. If after his request the superior's command remains the same, let the junior know that it is beneficial for him and let him obey in love, confident in God's help.[19]

Monks are to be obedient, not free to do as they please. But they are not automatons, mechanically following orders. Abbots and senior monks administer the rule but they are not free to be martinets, demanding unquestioned obedience. Yet they are not to be dupes, granting every excuse. Obedience is built on mutual honesty and shared stability, for it is the spiritual health of the community that is paramount.

---

[16]Venarde, *Rule of Saint Benedict*, prologue.

[17]Venarde, *Rule of Saint Benedict*, chap. 20.

[18]Venarde, *Rule of Saint Benedict*, chap. 48.

[19]Venarde, *Rule of Saint Benedict*, chap. 68.

PASTORS AS MONKS?

The Rule of St. Benedict deals with the nature and quality of ordered community by describing the roles and responsibilities of monks and abbots. The rule's depiction of their character and obligations is suggestive for the life of contemporary congregational pastors, but in an indirect and dual way. There is a sense in which pastors are analogous to both abbots and monks. Pastors are like abbots in their relationship to the congregation and like monks in their relationship to their bishop or judicatory, denomination, or (perhaps) a rule. It may be possible, then, to engage in a thought experiment, imagining Benedict's Rule as applying to pastors instead of monks and abbots, and to congregations and councils instead of monasteries.

Because community is so central to the Rule of St. Benedict, it makes sense to begin with the pastor as monk—that is, as one whose vocation is not confined to the congregation but is lived out within a denomination and a diocese, synod, presbytery, conference, or association. Some denominations and world communions are episcopally ordered, with a bishop in each diocese. While bishops might be thought of as abbots, it is more difficult to imagine councils as such. It may be even more difficult to imagine the denominational apparatus as an abbot. But before we dismiss these possibilities, our thought experiment should be played out. In what ways might the expectations of the monk's life suggest possibilities for the pastor's life?

The character of a monk. Benedict describes the desired character of monks early in the rule. First, monks are to love the Lord God with their whole heart, whole soul, and whole strength, and their neighbor as themselves. A rule would not be a rule if it simply cited the Great Commandment, however, so Benedict goes on to specify what love of God and neighbor means in the life of a monk: "Renounce yourself to follow Christ. . . . Give relief to the poor, clothe the naked, visit the sick, bury the dead. Help those in trouble, comfort those in mourning. Make yourself a stranger to the ways of the world, put nothing above the love of Christ."[20]

The rule indicates some characteristics that are familiar aspects of pastoral ministry, although its emphasis on self-renunciation and being a stranger to the ways of the world may appear excessive, perhaps appropriate to the cloistered life but not compatible with pastoral ministry in the twenty-first century. It is

---

[20]Venarde, *Rule of Saint Benedict*, chap. 4.

important, however, to recognize that Benedict is not speaking about generic self-denial and asceticism. Monks are to renounce themselves *in order to follow Christ*. Monks are to love Christ rather than the world. Pastors are also called to love and follow Christ rather than accede to contemporary society's emphasis on self-promotion and easy correspondence to "the way things are." As the rule progresses it is clear that self-renunciation means offering oneself to the Lord rather than centering on one's own preferences in pursuit of professional success and personal happiness. Similarly, being a stranger to the world is turning away from the indulgences of advancement and acquisition in order to follow Christ.

Benedict understands that it is not easy to follow Christ, which is why disciplined practices are necessary to undergird faithful discipleship. Benedict also understands that observing disciplined practices should not become a pursuit of spiritual merit badges. The rule calls monks to "put your hope in God. When you see good in yourself, attribute it to God, not yourself, but know that the evil you do is yours, and own up to it."[21] Contemporary missiology emphasizes the *missio Dei*, the work of God to bring about the reconciliation of all things. If this is to be more than a rhetorical cover for *our* mission and ministry, we might place more confident and active hope in God's work than in our abilities and skills. Honestly acknowledging our incapacities and shortcomings is also an aspect of reliance on God.

Where does hope in God come from? The rule requires that monks read Scripture and listen for God's leading, pray regularly and often, and confess sins in prayer daily, leading to amendment of life.[22] Once again, Scripture and prayer. This seems obvious, but it is part of the rule because it does not come naturally. Surveys consistently show that regular Scripture reading and prayer are difficult for pastors.[23] Pastors read the Bible, of course, but most often the reading is instrumental—to compose sermons and prepare for teaching. Reading Scripture as nourishment for one's soul and direction for one's life is only sporadic. Similarly, disciplined private prayer is intermittent, and confession of sin is atypical. "Look," says Benedict, "these are the tools of spiritual craft." They equip monks (and pastors) to hear and obey God's commands every day.[24] Obedience to the rule leads to obedience to God.

---

[21]Venarde, *Rule of Saint Benedict*, chap. 4.

[22]Venarde, *Rule of Saint Benedict*, chap. 4.

[23]Two identical surveys conducted ten years apart by Presbyterian Research Services show the same results.

[24]Venarde, *Rule of Saint Benedict*, chap. 4.

In all of this, however, monks have one great advantage over pastors. Benedict stresses the importance of the monastery as a place of mutual encouragement and support. The monastery is a community in which monks are not left to their own devices. The ordered life of communal Scripture reading and prayer shapes one's personal habit of Scripture reading and prayer. Disciplines are more readily observed in community than individually. Experience shows that contemporary pastors who seek others who will join them in prescribed daily disciplines of stipulated Scripture readings and regulated prayer, punctuated by weekly gatherings of the community, are those most likely to read and listen to Scripture gladly and to pray thankfully.

The monk in community. Most pastors already belong to a community, at least in theory. They are part of a judicatory or an association of denominational colleagues. Even nondenominational pastors are often part of a network of similar nondenominational congregations and their pastors. Whatever its character, there is often a broader ecclesial group that pastors "belong to." Historically, these ecclesial groups were conceived as communities of prayer, study, counsel, and mutual responsibility. Most have become administrative structures, complete with parliamentary procedures, committees and task forces, reports and organizational regulations. But even the most bureaucratized retain some measure of their original intent. It is unlikely that a council will easily move away from "doing business" to become a community of prayer and study. Yet it is likely that some pastors in every council yearn for a covenanted community that would observe daily disciplines and meet regularly for corporate prayer and study.

In community, obedience to a rule is bolstered through obedience to brothers and sisters in a pattern of mutual responsibility and accountability. In covenanted communities, each member is accountable to all. Such communities are not substitutes for faithful engagement in council and denomination, though. Pastors, like monks, are to be loyal and accountable to the wider church. Participation in a covenanted community should help pastors become more, not less, engaged in ecclesial service, lest they become an independent community of meandering gyrovagues, serving its own will.

The obedient monk. It is clear by now that at the heart of Benedict's Rule is a concept that is not valued by contemporary pastors: obedience. Obedience to God, obedience to the rule, obedience to one's fellow monks, and obedience to one's superiors are all of a piece. No one would deny that all Christians should be obedient to God, but obedience to earthly institutions is a far more ambiguous practice. Following the regulations and dictates of bishops, councils, and denominations is occasionally difficult, sometimes problematic, and, on rare occasions, intolerable. The ambiguity of obedience to the church was voiced dramatically by Dietrich Bonhoeffer. On the one hand,

> once the church has spoken authoritatively on, let us say, what it considers to be legitimate Protestant doctrine, then I as a theologian—and every Protestant Christian is a theologian—have only relative freedom with respect to this matter, within the framework of what the church has declared. . . . I owe relative obedience to the church; it has a right to demand a sacrifice of intellect, and on occasion perhaps even a sacrifice of conscience.[25]

But on the other,

> we Germans have had to learn the need for obedience. . . . Our gaze was directed upward, not in slavish fear but in the free trust that beheld a career in the commission and a vocation in the career. The readiness to follow an order from "above" rather than one's own discretion arises from and is part of the justified suspicion about one's own heart. . . . However, in doing so [we] did not reckon with the fact that the readiness to subordinate and commit [our] life to the commission could be misused in the service of evil.[26]

The first citation concerns obedience to the church and the second about civil (dis)obedience, but the contexts could be reversed without doing violence to the thought. In a civil democracy, citizens owe relative obedience to the state, and in the church, obedience can be misused in the service of evil. The ambiguity is always present in qualifiers—"relative" and "could be."

The Rule of St. Benedict does not eliminate the ambiguity, but it does moderate simple opposition between obedience and freedom. Benedict begins by assuming unanimous consent that all Christians are to be obedient to God. But how are we to know what God requires of us (and how are we to know what it is to do justice, love kindness, and walk humbly with our God)? Benedict believes that God's will is known through daily immersion in prayer and Scripture. It is in listening for and to God's Word that God's good will is heard. It is for this reason

---

[25]Dietrich Bonhoeffer, *Dietrich Bonhoeffer Works*, vol. 1, *Sanctorum Communio* (Minneapolis: Fortress Press, 1998), 251.

[26]Dietrich Bonhoeffer, "An Account of the Turn of the Year 1942-1943," in *Dietrich Bonhoeffer Works*, vol. 8, *Letters and Papers from Prison* (Minneapolis: Fortress Press, 2010), 41.

that obedience to the rule is crucial: "Everybody, therefore, should follow the Rule as a master in all things and nobody should rashly deviate from it. Nobody in the monastery should follow his own heart's will."[27] The rule sets out the means by which attention to Scripture and regular prayer become normal elements of daily life.

Scripture reading and prayer are not the province of solitary individuals, however. A monk's obedience to the rule immerses him in prayer and Scripture by engaging him in a community that prays and studies *together* so that discernment of God's commands is done communally. The rule stipulates that "whenever there is important business to do in the monastery, the abbot should call the whole community together . . . because often the Lord reveals what is best to a junior brother."[28]

"Important business" is business that affects the life of the whole monastery, and so all—from most senior to least—are to be involved in the discussion through which community discernment occurs. The matter is not decided by voting, for that would produce winners and losers; the decision is made by the abbot after hearing all comments. Lest we hastily criticize this for being undemocratic, we might note that this procedure follows the precedent of the so-called Jerusalem Council in Acts 15. Following much debate and testimony from Peter, Barnabas, and Paul, the gathering did not put the matter to a vote. Instead, James said, "I have reached the decision" (Acts 15:19 NRSV). His decision then became the decision of the whole: "It has seemed good to the Holy Spirit and to us" (Acts 15:28).

The quality that leads to appropriate rather than conformable obedience is humility. The longest chapter in the Rule of St. Benedict is on humility, which begins by making clear that the rule's commendation of this characteristic is found in the Lord's teaching that "everyone who exalts himself will be humbled, and he who humbles himself will be exalted" (Lk 14:11). Benedict notes that exaltation is a form of pride that focuses on oneself and one's capacities and achievements rather than on God's grace, the personhood of others, and the life of the community. Benedict's Rule does not counsel degraded self-effacement and groveling obedience but rather calls for discarding self-absorption by turning one's gaze to God and to the community. The rule outlines twelve steps on the

---

[27]Venarde, *Rule of Saint Benedict*, chap. 3.
[28]Venarde, *Rule of Saint Benedict*, chap. 3.

ladder of humility. Some of the steps are relevant only to the cloistered life, but others are pertinent for contemporary pastors:

◆ "Placing the fear of God before his eyes at all times, one should altogether shun forgetfulness and always remember everything that God commanded."[29]

Awe of the Lord is the beginning of humility as well as wisdom, for it turns vision away from self and toward the One who creates, redeems, and sustains the life of the world. Such awe is not an automatic human response, however, and pastors are as likely as anyone to constrict vision to self. Benedict's Rule holds that attention to what God commands—awareness of God's good will for human life—comes (not surprisingly) through Scripture and prayer. The rule's first step of humility makes clear that obedience to Scripture turns us from our will to God's will.

◆ "That one, not loving his own will, takes no pleasure in fulfilling his own desire, but in his actions mirrors the word of the Lord."[30]

The first step concerns the inner life while the second concerns actions. Benedict is aware that prayer and Scripture are not limited to worship and personal devotions but rather shape the way one lives, including how one lives out ministry. Contemporary pastoral life is surrounded by programs for leadership education, coaching, management training, and a host of other techniques for improving pastoral effectiveness. Many of these have merit, but without a clear sense of ministry's purpose and goal they do little to mirror the word of the Lord. Benedict, along with other faithful guides throughout the church's history, is convinced that reliance on oneself is insufficient and that living out God's will is essential.

◆ "When, for the love of God, one subjects himself to his superiors in all obedience imitating the Lord."[31]

If the first two steps appear reasonable as well as faithful, subjection to superiors may seem neither. How can superior/inferior distinctions be appropriate in Christian communities marked by mutuality and collegiality? Is subjecting oneself to another appropriate in Christian relationships? Benedict certainly had in mind the superiority of abbots and senior monks, and many contemporary pastors are just as certainly loath to think of themselves as submissive to councils

---

[29]Venarde, *Rule of Saint Benedict*, chap. 7.
[30]Venarde, *Rule of Saint Benedict*, chap. 7.
[31]Venarde, *Rule of Saint Benedict*, chap. 7.

or even to bishops. Yet councils and bishops are not free agents either, at liberty to impose their arbitrary will. Every denomination has doctrinal, moral, and procedural standards that are "superior" to the judgment of pastors, bishops, and church councils. In our time, too many pastors imagine themselves free from obligation to these standards, subjecting the church's norms to their private judgment. In our time, too many church councils and denominations use these standards to justify legalistic regulation of pastors and congregations. Application of Benedict's Rule unmasks the arrogance of pastors who subordinate the church to their theological and moral opinions as well as the condescension of churches that resort to theological and moral compulsion. Contemporary expression of the Rule of St. Benedict can lead pastors and councils to understand the ways in which they are mutually accountable to the whole church's developed faith and life.

♦ "If, when obedience involves difficulty, adversity, and even the infliction of certain injustices, one silently embraces suffering in his heart, and endures it, not growing tired or running away."[32]

Obedience to the church is often difficult. Denominations are not immune from error in doctrine and morality, and they are conspicuously prone to error in procedure. The rule acknowledges that obedience is sometimes challenging, can cause hardship, and may even seem unjust. Benedict's counsel of humility calls pastors not to assume that their every difference with the church indicates that it is wrong and they are right. Patience may lead to acceptance, but if difference remains, simply giving in out of weariness or leaving the church are ruled out.

♦ "In humble confession one reveals to his abbot any wicked thoughts entering into his heart and any wickedness done in secret."[33]

Most Protestant traditions reject forms of confession in the presence of another out of concern that forgiveness might appear to come from priests rather than from God. The result is a pattern of communal confession, usually read from a printed order of worship, together with silent confession in private prayer. The rule calls for accountability to God and to the community through personal confession of specific sin to the abbot. Confession is then followed by the abbot's counsel concerning amendment of life. In the absence of abbots, how might

---

[32]Venarde, *Rule of Saint Benedict*, chap. 7.
[33]Venarde, *Rule of Saint Benedict*, chap. 7.

pastors be held personally accountable, and where can they find counsel for the amendment of life?

♦ "The goodness of obedience is to be shown by all, not just the abbot, but the brothers should similarly obey one another."[34]

For Benedict, showing humility entails deep mutuality with fellow monks. Toward the conclusion of the rule, Benedict stipulates that:

♦ "The goodness of obedience is to be shown by all, not just to the abbot, but the brothers should similarly obey one another."[35]

Humility is not abasement and obedience is not servility, for both are expressions of loving God and loving others. A central task for contemporary pastors is to form covenanted relationships with other pastors in obedience to a rule that includes active accountability to and responsibility for one another. The nature of Christian community is seeking the good of the community and the persons within it, for obedience to one another through a common rule is an expression of obedience to the Lord.

PASTORS AS ABBOTS?

The Rule of St. Benedict gives careful attention to the character and role of abbots. The rule's call for monks to be obedient to superiors could become dangerous and destructive of community if the abbot were self-centered, arrogant, dictatorial, insensitive, or arbitrary. A good abbot must first be a good monk, embodying all the rule's wisdom concerning character and disciplines. Contemporary pastors, surrounded by disparate and conflicting expectations from congregation, denomination, other pastors, and the public, know that they are confronted with multiple, disparate "rules" seeking to govern their professional and private lives. The Rule of St. Benedict provides a more helpful approach to pastoral identity.

It is essential to remember that Benedict's wisdom about the character and role of an abbot is part of the rule. Abbots are as bound by the rule as novice monks, and it holds abbots accountable to the monastery. Contemporary pastors who are without a rule are unbound, free to follow plans of their own making. Even those pastors with a personal rule remain essentially unaccountable to a

---

[34]Venarde, *Rule of Saint Benedict*, chap. 7.
[35]Venarde, *Rule of Saint Benedict*, chap. 71.

community. Thus, the Rule of St. Benedict suggests the shape of an ordered pastoral life. The character and role of the abbot is explicit at several points in the rule and implicit throughout. The foundational elements are found in chapters two and sixty-four. A useful exercise might be for each pastor to identify pastoral attitudes and behaviors in congregational settings that correspond to the following elements in the Rule of St. Benedict.

♦ Shepherd: "An abbot who is worthy to lead a monastery should always remember what he is called and fulfill the name of 'superior' in his deeds."[36]

Pastors are not called "superior" (although some assume "senior" status), but they should remember what they are called—*shepherd*. Shepherds bear significant responsibility for the welfare of the congregation and its members. There is ample biblical indication of what it might mean to fulfill the name: avoiding the marks of a bad shepherd (Ezek 34:1-10) while embodying the marks of a good shepherd (Ezek 34:11-16; Jn 10:11-18).

♦ Steward: "The abbot should always be mindful of what a burden he has undertaken, and to whom he will render an account of his stewardship, and know that he should benefit the brothers rather than preside over them."[37]

The real burden of pastoral ministry is not located in managerial responsibilities, program development, or church growth expectations. Pastors undertake responsibility for the spiritual well-being of every member of the congregation, and Benedict's Rule understands that pastors will be held accountable for their fidelity to that responsibility. The primary pastoral calling is service for the benefit of the congregation and its members.

♦ Coach: "An abbot must always remember . . . what a difficult and demanding responsibility he takes up, to govern souls and be of use to many diverse dispositions, humoring one brother, scolding another, entreating another, thus shaping and adapting himself to all."[38]

The spiritual well-being of a congregation and its members is not a "one size fits all" matter. Knowing members of the congregation and understanding their abilities, needs, challenges, and problems is a difficult and demanding task. Even more so is discerning pastoral responses to diverse persons. Affirmation and

---

[36]Venarde, *Rule of Saint Benedict*, chap. 2.
[37]Venarde, *Rule of Saint Benedict*, chap. 64.
[38]Venarde, *Rule of Saint Benedict*, chap. 2.

admonition, support and challenge, confidentiality and confrontation—all of this and more is required of pastors.

+ Overseer: "An abbot must not favor any individual in the monastery."[39]

This is easier said than done, for some members are a joy to work with, others are difficult, while still others are virtually anonymous. Loving all equally is an ideal that is rarely achieved, but it remains the goal of pastoral life.

+ Role Model: "When anyone takes up the name of abbot he should show all good and holy things in deeds more than words, setting out God's commandments verbally for receptive disciples, but teaching the hard-hearted and less intelligent the divine precepts by his example."[40]

Many pastors chafe at the suggestion that they should be role models, maintaining that they should be treated like everyone else. Yet, like it or not, how a pastor lives is as important as what a pastor preaches and teaches. The content of sermons is quickly forgotten, and only a minority of the congregation will ever hear pastors teach, but members experience how a pastor acts, and many will learn the shape of Christian living in that way.

+ Accountability Partner: "Nor should he turn a blind eye to malefactors' sins, but pull them out at the root as soon as they spring up, as he is able."[41]

In an age when it is assumed that private and family life are no one else's business, the idea that the church can and should call people to account for sinful behavior is uncomfortable for pastors and inconceivable to members. Benedict's Rule assumes that avoiding accountability is not benign respect for privacy; rather, standing by while damaging, even dangerous situations persist inflicts harm.

+ Faithful Teacher: "The abbot must not teach or establish or decree anything that is outside the Lord's commands."[42]

Benedict understands the Lord's "commands" as the sum of the gospel in both Old and New Testaments. Pastors are called to teach the faith, not to espouse their personal opinions or promote their own agendas.

+ Scholar: "It is fitting that the abbot be learned in divine law."[43]

---

[39]Venarde, *Rule of Saint Benedict*, chap. 2.
[40]Venarde, *Rule of Saint Benedict*, chap. 2.
[41]Venarde, *Rule of Saint Benedict*, chap. 2.
[42]Venarde, *Rule of Saint Benedict*, chap. 2.
[43]Venarde, *Rule of Saint Benedict*, chap. 64.

Pastors who do not read deeply in the theological disciplines, engage in serious continuing education, or seek to understand cultural trends—to be learned in divine law—are guilty of pastoral malpractice. Reliance on one's own knowledge and wisdom alone is a strange kind of arrogance, the opposite of the humility required of abbots as well as monks.

♦ Pilgrim: "Above all, an abbot should not pay more attention to transitory, earthly, passing matters but should always be mindful that he has undertaken rule of souls."[44]

Pastoral ministry is easily consumed by transitory, earthly, passing matters. Managerial and administrative tasks seem to demand attention because they are immediate and specific. Too often the seemingly urgent buries the truly important.

OBEDIENCE TO A RULE TODAY

The Rule of St. Benedict is only suggestive for contemporary pastoral life. As a monastic rule, it cannot be imported wholesale into congregational settings. Furthermore, it cannot be adapted to devise a single modern rule for all pastors. But its insights into the nature of Christian faith and life, the need for community, and the responsibilities of leadership can provide possibilities for pastors to join in a covenanted community with a common rule. The Rule of St. Benedict concludes with the chapter "Not Every Practice of Justice Is Set Out in This Rule."

Benedict's intention can be paraphrased in contemporary idiom: *We are called to join with others in sketching out a pastoral rule so that we can practice it in community, striving for fidelity in the basics of Christian discipleship and in our pastoral vocation.*

I (Joseph) will confess that my attempts to live by a rule have been marked by many failures. Even the basic elements of a rule—daily Scripture reading and prayer—have sometimes eluded me. When I look back on my history of fits and starts, I recognize a pattern: when I have tried to live under a rule by myself I have been susceptible to negligence; when I have lived under a rule together with others I have felt encouraged by them and accountable to them, resulting in more faithful observance. My ruled communities have sometimes been close at hand, sometimes at a distance, but whether near or far, an intentional community has been key to my obedience to a pastoral rule.

---

[44]Venarde, *Rule of Saint Benedict*, chap. 2.

I came to the Rule of St. Benedict late in my ministry. I wish I had encountered it earlier. I find it helpful now to think of myself as a monk, taking Benedict's Rule as a helpful insight into my discipleship and a guide to the daily rhythms of life. I know I would have been a better pastor years ago if I had thought of myself as the abbot of the congregations I served.

The Rule of St. Benedict has become the model for monastic life throughout the Catholic Church and in Christian communities such as Taizé. It can also be a model for pastors who do not live in community but who can build community with one another in Benedictine patterns of mutual responsibility and accountability.

QUESTIONS FOR DISCUSSION

♦ How might a contemporary pastor become less like a sarabaite monk, and more like a cenobite?

♦ Is it helpful to imagine the pastoral vocation as analogous to a monk before thinking of the pastor as abbot?

♦ Why do so many pastors find disciplines of Scripture reading, prayer, and study difficult to maintain?

♦ Do you know two other pastors with whom you could join in "sketching out a pastoral rule so that we can practice it in community, striving for fidelity in the basics of Christian discipleship and in our pastoral vocation"?

FOR FURTHER READING

Boesak, Allan. *Walking on Thorns: The Call to Christian Obedience.* Geneva: World Council of Churches / Grand Rapids: Eerdmans, 1984.

Charry, Ellen T. *Psalms 1–50: Sighs and Songs of Israel.* Grand Rapids: Brazos, 2015.

Chrysostom, St. John. *Six Books on the Priesthood.* Crestwood, NY: St. Vladimir's Seminary Press, 2002.

Nouwen, Henri J. M. *Genesee Diary: Report from a Trappist Monastery.* New York: Doubleday, 1976.

Peterson, Eugene H. *Eat This Book: A Conversation in the Art of Spiritual Reading.* Grand Rapids: Eerdmans, 2006.

Weil, Simone. *Waiting for God.* New York: Harper Perennial, 2009.

3

The Holiness That Stoops to Serve

GREGORY the GREAT

G REGORY THE GREAT lived and recommended a Christian discipleship that is both active and contemplative. He argued and modeled that
the Christian life has two poles and pulls, each of which is essential to faithfulness
before God and usefulness to others. The one draws us to God—"Come unto
me all ye"; the other sends us out—"Go ye into all the world."

Gregory's life and work invite every Christian to think about discipleship and
ministry. Is my primary duty to contemplate God or to serve humanity? The
tension is heightened for those whom Christ calls to lead his people. Pastors may
struggle to know whether the contemplative or active life is more foundational
for their leadership of God's people. Some of us are by nature more easily disposed to one or the other. Our training may pull us more in one direction than
the other. At times a particular calling may require us to attend more to contemplation than action, or vice versa. By the end of our days, in which will we have
majored, and in which will we have minored?

Gregory was faced with these questions constantly. From his life, letters, and
legacy, we learn that the answers may not be an either-or matter. After all, love of
God and love of neighbor form one great commandment. And for the apostles,
Jesus' simple call, "Follow me," is paired with "I will make you fishers of men." The
question may be how each of us as a disciple and minister learns to be faithful to

both calls at once. Our task may be to integrate the two pulls and poles as best we can. The drive toward holiness is always and simultaneously a call to service.

TWO MEN

In the middle of the sixth century the first man was born into an aristocratic family with ties to well-known Roman leaders dating back several generations. The place of his infancy, a palatial estate on the Caelian Hill, situated him among the few, not the many. The family knew hardships but experienced them differently than most Romans of late antiquity. Famine was ever near, but no member of this family ever went hungry. The plague swept through and devastated nearby populations, but the family's social and physical location isolated them from it quite often. War was a constant presence—only its intensity varied—yet this family reported few battle deaths over these years.

By age thirty-three, young by contemporary standards, this man was named the prefect of Rome. This public office was a prized position, a super mayoralty of the ancient capital—at one time the world's center. During Rome's republic and the early years of its empire, holders of this office could be assured that their names would become part of Rome's written historical record. They spoke with senators and emperors daily. Now the position, though still highly competitive to achieve, was hard, thankless work.

The city's food supply came from distant Sicily and beyond. All the poor and a large part of the urban population depended on its uninterrupted delivery. War, plague, crop failure, corruption, and competition from other cities with hungry citizens to placate made this daily work burdensome.

Then the Lombards showed up. Described by contemporaries as more violent and less trustworthy than other Germanic tribes, they marched into the Italian peninsula and occupied the central valleys near Rome for a couple of generations. The city of Rome itself had changed hands at least three times between imperial forces and the Goths during this man's youth. In his early adult years, the Goths had become so sufficiently weakened and assimilated that peace had been rumored. This hope was dashed with the arrival of the Lombards and would not return in his lifetime. They did not want Rome—who wants to run the bureaucracy of an oversized, underfunded city? They wanted to plunder the city's remaining wealth and enslave its people. Constantly threatening violence, ever demanding tribute and ransom, and persistently disrupting Rome's attempts to keep connections with the rest of the empire, this tribe determined the annual peace and prosperity of the once eternal city.

And then all the principal and powerful partners of this first man died. Pope John III, more than an acquaintance to this man, died during the year of his prefecture, and a very long vacancy followed. The bishops of Rome in the sixth century could usually be counted on to be willing and able partners in pursuing the peace and prosperity of the city. The Christian religion united secular and sacred authorities in common causes for the common good. But not this year. With the papacy vacant, the church's resources—in material and personnel—were now lost.

Then the Byzantine general Narses died. He was the emperor's legate to the city and the whole Italian peninsula. He had the power of the sword in the field and around the city walls. The expected reward of mutual help for the Prefect from a personal friendship and partnership with the Roman High Command, ended with the general's death. Though the Prefect's pleas for a replacement legate were constant, it is not clear whether any of these messages got back to the emperor. The Lombards frequently and for long periods blocked all communications from the ancient capital Rome to the new capital Constantinople.

Further, Ravenna was considered the provincial capital of the Italian peninsula, not Rome, and it was favored by the emperor accordingly. It is not clear whether the emperor would be able or even willing to intervene for the prefect of Rome in this difficult time. In either case, he did not.

Yet, for all this, history tells us that the prefect did an admirable job. The citizens were fed more often than not, the walls of Rome were fortified, and the Lombards were sufficiently placated to prevent open attack without depleting Rome's material resources. Justice was administered in the courts, public works resumed, civil services were largely uninterrupted, and the city and its prefect survived this most terrible of years.

This first man's excellence in leadership and administrative abilities during difficult times would become part of his widespread reputation among his contemporaries and all historians of late Roman antiquity.

∽

The second man also lived in sixth-century Rome. His family had church ties, and it was rumored then and is generally accepted by historians now that Pope

Felix III was his great-great-grandfather. Certainly Agapetus, the pope in the years just prior to his birth, was his distant uncle. His father's three sisters gave up their family inheritance and lived as ascetics for all their adult years. His father was a Defensor of the Church of Rome and thus employed as a property and legal manager of ecclesiastical lands.

This second man followed his family's faith and devotion to the church. At age thirty-four he sold all that he owned to endow six monasteries in Sicily and establish the monastery of St. Andrew's near Rome. He then took the extraordinary step of appointing the monastery's abbot and entering as a novice under his authority.

The ascetic life would begin in earnest for him and continue until his death thirty years later. No private wealth would ever again be his, he would never marry or have children, his tasks would be assigned to him for the remainder of his life, and though he would be given tasks of great responsibility in his later years, he seems to have never sought them and often sincerely though unsuccessfully attempted to resist them.

Five years after beginning this ascetic commitment he would be ordained to the diaconate and be sent to the capital Constantinople as an apocrisiarius, a papal legate to the court of the emperor. He does not seem to have relished this assignment or even to have allowed himself to be influenced by this position of potential influence. He brought other ascetics from St. Andrew's with him, formed a community apart from the imperial court, and prayed, read, and wrote much.

Most of his later writings—and there would be many—seem to have been started or at least contemplated during this six-year posting in the East. Most importantly, he began his writing of *Moralia in Iob Libri*. This work is extraordinarily long but maintains one theme throughout—Job was a holy man, a man able to detach from the distractions of this life, and, unlike his friends and his wife, he was devoted entirely to the things of God. He could lose all things of this world and yet have all he would ever need or want—contemplation of and relationship with God. Has anyone ever been more steadfast in his love of God than Job? Is anyone more to be envied or emulated? Job, for this second man, is a paradigmatic contemplative who is also an active priest and pastor to his generation.

When this second man returned to Rome at the age of forty-five he would be the abbot of St. Andrew's and continue his ascetic life. He would never again be far from Rome. His contemporaries and later historians would read his works with great interest, which reveal the heart of a man whose persistent great love was the love of God, simply and wholly, and who effectively called many others to that same love.

The first and second man are the same person, Gregory. He will most often be called Gregory the Great, one of only two popes whose name is almost always accompanied by the title *Great*—great in part because he seems to have lived two extraordinary lives at once.

At age fifty, Gregory would become the bishop of Rome in an uncontested election. His contemporaries—seeking and needing a leader who would have great promise as both a skillful administrator in an era when the church could lose everything and as a man of deep spirituality in a city where it was all too easy to lose one's way—imagined no better candidate than the former first man of the city become beloved ascetic. Gregory protested this election, citing his desire and calling to attend to his prayers and studies. Though his early biographers may be reporting nothing more than the literary topos of feigned public humility—a recurrent theme in the celebrated lives of saints that was built on the narratives of Moses and Jeremiah—his own writings suggest sincerity in his initial reluctance and bear testimony to the continuing internal tension of the church's first monk-pope.

That internal tension—the contest within him for time and attention, the demands of the office vying with his ascetic calling for the prime moments of each day, the needs of his soul agonizing against the needs of the church for the next season of endeavor, the bucolic life of the shepherd confronted with the wolves that would ravish the flock—would be the central theme of his writing, episcopate, life, and legacy. Gregory would confide in a letter to a friend that all of this was a burden on his soul, but a burden given by God.[1]

Pope Gregory I was bishop of Rome for fourteen years until his death in 604. His writings speak to a life of the mind and spirit as pursued by the most dedicated of monks of his or any generation, and the accomplishments of his episcopacy are legendary.

Gregory wrote perhaps as many as twenty thousand letters, over eight hundred of which survive; his commentaries on Job and Ezekiel are still read with profit beyond the curiosity of papal historians; his written lives of the saints introduced

---

[1]Gregory, *Epistulae* 5.53. All translations of Gregory in this chapter are from the Latin and are my own.

a new brand of religious biography and moral/spiritual/theological argument into the Christian library—a participationist soteriology (somewhat versus Augustine), an appreciation of the mystical in the center of the practical, and an ecclesiology able to consider the church apart from its structures of power (unlike any other papal writer). All of this and more has won for Gregory a place next to Augustine as the most influential writer in the Western church. But the point here is not so much about the extent of his writing as it is about the thoughtfulness of a careful pastor writing to his flock of the things that mattered from the store of his rich interior life—a life only a monk could possibly live.

And what about the legend of his papal leadership? He would rebuild, even add to, the physical defenses of Rome—its walls and its sentries. He would rebuild the city's all-important aqueducts, perhaps the single most important contribution to the life and health of the Roman people in his generation. He would reestablish with unparalleled effectiveness the feeding of Rome's citizens, and this in an era of empire-wide famines. He would negotiate a necessary and advantageous settlement with the Lombards, with no help from and to the dismay of the distant emperor. He would advance the right and responsibility of preeminence of the Roman see when all things pointed east to Constantinople. And to top it all off (at least as judged by those of us who learned the faith in our native English language), he would send the monk Augustine (not to be confused with Augustine of Hippo) to the shores of the British Isles, resulting in an explosion of conversions.

In Edward Gibbon's *Decline and Fall of the Roman Empire*, the atheist historian argues at length that one of the causes for this fall, the greatest of all historical tragedies, is that the new Christian faith diverted the greatest minds of the times into the service of the church and away from the rightful claimant to their gifts, the empire and its culture. He spends considerable time on Gregory as an example and measure of such a waste and the eventual decline into the Middle (for Gibbon, "Dark") Ages.[2] Gregory is the first influential Christian writer who almost totally neglected the pagan classics. He spent his life teaching the population how to live for an invisible God rather than for the claims of empire and culture. Rome would have no better servant than Gregory, whether as prefect or pope, in his generation or perhaps ever again. But for him life was never first and foremost about Rome. For Gregory life was about his call as a servant of God.

---

[2]Edward Gibbon, *The History of the Decline and Fall of the Roman Empire*, ed. J. B. Bury (London: Methuen and Co, 1909-14), 5:34-41.

TWO CALLINGS

Gregory's personal calling and the one he extends to his contemporaries is best read in his short book *The Pastoral Rule*. This work, like almost all his writing, was published in the first years of his papacy. It is still somewhat unexplained how so much was produced in so little time. Most biographers conclude that the ideas, notes, even first drafts for some works were written in his community in Constantinople and during his later stay at St. Andrew's when abbot. But *The Pastoral Rule* seems to have been written from beginning to end shortly after his election to the bishopric. There is an urgency about it.

When you are pope, recruitment of pastors is pressing, the quality of the clergy is critical, and those appointed to office are expected to be effective. Gregory does not seem satisfied with any of this when surveying the priests he had inherited. He would call forth the gifts and lives of a whole generation of monks and priests, bishops, church workers, and leaders. He was actively involved in recruiting and elections and would famously remove bishops from office.

Nothing about Gregory's background would ever suggest ignorance of the church and its clergy, yet the monk had never pastored a parish or answered to any ecclesiastic other than the abbot of his own choosing and the pope himself. In this, Gregory was unlike the clergy of his day, and in *The Pastoral Rule* he shows little empathy for the common excuses and failings of his contemporaries.

The morale of those who bore the face of the church to the lay public was downcast in Gregory's day. The challenges cited above—famine, plague, war— would be sufficient to explain this, but there was more. Financially able families hired their own chaplains and provided for them quite generously; little was expected of their ministry other than their presence and loyalty. High offices in the church were openly contested (money and connections made a difference), while some poor parishes could not secure any clerical leadership. Those who accepted these lower positions were overwhelmed by the needs. Almost all were ill-equipped to pastor. Their recruitment was haphazard at best, with the majority being commissioned or ordained after following only their own sense of call and little confirmation of that call by others. Guidance was lacking on what manner of life this public servant of God was to live, and it showed. The simple skills needed to provide practical assistance to the genuine spiritual needs of the catholic laity were untaught and therefore rarely exercised. At least that is how Gregory saw it.

Qualifications for spiritual leadership. Gregory began his episcopacy with a strong sense of the need for reform, and *The Pastoral Rule* was written to meet that need. The first part sets forth the qualifications needed in one who is presented as a spiritual leader. It has common-sense suggestions so rudimentary that one wonders why they needed to be said at all as well as commands so surprising that we are left wondering what Gregory was facing.

He starts simply enough by considering who has come to church orders. "No one presumes to teach an art that he has not first mastered through study. How foolish it is therefore for the inexperienced to assume pastoral authority when the care of souls is the art of arts."[3] This reveals a tragic irony. The work of a church leader is humble work. Gregory views the pastor primarily as a teacher who must instruct the laity in what it means to live humbly. This teaching is to be offered humbly by the truly humble. Throughout the essay he assumes that this itself is the work of humility. But now that religion is highly valued by all throughout society, many, says Gregory, succumb to "the temptation of authority" and "aspire to the glory of honor," and thus put themselves forward as clerical teachers. "They lust to be superior to others," he says. This is vanity, humility's opposite. Arrogantly they claim the humble office. His condemnation is severe—"Those who do not know the Lord, the Lord does not know."[4]

Gregory will always applaud loudly the effort to perfect the heart by the contemplative life of the mind and the mortification of the flesh, but he will be relentless in his insistence that it is all for naught if those who are called to serve neglect that call. By this neglect, the contemplative will have failed to attend to a necessary part of sanctification—service to others for the common good. Just when they may think that they are serving God most, they are serving God least. The loss, therefore, will be theirs too.[5]

Others are even more at fault. They study humility, know its salutary effect, teach it with some skill, but do not practice it. They "corrupt the study of holy meditation with an evil life."[6] His analogy is apt. They are like the shepherd who drinks from the clearest waters yet steps in that same pool, thus muddying it

---

[3]This is a near quote from Gregory of Nazianzus who, in an earlier work, addressed some of the same needs. See Gregory of Nazianzus, *An Apology for His Flight to Pontus* Or. 2.

[4]Gregory, *Pastoral Rule* 1.1.

[5]Gregory, *Moralia Iob in Libri* 5.5.5-6.

[6]Gregory, *Pastoral Rule* 1.2.

before offering it to his sheep. "No one does more harm in the Church than he who has the title of holiness and acts perversely."[7] Their punishment would be less in hell if they had not caused the falling of others. Remember, this is the new bishop of Rome describing his own clergy.

The rest of the first section considers the troubles, trials, and temptations of those who, perhaps relatively innocent at their investiture, fall from the grace of humility during the years of their service in the church.

Jesus, he says, is the model for all of us. He, the Creator, declined an earthly kingdom that he might "redeem us by his suffering . . . teach us by his conversation . . . offering himself to us as an example."[8] This is not merely the experience of Jesus, it is his choice. Because it purges even long-standing faults, adversity is to be preferred over prosperity, for prosperity tempts us away from remembering who we are. We forget our calling. Think of David, who while on the run spared Saul and who, when in a palace, murdered Uriah: "This same man who had previously been known to spare the wicked learned afterwards to crave, without impediment or hesitation, the death of the good."[9]

The sheer multiplicity of concerns can distract us also. With authority comes broad responsibilities. Many petty matters may dissipate the attention that should be given to the singular and significant, and the never-ending concerns of this world always are at war with the peaceful contemplation of the self before the Savior. Think of Nebuchadnezzar, who, though he had acknowledged God to be God, later exalts himself as the greatest human when he considered all his varied kingdom; by God's just judgment he was made less than human—indeed, like an animal.[10]

So what kind of person did Gregory prefer for pastoral leadership, and how would he describe that person? Those fit for ministry are those who are:

♦ spotless in the pursuit of chastity,

♦ stout in the vigor of fasting,

♦ satiated in the feasts of doctrine,

♦ humble in the long-suffering of patience,

♦ erect in the fortitude of authority,

---

[7]Gregory, *Pastoral Rule* 1.2.
[8]Gregory, *Pastoral Rule* 1.3.
[9]Gregory, *Pastoral Rule* 1.3.
[10]Gregory, *Pastoral Rule* 1.4.

♦ tender in the grace of kindness,

♦ strict in the severity of judgment.[11]

Such people, while they may not abound, can be found. They can be found usually in libraries, and other such places, for the simple reason that they are people who have long practiced the disciplines of Bible reading, prayer, self-examination, and confession of sin and have spent their lives contemplating God. They, Gregory has no doubt, love God. But (and here is the difficulty) they are usually averse to accepting positions of authority. They know that by taking on these new responsibilities they will no longer be able to pursue their studies un-interrupted. The work that has made them what they are will diminish and may even come to end, so great are the distractions of pastoral work.

So, the misfits desire the offices, and those who are fit decline them. The latter prefer "the mysteries of stillness" to "preaching to their neighbors."[12] Alas, this sad fact is aggravated by the knowledge that those who are fit and therefore called to service will, if they do not accept the call, forfeit the gifts they have, for these gifts were given not for their sake but for the sake of others. And the greater their gifts, the greater the judgment on them. Jesus had given up so much more to lower himself so much further.

In their refusals they think themselves humble, and many truly are if they at first decline because of a sense of unworthiness yet soon accept out of a desire to be useful. But others—many others—sometimes think themselves even more humble for having refused entirely and finally. Not so, argues Gregory. They act without humility when they decline the wisdom of others and the call of God, refusing to serve others.[13]

Some who are fit for ministry answer the call immediately like Isaiah; others are compelled like Jeremiah. Both prophets had been formed by a love of God. Jeremiah, "who zealously clings to the Creator through the contemplative life, opposes being sent to preach." Isaiah volunteers to be sent because "he had pre-viously seen himself cleansed by a coal from the altar." It is this experience and contemplation of the Holy One that both provides a hesitation to leave his presence and compels one to be useful in his service.[14]

---

[11]Gregory, *Pastoral Rule* 1.5.

[12]Gregory, *Pastoral Rule* 1.5.

[13]Gregory, *Pastoral Rule* 1.6.

[14]Gregory, *Pastoral Rule* 1.7.

Speaking at once of several passages in the letters of the apostle Paul, Gregory says that for those called or seeking office, "this great master of pastoral care guides his listeners by encouragement and restricts them by fear."[15] Many offer themselves for the offices of the church, believing themselves to be dedicated to good works. Look at yourself now, Gregory counsels. If you are doing good works now, then you may be right about your motivation, but beware of the new temptations that inevitably come with new authority. It will more powerfully tax you. Some sailors who steer well in the calm are overwhelmed in the storm.

If, conversely, you are not doing good works now, do not think you will begin when in office, "for no one is able to acquire humility while in a position of authority if he did not refrain from pride when in a position of subjection."[16] Those who ail are not healed by pretending to cure the sick.

Again, we ask, just what kind of person does the bishop want serving with him? Let Gregory's own words describe the one who assumes spiritual leadership:

♦ he must be the model for everyone;

♦ he must be devoted entirely to the example of good living;

♦ he must be dead to the passions of the flesh and live a spiritual life;

♦ he must have no regard for worldly prosperity and never cower in the face of adversity;

♦ he must desire the internal life only;

♦ his intentions should not be thwarted by the frailty of the body, nor repelled by the abuse of the spirit;

♦ he should not lust for the possessions of others, but give freely of his own;

♦ he should be quick to forgive through compassion, but never so far removed from righteousness as to forgive indiscriminately;

♦ he must perform no evil acts but instead deplore the evil perpetrated by others as though it was his own;

♦ in his own heart, he must suffer the afflictions of others and likewise rejoice at the fortune of his neighbor, as though the good thing was happening to him;

♦ he must set such a positive example to others that he has nothing for which he should ever be ashamed;

---

[15]Gregory, *Pastoral Rule* 1.8.
[16]Gregory, *Pastoral Rule* 1.9.

◆ he should be such a student of how to live that he is able to water the arid hearts of his neighbors with the streams of doctrinal teaching;

◆ he should have already learned by the practice and experience of prayer that he can obtain from the Lord whatever he requests, as though it was already said to him, specifically, by the voice of experience: "When you are speaking, I will say 'Here I am.'"[17]

One becomes such a person by undistracted contemplation of the things of God. Such a person is evidenced by the discipline and the fruits in his life listed above. And, here is the rub, such a person will not want to give up such a life. Nonetheless, that is the person desired for spiritual leadership in the church.

The life of the spiritual leader. In the second part of his *Pastoral Rule*, after counseling who should and should not aspire to and accept spiritual leadership in the church, Gregory describes how the leader ought to live. Never at a loss for making lists in this short work, he starts with one and spends the remainder of this section enhancing the description of each and arguing from biblical examples:

◆ he should be pure in thought,

◆ exemplary in conduct,

◆ discerning in silence,

◆ profitable in speech,

◆ a compassionate neighbor to everyone,

◆ superior to all in contemplation,

◆ a humble companion to the good,

◆ firm in the zeal of righteousness against the vices of sinners.[18]

Notice that these things are a combination of the private life and public duties—the dual foundation of the pastor's life. Reading Gregory carefully reveals that this is not about the balance of the two, though balance is advised—after all, the pastor has only so many hours in a day, days in a week, and ultimately years in a life. But the mark of the righteous pastoral life is more about the quantity and quality of both aspects. A pastor, for example, is not to be only so pure in thought as the demands of work allow or only so effective in preaching as the time away from study permits; rather, a pastor is to be both pure in thought and

---

[17]Gregory, *Pastoral Rule* 1.10.
[18]Gregory, *Pastoral Rule* 2.1.

effective as a preacher. Pursuit of multiple virtues (though often Gregory will speak of dual virtues) is commanded; the pastor is not to be dedicated to only one or other of the poles as time and energy will permit.

This may or may not be Gregory at his best, but it is Gregory at his heart. When the Savior says, "Love the Lord your God with all your heart and with all your soul and with all your mind. . . love your neighbor as yourself" (Mt 22:37-39), it is doubtful that he meant us to balance the two. When the Savior says, "If you love me, then feed my sheep," he seamlessly connects the two, Gregory argues. It is not helpful to conclude that one is to do them best by alternating between them. Gregory, I think we would say, got this perfectly right. This is the heart of the pastor's heart—loving God, loving neighbor; loving Jesus, serving the sheep.

Sometimes the advice is clearly meant to clarify the expectations of one of these pursuits rather than both simultaneously, but this is made necessary by the restrictions of language, which permit us to consider only one virtue at a time in depth. Thus, in this section on the life that the pastor is to live, Gregory advises (or since he is bishop, should we say, "commands"?), in no particular order, things that tend toward one or the other but not both at the same time. On the one hand, the pastor is to "meditate on the life of the ancients," "admire the examples of the fathers," and "consider unceasingly the footsteps of the saints."[19] On the other, he says, "Be first in service" and "put your shoulder to good works."[20]

At other times, he speaks of the ends—contemplative love of God and active service to congregation—in one sentence, intentionally combining them to show the necessity of both: "The spiritual director should be a compassionate neighbor to everyone and superior to all in contemplation . . . otherwise in pursuing high things he will despise the infirmities of his neighbors, or by adapting himself to the infirmities of his neighbors he will abandon the pursuit of high things."[21] Think of Paul, he says. Was anyone more knowledgeable, thus showing the excellent fruits of study? Or was anyone ever more useful in the building up of the church than was Paul by his direct engagement with the people of God?[22] At his best, and perhaps most inspiring, Gregory attempts to think through the relation of the two—"love God, *and* love neighbor"; "love me, *then* feed my sheep."

---

[19] Gregory, *Pastoral Rule* 2.2.

[20] Gregory, *Pastoral Rule* 2.3.

[21] Gregory, *Pastoral Rule* 2.5, 7.

[22] Gregory, *Pastoral Rule* 2.5.

Gregory may have been uniquely positioned to think through these matters. He had been the first man of Rome, both as prefect and as bishop. The monk, fully dedicated to pursuit of the holy in his studies and prayers, was now again negotiating treaties with the hostile Lombards. Feeding the citizens and feeding his soul, he began to think, were connected in such a way that one was not to choose between them or balance them (though this is somewhat better). Rather, he now thought that one could not choose either one without the other.

Consider Christ's call to the fishermen on the shores, specifically the command to drop the nets. These texts had been interpreted by earlier preachers as calls to abandon the world and its cares—such as running the family fishing business—in order to contemplate Christ. To follow Jesus, they preached, was to let go of all other things. Monasticism (and Gregory's life) was built on such ideas and practices. But when preaching on this text (Mt 4:18-22) at the Feast of St. Andrew, he asks, How do we know if we have dropped our nets and followed? We can know, he argues, if we can answer yes to these questions: Have we learned to fear for the well-being of our neighbor more than for ourselves? Do we seek their gain (yes, worldly gain included) and not our own? Do we desire the suffering of our enemies to become our own (he thinks here more of church-based opposition than the Lombards)? And do we offer our souls to God as sacrifice for them? There is no better way to do these things than to leave the nets of our self-serving, self-edifying, self-satisfying study of the Savior and instead to follow him into the world of worldly cares. Gregory turned the long-standing interpretation on its head. After all, did not the Savior say, "And I will make you fishers of men"?[23]

Just as interesting as the fresh interpretation is the audience—the laity. While sermons by monks (rare entities) and priests (more common) always exhorted the laity to aspire to the contemplative life, holding that out as the (near impossible) goal, Gregory invites the laity to live fully in service to each other. Contemplate God in his beauty and engage neighbors in their need. As Gregory points out, Jesus is a man of prayer and action. What is required is the grace of God and then both the motivation (love of God) and the action (love of neighbor) that it fosters.

Gregory's contemporaries most often interpreted Scripture to inspire asceticism. Gregory did this too, but the social dimensions he consistently points out are unique. On Trinity Sunday, with a trinitarian text before him (Jn 15:12),

---

[23]Gregory, *Homiliae in Evangelia* 5.2, 3.

Gregory preached on envy, greed, spiritual contest, and becoming indifferent to material loss—all in a context of the harm to neighbor that comes from inattention to these vices and virtues. The work of spiritual improvement is for the sake of the other, not for self.

The two ends of the pastor's life reinforce rather than oppose each other. Gregory argues in his exhaustive commentary on Ezekiel that the carnal reading serves self and the spiritual reading serves neighbor. Ascetic practice aids us in seeing the spiritual text because the ascetic has become accustomed to the things of God. Ascetic practice is therefore necessary; the laity, who lack this practice, will never be able to interpret a text well. But the truly spiritual man uses his superior reading to aid the neighbor.[24]

A further aid to the exegete and ascetic is active service. Activity helps the memory, and learning spiritual principles is deepened by exercising the principles. Learning is retained by doing.

The activities that Gregory suggested (and perhaps commanded) are varied and often highly specific. The remainder of the second section of *The Pastoral Rule* describes and argues for them. But, again, the life of pastor is to be the constant (even daily) movement from the one to the other—the vertical and the horizontal; the inward and the outward; God and neighbor; Jesus and his flock.

The pastor should be a humble companion to the good yet exercise his authority against sinners: equal to the good, authoritative over the perverted. The Fathers are remembered not because they were rulers but because they were shepherds: "A mother with respect to kindness and a father with respect to discipline."[25] How does the active shepherd know these things? By previous and serious study of the holy.

Again, Gregory points out the fault of some of his clergy. They seek secular assignments, are depressed in their absence, and do not know what to do with quiet, which wearies them. What is worse, by their non-contemplative life they spoil any desire the laity has for spiritual things. Such pastors are abandoning the flock.[26]

And he points out the opposite fault—those who attend exclusively to their spiritual life. These pastors discover that the laity do not listen to sermons

---

[24]Gregory, *Homiliae in Hiezechihelem* 1.5.3; 1.8.17; 1.6.2-4.

[25]Gregory, *Pastoral Rule* 2.6.

[26]Gregory, *Pastoral Rule* 2.7.

because they do not respect or trust those who do not attend to their needs. "Doctrine does not penetrate the mind of the needy if the hand of compassion does not commend it to the soul."[27] This is a painful lesson many of us learned early, and it was most wise of Gregory to warn us.

A spiritual director will meet the needs of the people, and that will please them, but their sense of their needs may be mistaken. The spiritual director must know what *ought* to please them. But not pleasing them has its own troubles too. So what is one to do? Love them, occasionally concede to them, let them speak, win them over, and then use their affection for you to turn them toward the Truth (capitalized almost always by Gregory).[28]

This nurture and discipline of the flock is difficult, and it is made more difficult when, as often happens, a vice masquerades as a virtue. The spiritual leader must be able to detect this in order to benefit the laity, who must be encouraged in some things and dissuaded from others. The pastor gains this knowledge both by contemplation of the holy and by knowledge of the flock.[29]

Nurture and discipline of the flock is further complicated by needing to know when to discipline with gentleness and when to do so with severity. Sometimes there should be a judicious tolerance of known vice; sometimes there should be a keen investigation into concealed vice. The readiness and ability of the laity to be disciplined largely determines this. Are they ready to be corrected? Will they receive the correction with good result? In these matters, the two commitments of the pastor help each other. From their own experience as disciples, pastors can know how well discipline will be tolerated in others. And they must remember their own vices, known only by self-examination, when correcting the vices of others. Moreover, it is beneficial if pastors restrain their tongue from the things they want to say when saying the things that need to be said.[30] All of this is the result of the pastor's study of Scripture, "meditating daily on the precepts of the sacred Word."[31]

The spiritual leader as guide. The third section, by far the longest, tells with exacting detail how spiritual guides should guide. The details need not concern us here, but reading this will be a delight to anyone interested in the care and cure of souls. It is still good advice.

---

[27]Gregory, *Pastoral Rule* 2.7.
[28]Gregory, *Pastoral Rule* 2.8.
[29]Gregory, *Pastoral Rule* 2.9.
[30]Gregory, *Pastoral Rule* 2.10.
[31]Gregory, *Pastoral Rule* 2.11.

What interests us in this section is Gregory's insistence that great care must be given to knowing well the person to whom one is offering spiritual advice. The differences among congregants are great, so it is important to counsel each one differently. What is more, even in teaching larger groups it is important to know each one who is present so that one sermon can reach all the listeners equally well. Here is the prologue of his argument:

> Because we have already shown how the pastor should live, let us now demonstrate what he is to teach. Indeed, long before us, Gregory of Nazianzus of blessed memory taught that one and the same exhortation is not suited for everyone because not everyone shares the same quality of character.[32] For example, what often helps some people will cause harm in others, just as herbs that are nutritious to some animals will kill others or the way that gentle hissing will calm a horse but excite a puppy. Likewise, the medicine that cures one disease will spur another, and the bread that fortifies a grown man can kill a young child. Therefore, the discourse of the teacher should be adapted to the character of his audience so that it can address the specific needs of each individual and yet never shrink from the art of communal edification.[33]

A list follows of thirty-six differences—often posed as opposite qualities and tendencies—of which the spiritual counselor must be aware and reminded when ministering to the laity. Some of the pairs listed are obvious—men and women; young and old; poor and rich. Some are less obvious and more nuanced—those who fear punishment and therefore live innocently, and those who have become so hardened in iniquity that they cannot be corrected by punishment; those who deplore the sins of action and those who deplore sins of thought; those who are overcome by unexpected desires and those who bind themselves deliberately in sin; and (my favorite) those who misinterpret the words of sacred Scripture and those who understand them but do not speak about them with humility.[34]

The long remainder of the third section is an explication of how best to approach, speak to, entreat, admonish, warn, encourage, absolve, and condemn each person and each proclivity. Again, this is best read for oneself (or perhaps I should say, influenced by Gregory, read for the sake of others).[35]

---

[32]Gregory is paraphrasing Gregory of Nazianzus, *An Apology for His Flight to Pontus* Or. 2.
[33]Gregory, *Pastoral Rule*, prologue to book 3.
[34]Gregory, *Pastoral Rule* 3.1.
[35]Gregory, *Pastoral Rule* 3.2-40.

The final very brief section is a warning. Simply put, the one who practices these things and even masters these things is at risk of pride—a pride that will disqualify the pastor from the work of spiritual leadership. Alas, the congregation will grow healthy from the sermons but the preacher will become ill. The seducer flatters. What to do?

> Thus it is necessary that when we are flattered by a wealth of virtues, we must turn the eye of our mind to our infirmity and allow it to humble itself. It should not look at the good things that it has done, but at those things that it has neglected, so that when the heart reflects upon its infirmity, it will be all the more strongly established before the Author of humility.[36]

The picture of the pope's preferred partners in gospel ministry has now been painted fully. Humility is central in that portrait—painted by Gregory with shades and tones unused by his predecessors. The humble act of the one who pleases God is not only in the denial of the world by pursuit of the contemplative life but also in the denial of the contemplative life to reenter the world and offer the self in service. Gregory will tenderly conclude *The Pastoral Rule* with these words:

> Behold, good man, being compelled by the necessity of your request, I have tried to show what the qualities of a spiritual director ought to be. Alas, I am like a poor painter who tries to paint the ideal man. I am trying to point others to the shore of perfection, as I am tossed back and forth by the waves of sin in the shipwreck of this life, I beg you to sustain me with the plank of your prayers, so that your merit-filled hands might lift me up, since my own weight causes me to sink.[37]

The Pastoral Rule has become the most widely read and influential work of pastoral care and spiritual direction in the history of Christendom. Gregory will be the only Latin author in late antiquity to have a work translated into Greek during his lifetime. There had been earlier important authors who wrote on the subject—Ambrose, Augustine, Chrysostom, Gregory of Nazianzus. They too spent time discerning who should and should not assume the offices. But Gregory will offer the most detailed description of the skills needed in the one who is called. He will be the only one to argue at length, so persistently and effectively, that the call, given to the contemplative, must be lived out in active service in the church—for the sake of others as well as for the sake of the one called.

---

[36]Gregory, *Pastoral Rule* 4.
[37]Gregory, *Pastoral Rule* 4.

TWO BROTHERS

Gregory is faulted by our contemporaries for writing the *Dialogues*, a compendium of stories of the saints. They are without intellectual challenge and lack careful research or even critical judgment, it is said—just stories, of which the Middle Ages will tell too often. But Gregory used the form of hagiography to teach what he had more rigorously expounded in sermons, letters, commentaries, and *The Pastoral Rule*—the values of the active life among the ascetics. By the *Dialogues*, Gregory will show, like no hagiographer before him, both virtue and vice in the lives of saints, thus showing the distinction between those lives—holy though they may be—that were expended on the self and those expended for others.

Let this one story illustrate and conclude: Two men in Nursia, Euthicius and Florentius, brothers perhaps, were both holy, says Gregory as he tells this story to his deacon, Peter. Euthicius was called to be the abbot of the local community. He was faithful to his task of serving others, laboring by exhortation constantly to win souls to God. Florentius, free from such obligations, developed an extraordinary spirituality. As Gregory tells the story, a bear bowed before him and, on assignment from the spiritually great Florentius, this bear became the shepherd of the same flock of sheep that he formerly had been devouring. The fame of Florentius, living a strictly contemplative life, grew far and wide. But jealousy in the abbot's community grew; four monks slew the bear. Florentius was so angry that he cursed the four monks. They died shortly after, and miserably, from leprosy. The hermit Florentius had acted badly. Euthicius, however, counseled Florentius wisely and did not curse in return. The abbot long had practiced the humility of serving others. He had been engaged in the active life and thus developed additional graces that Florentius had not, like patience with others, suppressing the need for revenge, and being sympathetic to sinners. Gregory is sure to add that Euthicius also was able to perform miracles—miracles of greater meaning because of greater service to the people (not just sheep), miracles that have continued to protect the citizens of the city even into his day of the Lombards, he notes with great care. Here at the story's end, Gregory gives the highest praise to the active abbot—highest praise because his holiness stooped to serve.[38]

---

[38]Gregory, *Dialogorum* 3.15.

CONTEMPLATION AND ACTION TODAY

Gregory the Great lived and recommended an active contemplative discipleship (Or is it a contemplative active discipleship?). He argues and models that the Christian life has two poles and pulls, each of which is essential to faithfulness before God and usefulness to others. The one draws us to God—"Come unto me all ye"; the other sends us out—"Go ye into all the world." Gregory was faced with these questions constantly. In his life, letters, and legacy he leaves us well-argued answers. Our calls given by Christ to come to him and to minister to others can be made more clear, and we can respond clearly with Gregory's help. I have found this to be so in life and ministry.

Gregory's challenges as pope only somewhat parallel my (Jerry) own calling. His calling was to invite/command those who had long and sincerely committed to a contemplative life to give up a portion of it in order to become active in the life of God's saints—encouraging monks to take on the assignment of abbots or parish priests. My call to active ministry preceded my life as an avid reader, practicing thinker, and sometime writer, but contemplation soon followed. I still lament my poor prayer habits. In late college I learned the joy of reading significant authors—reading beyond classroom assignments. In seminary I first began to contemplate at length while reading closely great texts. My first pastorate included a requirement to be in every home every year—a full engagement with real people with an acknowledged real need for a pastor to be close to them. Soon the two developed in tandem.

Among my contemporaries, the call to an active pastorate is often better developed and practiced than is sustained study and committed contemplation. The call now, it seems to me, is to effectively attract the busy pastor into a sabbath rest with Christ. The public too often trumps the intimate and the urgent takes precedence over the important.

I found Gregory to be helpful in persuading me that I may not neglect one for the sake of the other. Further, the pastoral call is not so much about balance (inevitably attempted by less of the one, then less of the other) as it is about pursuing both the active ministry and the contemplative life. On the one hand, pastors are to emerge from their study (but must be in their study in the first place); on the other hand (and here I regard Gregory as speaking to me), they cannot retreat to the prayer room if they have not engaged the battles of the day. Or, as my father would say, sabbath is only for those who work six days a week.

I confess that I would quickly retreat to the study whenever there was perplexity in ministry or failure, especially if there was a wound. Sometimes I simply did not know a sure way forward with a person or program, so I picked up another book and read until . . . well, until it was no longer possible. It was unimaginative, lazy, and cowardly of me. The grace of God toward me includes not only that I did not develop a worse recourse, and that this fault was shown to me and was challenged until it diminished, but that God used my fault to his own pleasure to form me as a reader of his Word and as one glad to engage in conversations with those who have lived and died the faith before me.

Reading Gregory has persuaded me that I cannot get more of Jesus by contemplation of him alone. I must engage others. The classroom of Christ is no less in the street and suite—with the pagan neighbor and the church member, by conversing with those who will live and die in the faith after me—than it is when alone with Christ, the psalmist, or Gregory.

Yes, my meditating on the things of God blesses me, and yes, Christ has called me to be a blessing to others. The story of Job worked for Gregory; Jonah works well for me. In Nineveh, at the story's end, he finally contemplated after becoming exhausted by the work of the ministry. The story of Mary and Martha also works especially well for me. While I may have learned and long cherished what is "the better part," people also need to eat. The kitchen is not to be despised.

From the heights of conversation with Christ, I must converse with my neighbor for whom Christ died and now lives: a holiness, such as it is, that stoops to serve.

When we read about Gregory's life and work, we are invited to ask many foundational questions about our own discipleship of following Christ and our own ministry in his name.

QUESTIONS FOR DISCUSSION

♦ Do you think of Christ's call to you as first to himself, then to his mission? Love of God and love of neighbor are positioned together by Christ. How can you, called by Christ, be faithful to both calls all at once?

♦ Tension is heightened in the life and work of those whom Christ calls to lead his people. Even the simple call to "follow me" is paired with "I will make you fishers of men." Is the contemplative life or the active life more foundational for you as a leader of the people of God?

- To which—the active or contemplative—are you by nature more easily disposed? By training more prepared to do well? By particular calling more required to perform daily? At the end of your days, in which will you have majored; in which will you have minored?

- Where in your life and ministry are the two pulls and poles best integrated? Where least?

- What commitments can you make now, and what disciplines can you begin immediately, that will best form you to follow through fully on the dual invitation of Christ to come and follow him?

FOR FURTHER READING

Baxter, Richard. *The Reformed Pastor*. Carlisle, PA: Banner of Truth, 1974.

Dawn, Marva. *The Sense of the Call: A Sabbath Way of Life for Those Who Serve God, the Church, and the World*. Grand Rapids: Eerdmans, 2006.

Ferguson, Sinclair. *Some Pastors and Teachers: Reflecting a Biblical Vision of What Every Minister Is Called to Be*. Carlisle, PA: Banner of Truth, 2017.

Lathrop, Gordon. *The Pastor: A Spirituality*. Minneapolis: Fortress Press, 2011.

Peterson, Eugene. *The Pastor: A Memoir*. New York: HarperOne, 2011.

4

" *All the* 𝕸inisters *Shall* 𝕸eet Together"

JOHN CALVIN

𝖂HEN MARTIN LUTHER posted his Ninety-Five Theses on true repentance at the Wittenberg Castle church in 1517, John Calvin was an eight-year-old French schoolboy. He was first introduced to the Reform movement sparked by Luther during his university studies at Paris and Orléans, eventually leading to what he called a "sudden conversion" to the Reformation movement. Calvin's active commitment to the cause of the *évangéliques* made life in Catholic France risky, necessitating periodic withdrawals to the Swiss cities of Basel and Strasbourg.

Three crucial events in 1536 shaped the future of Reformed Protestantism. First, John Calvin published a small, pocket-sized book, *Institutes of the Christian Religion*, which he would revise and expand in subsequent Latin and French editions in 1539, 1543, 1550, and 1559. Second, a public assembly of the citizens of Geneva voted in May to "live henceforth according to the law of the gospel and the word of God, and to abolish all papal abuses." Finally, in August, John Calvin arrived in Geneva, intending to stay the night before continuing his journey to Strasbourg.

Calvin's little *Institutes* had not received wide recognition, but it was known to Guillaume Farel, the leading Reformer in Geneva, who prevailed on Calvin to remain in the city to help consolidate the new religious situation. Consolidation was an urgent necessity, for the citizens of Geneva had rejected the Catholic

Church without affirming anything definite. Living according to the gospel and the Word of God required a new form of church, but all Geneva had was a reform-minded void.

In this novel situation, the city council assumed ecclesiastical as well as civil authority. It was the council, not Farel and certainly not Calvin, that controlled the religious affairs of Geneva. It soon became apparent that the council was not amenable to many of Calvin's proposals for reforming the church, and it further asserted its right to shape ecclesial life. Calvin's forceful counterassertions that the church, not the civil government, had jurisdiction over sacramental practice, church discipline, and ministerial appointments led the council to expel Calvin and Farel in the spring of 1538. Calvin's three-year exile in Strasbourg, where he became pastor of the French-speaking Reformed congregation, deepened his views on church reform and enhanced his reputation. Geneva invited him back to stay in 1541.

Calvin was a second-generation Reformer, an inheritor of the Reformation's central theological trajectories. Among the remaining tasks, however, was the shaping of Christian communities that would be capable of ensuring the proclamation of re-formed faith and the nurturing of re-formed faithfulness. Thus, the nature and purpose of the church and its ordered ministries endured as a central concern throughout Calvin's life. The church was central in all his writing, and the task of giving new shape to the life of the church was central to his labors in Geneva.

The nature and purpose of the church and its ministries is an issue in every time and place. What do *we* mean by the word *church*? Everyday speech gives voice to a jumble of meanings tumbling over one another: buildings, people, congregations, organizations, judicatories, denominations, world communions, all Christians everywhere, and more, all with variations that further complicate the sense of *church*. What we mean by *church* is more than a matter of vocabulary, for the church is central in the reception, preservation, and transmission of Christian faith and faithfulness. Following Cyprian and Augustine, John Calvin spoke of the church as "the common mother of the godly": "There is no other way to enter into life," said Calvin, "unless this mother conceive us in her womb, give us birth, nourish us at her breast, and lastly, unless she keep us under her care and guidance . . . until we have been pupils all our lives."[1]

---

[1] John Calvin, *Institutes of the Christian Religion*, ed. John T. McNeill, trans., Ford Lewis Battles (Philadelphia: Westminster Press, 1960), 4.1.4.

What do we mean by *church*? Answering this is the work of ecclesiology—the doctrine of the church—which is not confined to academic theologians or ecumenical enthusiasts. Understanding the "who, what, when, where, why, and how" of the church is a critical, often-neglected practical theological task of pastors, who bear significant responsibility for shaping patterns of congregational faith and life. While most pastors labor to develop congregational faith and mission, the basic given-ness of the church is simply assumed. Pastors may assess its spiritual health, appraise its missional fidelity, and evaluate its management, but what "it" is remains elusive.

Pastoral attention that focuses simply on improving what *is* becomes vulnerable to religious market forces, catering to real or imagined needs. Needed in every age is serious, sustained attention to the fundamental nature and purpose of the people of God in the world. Similarly, apart from an understanding of the church's character and intention, members will be set adrift to engage in comparison shopping, measuring churches by their capacity to provide appealing and satisfying religious goods and services. Understanding what the church is and what it is intended to be is not only an academic but a spiritual matter for all Christians.

In our time of ecclesial disarray, marked by denominational divisions and cultural disestablishment, it may be worthwhile to give renewed attention to Calvin's reform of the church's character and structure, especially to his formation and cultivation of the church's *ministries*. Calvin's understanding of the pastor's vocation cannot be appreciated apart from his conviction that pastoral ministry within the congregation is to be lived in collaboration with two other ordered ministries—elders and deacons—within the ministry of the whole people of God. Furthermore, Calvin believed that pastoral ministry is to be lived within relationships of mutual responsibility and accountability among pastors.

Calvin did not write a formal pastoral rule. Nevertheless, the elements of his hopes and expectations for pastors are evident throughout his writings and in the practices of the church in Geneva. Calvin's pastoral "rule" is best appreciated within his understanding of the faith and life of the whole people of God. The starting point, then, is his conviction that Word and sacrament are the core of the church's life, followed by his insight into the unified plural ministry of the church, and concluding with his rule for pastoral ministry.

A CHURCH OF THE WORD AND SACRAMENT

The sixteenth-century Swiss Reformation's distinct approach to the nature and purpose of the church began with Christ, not with the church itself.[2] According to the Ten Theses of Berne (1528), an early Reformed confession of faith, "The holy Christian Church, whose only head is Christ, is born of the Word of God, and abides in the same, and listens not to the voice of a stranger."[3] For Calvin, the church's meaning begins with Jesus Christ, revealed to us in Scripture. As a creation of the Word, the church comes into being continuously through the real presence of the living Christ in the power of the Holy Spirit.

How do we know this creature of the Word when we see it? Together with Luther, Calvin said that the church becomes visible through the Word and sacrament—preaching and teaching, baptism and Eucharist: "Wherever we see the Word of God purely preached and heard, and the sacraments administered according to Christ's institution, there, it is not to be doubted, a church of God exists."[4] The right proclamation and hearing of God's Word and the faithful celebration of baptism and the Lord's Supper are clear indicators of the one, holy, catholic, and apostolic church. Although churches engage in many other forms of ministry and mission, Calvin was convinced that at the heart of it all, shaping and animating everything else, must be God's living and present Word in the means of grace.

Calvin's two marks of the church center on lived faith within congregations. He validates a church's fidelity not by its orthodox doctrine or its sacramental theology, much less by its ecclesiastical structures, but by the presence of faithful proclamation, reception, and sacramental life. His marks of the church point us to congregations, not academies; to assemblies of people, not libraries; to worship, not books. For Calvin, doctrinal purity and sacramental precision are subordinate to our fundamental ecclesial faithfulness that allows the gospel to be received, believed, and lived by ordinary men and women. Proclamation and sacraments are more than liturgical activities and certainly more than the memory of a long ago and faraway Jesus; they are the primary means of uniting with Christ.

---

[2]Much of this section first appeared in Joseph D. Small, "A Call and Response Ecclesiology," https://pres-outlook.org/wp-content/uploads/2013/12/www.pcusa.org_media_uploads_oga_pdf_call_and_response_ecclesiology.pdf.

[3]"The Ten Conclusions of Berne," in *Creeds of the Churches*, 3rd ed., ed. John A. Leith (Louisville, KY: Westminster John Knox, 1982), 129.

[4]Calvin, *Institutes* 4.1.9.

In Calvin's understanding, Word and sacrament share precisely the same function: they are the clearest means by which the risen, living Lord reveals himself to us. "Therefore, let it be regarded as a settled principle," says Calvin, "that the sacraments have the same office as the Word of God: to offer and set forth Christ to us, and in him the treasures of heavenly grace."[5] In baptism, Eucharist, and Scripture preaching and teaching, "it is therefore certain that the Lord offers us mercy and the pledge of his grace both in his Sacred Word and in his sacraments."[6] Word and sacrament are identifiers of the church because they are the action of Christ for us in the power of the Holy Spirit. The church flourishes when the living Word of God—preached, taught, heard, seen, felt, tasted—is unconstrained. Conversely, when the means of grace are suppressed, distorted, veiled, or marginalized, the church is deformed, even if its ordered structures endure.

We should not imagine that in marking the church by Word and sacrament Calvin was thinking only of the church's worship—the Sunday sermon, the baptism of an infant, and the celebration of the Lord's Supper. Proclamation of the Word includes multiple forms of teaching and study: studying the Bible, reciting catechisms, singing psalms, and learning the church's creeds, commandments, and prayers "by heart" are all instances of the Word's daily presence in the body of believers. Perhaps most significantly, Calvin added two little words, "and heard," to the pure preaching of the Word, making explicit his intention that all forms of proclamation should be received and lived by God's people. Proclaiming the Word leads to living the Word, and both together are a mark of ecclesial faithfulness.

Similarly, baptism and Eucharist encompass patterns of life beyond the church's walls. The Calvin-inspired confession of the French Reformed churches declares that "In Baptism we are grafted into the body of Christ, washed and cleansed by his blood, and renewed in holiness of life by his Spirit. Although we are baptized only once, the benefit it signifies lasts through life and death."[7] Correspondingly, the confession declares that "the holy Supper of the Lord is a testimony of our unity with Jesus Christ. He died only once and was raised for our

---

[5] Calvin, *Institutes* 4.14.17.
[6] Calvin, *Institutes* 4.14.7.
[7] The French Confession of 1559, trans. Ellen Babinsky and Joseph D. Small (Louisville, KY: Office of Theology and Worship, 1998), §35, p. 16.

sake, yet we are truly fed and nourished by his flesh and blood. Thus, we are made one with him and his life is communicated to us."[8] The sacraments' power to unite us to Christ extends beyond the moment of their administration and into our continuing sanctification.

More than mere nostalgia for Reformation clarity, the application of Word and sacraments provides the twenty-first-century church with foundational identifiers of ecclesial faithfulness. Each congregation (and denomination) should ask whether Word and sacrament are found at the heart of its common life. Other church activities are important, of course, but they must not bury these means of grace or push them to the periphery. Furthermore, the whole range of church programs must remain subject to authentication by Word and sacrament, for these crucial realities are the embodiment of the gospel of Christ in the life of his people. For Calvin, and for us, Word and sacrament stand as the controlling core and marks of the church's true life.

UNIFIED PLURAL MINISTRY

Churches of the Word and sacrament do not happen automatically, nor is their continuing faithfulness assured.[9] Calvin was clear that the necessary, continual reform of the church is based on the three pillars of "doctrine," "administering the sacraments," and "governing the church."[10] It is important to note that Calvin employs *doctrine* and *preaching* interchangeably. He understands doctrine not as a set of abstract formulations but as truth best known in faithful proclamation, which is why he was also clear that ministry—the pastoral office—is essential to the revival and maintenance of the church's faithful theology, worship, and order. "Neither the light and heat of the sun, nor food and drink, are so necessary to nourish and sustain the present life," Calvin asserted, "as the apostolic and pastoral office is necessary to preserve the church on earth."[11]

Calvin and other sixteenth-century Reformers held pastoral ministry in high regard because they were convinced that the church's fidelity to the gospel

---

[8]French Confession of 1559, §36, p. 16.

[9]A more detailed treatment of "unified plural ministry" is found in Joseph D. Small, "Undivided Plural Ministry: Ordered Ministries and Episcope in the Reformed Tradition," *Ecumenical Trends* 32.1 (2003).

[10]John Calvin, "The Necessity of Reforming the Church," in *Calvin: Theological Treatises*, ed. and trans. J. K. S. Reid (Philadelphia: Westminster Press, 1964), 184-216.

[11]Calvin, *Institutes* 4.3.2.

depends on proclamation of the Word in preaching, teaching, and sacramental life; on worship that glorifies God; and on church order that honors the Spirit's leading. By virtue of its vocation to proclaim the Word and teach the faith, the ministerial office was "the chief sinew by which believers are held together in one body."[12]

Therefore, the foundational elements in Calvin's pastoral rule emerge from the centrality of Word and sacrament. First, pastors must engage in continual study of Scripture and the faith of the church so that they are equipped to preach and teach the gospel with integrity. Study is not preparation for ministry, it is central to ministry itself. Second, pastors must celebrate the sacraments with theological integrity and pastoral sensitivity so that the presence of Christ is perceived, received, and lived by the congregation. Third, pastors must ensure that Word and sacrament live beyond the Lord's Day worship, animating the church's other ministries and missions.

As essential as pastors are to ministry, Calvin does not confine his understanding of the church to this office alone. His reading of the New Testament led him to commend four offices of ministry: pastors, teachers, elders, and deacons. Rather than thinking of these ministries as a differentiated quadrilateral, Calvin understood them as plural offices within two ecclesial functions: ministries of the Word performed by presbyters (pastor-teachers and elders) and ministries of service performed by deacons (caring directly for refugees, the poor, sick, and dispossessed). He further held that these presbyterial and diaconal ministries are plural expressions of the church's one undivided ministry.

Calvin's distinctive approach to the church's ordered ministries is clearly seen in his transformation of the office of deacon. The Catholic Church's deacons were future priests, distinct from the laity. In the emerging Lutheran churches, deacons were now laity—usually civil servants—charged with care for the poor. But for Geneva's Reformed ecclesiology and practice, deacons were church members who held ecclesiastical office as an essential component of the church's ministry. Although all Christians share diaconal responsibilities, Calvin charged ordered deacons with leading the whole church in works of mercy and justice. They were no longer a subset of another order of ministry, nor were they removed from the church's orders of ministry. Instead, they held

---

[12]Calvin, *Institutes* 4.3.2.

dual vocations—secular and ecclesial. Deacons were church members called and ordained as one of the "orders of office instituted by our Lord for the government of his Church."[13]

Calvin's understanding of the deacon reflects two key features of his approach to the church's ordered ministries. First, he resisted clericalism and constructed a pattern of ministry that breaks down the distinction between clergy and laity by instituting two so-called lay ecclesial ministries—deacon and elder. Second, the church's various ministries are corporate, both within and among the orders. No person or order of ministry can function apart from its essential relationship to other orders. For instance, the corporate character of Calvin's orders of ministry is evident in the exercise of ecclesial discipline. Pastors are called "to proclaim the Word of God, to instruct, admonish, exhort and censure, both in public and in private, to administer the sacraments and to enjoin brotherly correction *along with the elders and colleagues*."[14] Discipline—a combination of church governance and pastoral care—is a corporate responsibility shared within a council of pastors and elders.

Calvin's plurality of ministries seeks to break open the ministry of the whole people of God. His ordering of ministry in the church gives visible form to the "priesthood of all believers" while protecting the church against the potential abuses of clericalism. Distinctions between clergy and laity are so deliberately broken down that these very terms are ill-suited to Calvin's ecclesiology. All ordered ministries are exercised in, with, and for the whole church, and all are bound together in the common task of ensuring the church's fidelity to the Word. Furthermore, the church's ministries remain undivided. Any ministerial act performed by a pastor, elder, or deacon is done on behalf of the whole ministry; no one may act independently as the representative of Christ.

Contemporary Reformed and Presbyterian churches retain the form of Calvin's unified plural ministry, although not always its substance. While other ecclesial traditions embody different forms of ordered ministry, Calvin's insight of pastoral ministry as a shared vocation is directly relevant to the life and work of all pastors, whatever their church's polity. Today, in far too many congregations, pastors act as CEOs of an organization, working to rationalize mission, enhance efficiency, and increase market share. Elected congregational councils act as a

---

[13]John Calvin, "Draft Ecclesiastical Ordinances" in Reid, *Calvin: Theological Treatises*, 58.
[14]Calvin, "Draft Ecclesiastical Ordinances," 58 (emphasis added).

board of directors that reviews and approves management's programs and strategy and monitors financial and property assets. Diaconal ministries are often confined to personal services within the congregation.

Calvin's understanding of the shape of pastoral ministry assumes that pastors are never unaccompanied in their calling. Whatever the specific shape of a church's governance, Calvin's vision presupposes that pastoral ministry is lived out in deep, abiding companionship with others. Partnership within the congregation means far more than an obligatory bow to "the ministry of the laity." Rather, Calvin's pastoral rule insists that ministry takes place among those whom a congregation has called to specific forms of service, whether administrative, educational, liturgical, or missional.

Calvin's vision also assumes that each pastor will live out ministry in deep, abiding companionship with neighboring pastors, which means far more than common service in a judicatory. Rather, ministry is to be lived within a shared vocation marked by regular study, prayer, mutual accountability, and common mission. Both within and beyond the congregation, all are to act as "good stewards of God's varied grace" (1 Pet 4:10). Their mutual calling is to proclaim clearly the grace of the Lord Jesus Christ, the love of God, and the communion of the Holy Spirit, nurturing congregational fidelity to God's new Way in the world. Calvin's pastoral rule requires that ministry be lived collegially with other pastors as a demonstration of the church's unity.

THE GENEVA CONSISTORY AND
THE COMPANY OF PASTORS

Restored unity of the whole church was beyond Calvin's reach, and the Reformation churches themselves were embroiled in divisive doctrinal disputes. It was possible, however, to ensure the unity of the Geneva churches. Calvin understood that "some form of organization is necessary in all human society to foster the common peace and maintain concord." He went on to say that "this ought especially to be observed in churches, which are best sustained when all things are under a well-ordered constitution, and which without concord become no churches at all."[15] Thus, the organization of the church in Geneva included ecclesiastical ordinances, provision for the visitation of churches, a common catechism,

---

[15]Calvin, *Institutes* 4.10.27.

liturgy, the Psalter, the Geneva Academy, and two quite remarkable institutions, the Geneva Consistory and the Venerable Company of Pastors. Both the consistory and the Company of Pastors are corporate embodiments of Calvin's pastoral rule. Their shape was set out by Calvin in his ecclesiastical ordinances of 1541.

The Geneva Consistory. The Geneva Consistory was composed of twelve elders together with the pastors of Geneva and the surrounding villages (beginning with nine and growing over the years to nineteen). It was responsible for church order and discipline. The consistory's composition freed church affairs from exclusive control by pastors, and it progressively liberated the church from the jurisdiction of the magistracy.

Community governance. "The elders are to assemble once a week with the ministers, that is to say on Thursday morning, to see that there be no disorder in the Church and to discuss together remedies as they are required."[16]

Popular mythology portrays Calvin as "the dictator of Geneva" who instituted a "reign of terror," policing every aspect of civil and personal life. This characterization has been debunked repeatedly, but it persists nevertheless. Actually, throughout Calvin's service in Geneva, church discipline—a combination of governance and pastoral care—was the responsibility of the pastors and elders together, meeting weekly as a council. Recent publication of the consistory minutes shows that the body dealt sensitively with most matters coming before it.[17] The pastors and elders devoted much of their time to family disputes, mistreatment of wives by their husbands, public flouting of civic and ecclesial authority, marital infidelity, and family disputes over inheritance.

The consistory was composed of elders and ministers from the three churches within Geneva proper. Other churches were scattered in small country villages throughout greater Geneva. Each of the country churches was visited annually to inquire into the well-being of the congregation and the fidelity of the minister. Among the matters explored in the visitation was attendance at worship and whether the people "found profit in it for Christian living."[18] The people of the church were asked "whether the Minister preaches edifyingly, or whether there be anything . . . unfitting to the instruction of the people because it is obscure, or

---

[16]Calvin, "Draft Ecclesiastical Ordinances," 70.
[17]Cf. Robert M. Kingdon, ed., *Register of the Consistory at Geneva in the Time of Calvin* (Grand Rapids: Eerdmans, 2000).
[18]John Calvin "Draft Order of Visitation of the Country Churches," in Reid, *Calvin: Theological Treatises,* 74.

treats of superfluous questions, or exercises too great rigour."[19] The purpose of the visitation was to affirm evidence of fidelity and to remedy any defects in faith and life.

The consistory's aim was not punishment but rather resolving conflicts, reconciling disputants, and strengthening personal and congregational faith and faithfulness. When punishment was levied, always as a last resort, it was most often exclusion from the Lord's Table until repentance and restoration were accomplished. Historian Robert Kingdon's detailed review of the consistory's minutes led him to conclude that the body "reflected a real concern for other people. . . . There were many signs of real caring, of a desire to help those in need of help in resolving their personal problems, including their most intimate family problems. To a degree, then, the consistory of Geneva incorporated a real Christian concern, a desire to help one's neighbor."[20]

The Geneva Consistory gave substance to Calvin's conviction that ministering to the people of God is not the sole preserve of clergy and that a functional renewal of clergy-laity partnership in pastoral care is an essential component of faithful church life. Collaboration took form in council, which exercised governance and pastoral care for persons, pastors, and congregations. In many contemporary American congregations, church councils (sessions, vestries, etc.) function as management committees, focusing primarily on budgetary and facility issues. Similarly, judicatories (dioceses, presbyteries, conferences, etc.) tend to deal with organizational, administrative, and business matters. Both congregational councils and judicatories shy away from addressing personal, family, and group beliefs and behaviors, showing more concern for individual rights of privacy than for personal faith and faithfulness.

Calvin understood that reformation of church life is not the right or responsibility of pastors alone. They are not the rescuers of ailing congregations, the renewers of moribund churches, the entrepreneurial managers of thriving congregations, or the sole providers of pastoral care. Calvin's vision of governance entailed shared responsibility for the spiritual health of congregations and their members. His concerns could be ours as well: What is the condition of Word and sacrament in the church? What is the relationship of other church programs

---

[19]Calvin, "Draft Order of Visitation," 74.

[20]Robert M. Kingdon, "Calvin and the Family: The Work of the Consistory in Geneva," *Pacific Theological Review* 17, no. 3 (1984): 18.

and activities to Word and sacrament? Is Christ the living, present Lord of the church? In what ways are members helped to shape Christian lives in families, occupations, and society, and how are they helped to alter destructive behavior?

The church's spiritual leadership should open beyond pastors to encompass a body of church members charged with responsibility for the ministry of God's people in a particular Christian community.

Community faith. "If there be anyone who dogmatizes against the received doctrine, conference is to be held with him. If he listens to reason he is to be dismissed without scandal or dishonor."[21]

The consistory was responsible for the maintenance of evangelical truth. Both Catholic "errors" and enthusiasts' "excesses" were subject to correction through instruction. The principal means of strengthening devotion to evangelical truth were regular preaching, the Catechism of the Church of Geneva, and the Geneva Academy. The consistory required everyone to participate in worship so that they would hear the fullness of the gospel. Sunday and Wednesday worship were strongly encouraged, although provision was made among the three city churches for daily worship, with twenty sermons each week. For his part, Calvin worked to ensure that preaching and teaching in the Geneva churches centered on careful exposition of the biblical text, communicated with sensitivity to the context of the people.

Pastors' responsibility to proclaim the Word of God is central to their calling as "ambassadors of Christ." In a comment on 2 Timothy 2:15, Calvin noted that Paul's metaphor, "rightly handling the word of truth," captures the central purpose of proclamation. He asked what purpose sermons serve if people could read the Bible for themselves. Calvin answered that "Paul assigns to teachers the duty of dividing or cutting, as if a father, in giving food to his children, were dividing the bread, by cutting it into small pieces." Thus he advises Timothy to "cut aright," by which he means "an allotment of the word which is judicious, and which is well suited to the profit of the hearers. Some mutilate it, others tear it, others torture it, others break it in pieces, others, keeping by the outside, (as we have said,) never come to the soul of doctrine." To all these faults Paul contrasts "dividing aright, that is, the manner of explaining which is adapted to edification; for that is the rule by which we must try all interpretation of Scripture."[22]

---

[21]Calvin, "Draft Ecclesiastical Ordinances," 70.

[22]Calvin, *Commentaries on the Epistles to Timothy, Titus, and Philemon* (Grand Rapids: Christian Classics Ethereal Library), 178-79.

Christian doctrine found concise explication in the Geneva Catechism, a "Plan for Instructing Children in the Doctrine of Christ." The catechism rehearsed faith (Apostles' Creed), law (Ten Commandments), prayer (the Lord's Prayer), and sacraments (baptism and the Lord's Supper). It was taught to all children as a way of transmitting evangelical faith to coming generations. The academy, forerunner of the University of Geneva, was established to regularize the training of pastors at the highest theological and pastoral level. The education of both children and pastors was a principal means of establishing and sustaining the young Reformation. The consistory bore special responsibility for dealing with breakdowns in religious education such as absence from worship; failure to learn the creed, commandments, and Lord's Prayer; and neglect of the catechism. The typical remedy was exhortation, repentance, and tutoring rather than punishment. The consistory functioned more like a department of education than a Protestant inquisition.

Contemporary congregations and denominations value diversity. The diversity of the Christian community in age, gender, race, ethnicity, and other natural characteristics is an imperative of the gospel, so the church should strive to make actual commitments to diversity. But many congregations and denominations also value a different kind of diversity—variety in Christian belief. Welcoming wide theological diversity among members is often accompanied by embracing the same among ministers. Our celebration of theological diversity may spring, in part, from a fear of rigid orthodoxy, demanding that everyone march in lockstep. But it also springs from a cultural assumption that religious belief is a private matter and that no one should presume to question another's personal faith. Reducing Christian faith to private opinion was anathema to Calvin, who sought to build a loving community that was grounded in common trust in the gospel and shared patterns of Christian living.

Calvin's understanding maintains that the church's ministry is responsible for teaching the shape of Christian faith. Pastors are not theological free agents, released from obligation to the deep patterns of Christian faith and faithfulness. Expecting pastors and other church officials to teach the faith through preaching, liturgy, educational programs, and other means of witness to the gospel does not mean requiring narrow, severe uniformity. However, expecting that the faith will be taught recognizes that diversity of belief is not always benign. Some church members harbor beliefs about "god," sin, heaven and hell, spirits, prayer, and a host of other "religious" matters that are not only outside the bounds of historic Christian faith but are also harmful to personal and communal well-being. Calvin set a high value on right understanding of God's Way in the world, and he places responsibility for ensuring fidelity to gospel truth in the hands of a corporate body, not the pastor alone.

Community worship. "If anyone is negligent in coming to church, so that a noticeable contempt of the communion of the faithful is evident, or if any show himself contemptuous of the ecclesiastical order, he is to be admonished, and if he prove obedient dismissed in friendliness."[23]

Calvin believed that participation in worship was the chief means of glorifying God, knowing the real presence of Christ in Word and sacrament, and receiving instruction in the faith. He was also clear that worship was the chief means of establishing a *community* of faith, for neglect of worship evidenced contempt for both God and neighbors. Worshipers were expected to learn by heart the Apostles' Creed, the Ten Commandments, and the Lord's Prayer. In a society in which only few could read, knowing these three enabled full participation in worship and provided the essential truths of Christian faith and life.

Consistory registers show that when worshipers did not know the creed, commandments, or Lord's Prayer, they were not punished but rather assigned a tutor, often a child, because children had studied the full catechism. The consistory also required that baptisms occur in public worship (no "emergency" baptisms by midwives) and that both parents be present (previously, fathers had been noticeably absent). For Calvin, common worship was the principal means of shaping a faithful Christian community, so it was essential that the whole community participate actively in all elements of the service.

In our time, worship is an optional activity for many church members. Typically, less than half of a congregation is in the pews on a given Sunday. In an increasingly unchurched American society, dwindling worship attendance produces anxiety among church leaders. This leads, in turn, to a search for ways to make worship more appealing. Strategies tend to focus on matters of style—contemporary music, casual dress, and folksy sermons. Matters of style are not unimportant; Calvin's reformation of worship included "stylistic" innovations such as using the language of the people instead of Latin, dispensing with side chapels

---

[23]Calvin, "Draft Ecclesiastical Ordinances," 70.

that encouraged private devotion rather than corporate worship, initiating congregational singing, and introducing the practices of reciting the creed, singing the Ten Commandments, and praying the Lord's Prayer in common.

Style must not devolve into mere stylishness, however. The question is always whether the form of congregational worship directs persons and the congregation itself to the one God—Father, Son, and Holy Spirit—or diverts attention away from God to worshipers themselves. Concentrating on what people are thought to want or need may result in making worship about us rather than about the grace of the Lord Jesus Christ, the love of God, and the communion of the Holy Spirit.

Calvin understood that worship is the single most powerful shaper of congregational and personal faith and faithfulness, for it is the time in congregational life that the most people are gathered together. The substance of Scripture and prayers, hymns and preaching, sacraments and announcements, children's sermons and choir anthems all form or malform Christian faith and life. That is why Calvin gave exceptional attention to the order, content, and design of worship and why he insisted that people were obligated to gather as a community of faith in grateful worship of God. Calvin's concern for worship cuts against the grain of our individualistic, free choice culture when he equates "negligence in coming to church" with "contempt of the community of the faithful." Regular participation in worship is a mark of love of neighbors as well as love of God. Few contemporary American churches will call persons and families to account for neglecting worship, but it is possible to convey the Christian responsibility to worship God rather than promote stylistic inducements.

Community discipline. "As for each man's conduct, for the correction of faults, proceedings should be in accordance with the order which our Lord commands. Yet all this should be done with such moderation, that there be no rigour by which anyone may be injured; for even the corrections are only medicine for bringing back sinners to the Lord."[24]

Consistory registers disclose that the most common reasons for appearing before the elders and pastors were domestic conflicts—spousal abuse and quarrels over inheritances, for example—and failure to learn the creed, commandments, and Lord's Prayer. The most common outcomes were reconciliation

---

[24]Calvin, "Draft Ecclesiastical Ordinances," 70.

and instruction. It is notable that domestic disputes, public drunkenness, adultery, and similar matters were dealt with by the church, not the civil authorities, and that, consequently, the aim was personal reformation, not municipal punishment.

There was a time, in the not-too-distant past, when church boards—sessions, vestries, councils—took responsibility for the faith and morals of church members. Regular visitation and periodic intervention was the norm. Today, in most congregations, such a practice would be unthinkable. It is assumed that our life outside of church activities is nobody's business but our own. Our personal, family, and occupational lives are private, immune from the meddling of the church. If we seek counseling from the pastor, this should be confidential. Unspoken "privacy laws" are characteristics of congregational life, and explicit privacy protections for pastors are regularized in judicatories. "The correction of faults" by church councils may not be a possibility in most congregations, but this must not imply indifference to the moral life of persons.

Calvin's ordering of ministries assumes that how Christians live is as crucial as what they believe. Faith and faithfulness are interrelated aspects of lived discipleship, so reformation of personal and corporate *living* and *believing* are equally important. How spouses treat one another and how parents and children relate are central to Christian faith. Individual captivity to alcohol abuse or gambling addiction are moral issues that are the proper concern of the Christian community. Teenage girls' struggles with cultural images of ideal body types and teenage boys' fascination with violent, often misogynistic video games call for pastoral care. Church members' work lives—where they spend far more time than in church—are central to their *Christian* vocation. The Geneva Consistory was an appropriate communal vehicle for encouraging personal and corporate morality. The ministry of the consistory demonstrates Calvin's rule that pastoral care is not the sole province of the pastor but must become an explicit ministry shared with the congregation's elders and deacons.

The Venerable Company of Pastors. When Calvin returned to Geneva from Strasbourg in 1541, he set out to assemble and maintain a company of ministers who were committed to Reformed evangelical faith, competent interpreters of Scripture, and dedicated to pastoral duties. Central to this undertaking was his conviction that committed, competent, and dedicated individuals serving unconnected parishes would not sustain reformation of faith and life in Geneva. If the gospel were to take root among the people, the Geneva parishes—three within the walled city and sixteen in the surrounding countryside—had to share a common life, and their pastors had to share a collegial ministry.

Calvin was certain that faithful Christian faith and life within and among congregations depended on faithful Christian community among their pastors. What he understood about life within a congregation applies equally to his understanding of pastors' lives:

> For if anyone were sufficient to himself and needed no one else's help (such is the pride of human nature), each man would despise the rest and be despised by them. The Lord has therefore bound his church together with a knot that he foresaw would be the strongest means of keeping unity, while he entrusted to men the teaching of salvation and everlasting life in order that through their hands it might be communicated to the rest.[25]

Geneva's Company of Pastors was Calvin's instrument for ensuring that pastors joined one another in bonds of mutual responsibility and that through them Geneva's congregations joined in communion with one another. The Company of Pastors met together regularly to engage in biblical and theological study, encourage and challenge one another on their preaching and pastoral conduct, examine and recommend placement of ministers, and make provision for missionary work in neighboring countries. Together with the consistory, the Company of Pastors formed the reformation nucleus of the church in Geneva.

Corporate Scripture. "First it will be expedient that all the ministers, for preserving purity and concord among themselves, meet together one certain day each week, for discussion of the Scriptures."[26]

Geneva's Venerable Company of Pastors embodied Calvin's commitment to collegial leadership. Pastors and their congregations were not to be autonomous but rather bound together in a multifaceted pattern of mutuality. Notably, pastors were responsible for and accountable to one another in all aspects of their ministry. Pastors' accountability began with their capacity to read, interpret, and employ Scripture in service of their congregations. Thus, when the company met each Friday morning at 7:00 in the Cathédrale St. Pierre or the adjacent Auditoire (formerly the Notre-Dame-la-Neuve Chapel), portions of Scripture were discussed in systematic order, led by one of the pastors. Variously called the

---

[25]Calvin, *Institutes* 4.3.2.
[26]Calvin, "Draft Ecclesiastical Ordinances," 60.

congrégation, conference des Escriptures, or *colloque,* the weekly Bible study may have been ordered according to Calvin's lectures on Scripture, but leadership was shared by all pastors.

The Scripture study portion of the weekly meeting was open to the public—and people came, listening to their pastors expound Scripture, even participating in the discussion following the initial presentation. A contemporary description by a visitor to the city in 1550 provides a glimpse into this remarkable gathering:

> Every week, on Fridays, a conference is held in which all their ministers and many of the people participate. Here one of them reads a passage from Scripture and expounds it briefly. Another speaks on the matter what to him is according to the Spirit. A third person gives his opinion and a fourth adds some things in his capacity to weigh the issue. And not only the ministers do so, but everyone who has come to listen.[27]

Although some contemporary pastors participate in lectionary study groups as a resource for the preparation of sermons, it is intriguing to imagine today's ministers participating in something like Geneva's *congrégation.* It would be a weekly gathering of all pastors in a locality, one of whom would be responsible for presenting a portion of Scripture. All pastors would have studied the text in advance, and some would be designated respondents. The presentation and discussion would take place amid a hundred or so church members, who would also be invited to ask questions and share their views on the passage. The ministers would be responsible to one another and to church members for their knowledge and pastoral application of the Bible.

In one of his many letters, Calvin wrote about the *congrégation,* "Not only for ministers is such training useful, but a number of the people who are led by an outstanding zeal to understand the Scripture experience part of its usefulness. . . . I know there are here pious men, who have no reason to be humble about their learning, who would rather miss two sermons than one exposition of Scripture like those heard here."[28]

---

[27]Pier Paolo Vergerio, as quoted in Eric A. de Boer, "The *Congrégation*: An In-Service Theological Training Center for Preachers to the People of Geneva," in *Calvin and the Company of Pastors,* ed. David Foxgrover, Calvin Studies Society Papers 2003 (Grand Rapids: Christian Reformed Church in North America, 2004), 59.

[28]Calvin, letter to Wolfgang Musculus, quoted in de Boer, "The *Congrégation*," 82.

Corporate theology. "If there appear differences of doctrine, let the ministers come together to discuss the matter. Afterwards, if need be, let them call the elders to assist in composing the contention."[29]

Following the public study of Scripture, the Company of Pastors met in private to discuss scriptural, theological, pastoral, and ecclesiastical matters. Exposition and discussion in the *congrégation* was intended to be edifying to ministers and people alike, so contention was discouraged. In private, however, discussion could be more focused on ministers' doctrinal understanding, including the character and quality of their preaching. It is important to remember that Calvin used *preaching* and *doctrine* interchangeably. Unlike current understanding, in which the relationship of doctrine to preaching is tenuous, Calvin believed that doctrine informs the study of Scripture and that both shape proclamation. Doctrine, Scripture, and proclamation are all mutually enriching expressions of the gospel.

Calvin's preface to the *Institutes* sets out his understanding of the relationship of theology and Scripture: "It has been my purpose in this labor to prepare and instruct candidates in sacred theology for the reading of the divine Word, in order that they may have easy access to it and advance in it without stumbling."[30] The current division of ministerial education into self-contained "departments" of study, separating biblical studies from theology, is foreign to the integrated sense of faith and life that characterized the Geneva Reformation.

Calvin understood that just as it was necessary to examine ministers when they were ordained or elected, "so also it is necessary to have good supervision to maintain them in their duty."[31] "Supervision" was the ongoing responsibility of the company's exercise of collegial discussion, affirmation, and admonition. Discussion among the pastors was not an abstract academic exercise, for the church's faith and life were tied to that of its pastors. The search for truth required the company of pastors to engage in analysis, discussion, and debate and mutual critique because biblical, theological, and moral affairs were not private concerns or merely matters of personal opinion.

Company meetings were sometimes contentious. At one point the pastors became so weary of "the torrent of inept, erroneous, and absurd statements" of

---

[29]Calvin, "Draft Ecclesiastical Ordinances," 60.
[30]Calvin, *Institutes*, "John Calvin to the Reader," 4.
[31]Calvin, "Draft Ecclesiastical Ordinances," 60.

one of their colleagues that they censured him and prohibited him from speaking (but not from listening!).[32] Perhaps more serious was the outbreak in the *congrégation* of a serious controversy. Jerome Bolsec, a former monk who practiced medicine in Geneva, issued a rude, slanderous, public challenge to Calvin's teaching on predestination. His outburst led to his arrest and expulsion from the city. These incidents were the exception, however. The Company of Pastors was characterized by mutually helpful deliberation, discussion, debate, and deepened ministry.

Theological work of the Company of Pastors included "ecumenical" discussion and action. Led by Calvin, pastors analyzed differences among Reformed churches in Switzerland, searching for resolution. Deepening divides between the Reformed and Lutheran churches over the Lord's Supper were also examined in hopes that a way could be found to reach agreement. Conversely, the Catholic Council of Trent elicited harsh critique rather than a quest for common ground. In all cases, however, the Company of Pastors was concerned with the whole church, not restricting its scope to Geneva, particular parishes, or themselves.

Corporate faithfulness. "To obviate all scandals of living, it will be proper that there be a form of correction to which all submit themselves. It will also be the means by which the ministry may retain respect, and the Word of God be neither dishonoured nor scorned."[33]

The Venerable Company of Pastors was a disciplined community. Its meetings were more than conversation about abstractions, for their purpose was to encourage pastors to grow in faith and faithfulness. Once every three months the company engaged in a session of mutual support and correction. Among the faults that required correction were lack of zeal for study and an undisciplined life. All of this was for the sake of the gospel—its proclamation, reception, and fulfillment.

Because "true and faithful" doctrine found expression in pastors' preaching, teaching, and pastoral care, each minister was accountable to the body for his understanding of Scripture, doctrine, and the exercise of pastoral duties. Pastors regularly heard each other preach in their congregations, so all were in a position to evaluate the relationship between doctrinal matters and pastoral practice. Among the faults that might need correction were heresy, fomenting schism,

---

[32]Scott M. Manetsch, *Calvin's Company of Pastors: Pastoral Care and the Emerging Reformed Church, 1536–1609* (New York: Oxford University Press, 2013), 135.

[33]Calvin, "Draft Ecclesiastical Ordinances," 60.

agitation against church order, blasphemy, simony, lack of zeal for study, a way of treating Scripture that gives offense, the pursuit of idle questions, and an undisciplined life. The company's exercise of mutual critique was not an inquisition but rather an honest and serious mutual supervision, necessary because the faith and life of pastors had an impact on that of the whole people of God. Yet the company did impose restrictions on mutual critique, limiting it to once every three months so that it did not assume disproportional importance.

Calvin's pastoral rule was to be lived out corporately. Individual attention to study, sacramental fidelity, pastoral care, and congregational ministries was insufficient. Pastors must be responsible for and accountable to one another regarding their fidelity to Word and sacrament and the conduct of ministry in their congregations.

MUTUAL SUPERVISION TODAY

It is worth pondering the contrast between Geneva's Company of Pastors and the current reality of pastoral life. A pattern of weekly half-day meetings of pastors for prayer, serious biblical and theological study, and mutual accountability for their practice of ministry seems almost unimaginable in the contemporary church. Lectionary study groups, while valuable, are too narrowly focused on sermon preparation. Pastoral support groups often lack the honesty of mutual critique. Difference of doctrine is not in short supply among us, but coming together to discuss a matter is too often reduced to exchanging slogans and voting in an essentially political context. While historical experience shows that the practice of mutual affirmation and admonition can become harmful, ministers who live as theological and ethical free agents present a clear and present danger to the whole church.

Calvin's ordering of the church's ministries and his provision for patterns of mutuality among pastors were not designed for heresy hunting or moral policing. Calvin was concerned about the ordinary, week-to-week life of pastors and how the rhythm of their lives would honor God and serve their congregations and the wider church. The Company of Pastors embodied three practices designed to enhance fidelity to the Lord and the Christian community that are just as foundational today.

First, regular, ongoing, in-depth study of Scripture remains fundamental to pastors' capacity to proclaim the gospel. Proclamation is not confined to preaching and teaching, although it is essential to both. Proclamation of the gospel encompasses witness to Christ in all facets of personal and communal life, and certainly throughout the whole range of pastoral life. Confining biblical study to private sermon preparation may lead to secondhand reliance on the work of others or to idiosyncratic interpretations that draw congregational attention away from the good news of Christ's grace, God's love, and communion in the Holy Spirit. More broadly, restricting study of Scripture to solitary consideration deprives a pastor of the insights and the corrections of others.

Second, serious and sustained theological study is an essential component of veracity in preaching, teaching, pastoral care, and mission. Continual theological engagement is necessary in building the pastoral capacity to understand contemporary culture and respond faithfully to its challenges, to deal knowledgeably with church members' doubts and questions, to encourage faithful mission initiatives, and to wrestle with difficult moral issues. All of these normal pastoral activities require theological knowledge and insight; reliance on past seminary education and occasional continuing education seminars will not sustain pastors over the course of ministry. None of us possesses the rich theological wisdom necessary for the task. We need colleagues—both books and fellow pastors—as companions in the ongoing engagement with "the depth of the riches and wisdom and knowledge of God" (Rom 11:33).

Third, biblical and theological wisdom is a necessary element in pastoral care. Church members deserve the truth of the gospel at all times, but certainly in moments of deep personal and communal significance—birth, baptism, confirmation, dating, marriage, hospitalization, death, funerals. People need the truth of the gospel in times of crisis—unintended pregnancy, birth defects, addiction, accidents, crime and imprisonment, marital infidelity, divorce. In moments such as these, pastors cannot fall back on pop therapy or religious clichés. Only constant probing of the deep mystery of God with us and for us in the dying and rising Christ can prepare pastors to serve the personal needs of congregations and members.

The ministry of pastoral care is in constant need of the wisdom of other pastors, and also in need of challenge and correction. Are we saying our prayers? Attending to the sick and lonely? Being with grieving family members after a funeral? Confronting church members who abuse alcohol or mistreat their children?

The reality of pastors' lives is that none of this can be done alone. Only sustained, honest relationships with colleagues in ministry can provide pastors with patterns of mutual responsibility and accountability that ensure consistent engagement with Scripture, openness to think through the faith together with theological forebears, and the pastoral imagination and wisdom that fully serves congregations and members. The Geneva Consistory, Calvin's Company of Pastors, and his comprehensive understanding of the church's ministries were elements in a re-formed ecclesiology. While the particular forms instituted in sixteenth-century Geneva could not be duplicated in the contemporary church, Calvin's animating insights into the nature of the church and the purpose of pastoral ministry can find an appropriate form in twenty-first-century North America.

> Many are led either by pride, dislike, or rivalry to the conviction that they can profit enough from private reading and meditation. . . . In order, then, that pure simplicity of faith may flourish among us, let us not be reluctant to use this exercise of religion which God has shown us to be necessary and highly approved.[34]

I (Joseph) did not grow up in the church. My Sunday mornings were spent riding my bike on country roads in western Massachusetts delivering thick New York, Boston, and Springfield newspapers. I came to faith in my early twenties, and when I entered seminary I was woefully ignorant about Scripture, the history of the church, theology, and everything else. For three years, I was dependent on fellow students as well as professors for facts, knowledge, and wisdom.

My dependency did not end with a seminary degree. During my pastorates in Maryland, Ohio, and New York I continued to read because the more I learned, the more I understood there was yet more to understand. But I also sought out other pastors with whom I could talk about what we were reading and how that shaped our understanding of Christian faith and life, and what that meant to our pastoral vocation. Twenty-three years of my ministry were spent with marvelous colleagues in the Presbyterian Church's Office of Theology and Worship. Daily conversations, times of prayer, reading in common, and mutual affirmation and correction all deepened my faith and enhanced my ministry.

My theological and pastoral need for the company of others is as real now as it was on my first day in seminary. Calvin's pastoral "rule" is significant because of its thoroughly corporate character. He understood that spiritual, intellectual,

---

[34]Calvin, *Institutes* 4.1.5.

and pastoral disciplines are never merely personal but are to be lived in company with other congregational leaders and fellow pastors, all within the ministry of the whole people of God. In our time, his insights offer good guidance for the re-formation of pastoral ministry.

QUESTIONS FOR DISCUSSION

♦ Does Calvin's vision of the ministry of the whole people of God (and "unified plural ministries") suggest possibilities for the life of your congregation?

♦ For Calvin, Scripture and theology were intertwined and complementary. How might your study of Scripture be enriched by ongoing theological study?

♦ Does the celebration of the sacraments in your congregation "offer and set forth Christ to us, and in him the treasures of heavenly grace"?

♦ How might you approach other pastors about establishing a "company of pastors" among you?

FOR FURTHER READING

Bucer, Martin. *Concerning the True Care of Souls.* Carlisle, PA: Banner of Truth, 2009.

Calvin, John. *Commentaries on the Epistles to Timothy, Titus, and Philemon.* Grand Rapids: Eerdmans, 1959.

Dawn, Marva J. *The Sense of the Call.* Grand Rapids: Eerdmans, 2006.

Jones, Serene. *Calvin and the Rhetoric of Piety.* Louisville, KY: Westminster John Knox, 1995.

Leith, John H. *John Calvin's Doctrine of the Christian Life.* Louisville, KY: Westminster John Knox, 1989.

Torrance, James B. *Worship, Community and the Triune God of Grace.* Downers Grove, IL: InterVarsity Press, 1996.

5

Choosing *Your* Words Carefully

JOHN WESLEY

MINISTERS, ESPECIALLY PREACHERS, are called to handle words with all the care that a banker counts money or a surgeon wields a scalpel. Words are the currency in which the gospel has come to us and in which we offer it to others. But words can become inflated or devalued; they can promise too much or too little; they can hurt others or fail to connect. Ministers work with words all the time, but we are also aware of how difficult it can be to find the right words for the situation. As the apostle James warns, "Not many of you should become teachers, my brothers, for you know that we who teach will be judged with greater strictness. For we all stumble in many ways. . . . no human being can tame the tongue. It is a restless evil, full of deadly poison. With it we bless our Lord and Father, and with it we curse" (Jas 3:1-2, 8-9).

John Wesley loved words. He read widely and immersed himself in Scripture and the writings of the great teachers of the Christian faith going back to the church fathers. He wrote constantly, producing journal entries, letters, tracts, translations of classic Christian texts, commentaries on Scripture, and sermons. For much of his life, he preached four to five times a day; the most recent edition of his collected works comes to twenty-seven volumes. And many other of Wesley's words were never recorded, such as the spiritual advice that he gave to thousands of people, as he came into their homes, attended their small group meetings, or met them on the road. He rode on horseback across Britain perhaps as many as 250,000 miles over his lifetime and visited more of England's towns and villages than anyone else in history. He once declared,

> I look upon all the world as my parish. I mean, that, in whatever part of it I am, I judge it meet, right, and my bounden duty to declare unto all that are willing to hear, the glad tidings of salvation. This is the work which I know God has called me to; and sure I am that His blessing attends it. Great encouragement have I, therefore, to be faithful in fulfilling the work He hath given me to do. His servant I am, and, as such, am employed according to the plain direction of His Word.[1]

Words mattered deeply to Wesley, for he believed that God had called him to declare the gospel to renew an English church that had become spiritually moribund. Today, three centuries later, we too will need to find the right words to proclaim the gospel to a world—and often a church—that has grown weary of "God-talk."

A LIFE JOURNEY

Wesley's life was marked by an ongoing search for personal holiness. Born to a father who was a village Anglican priest and to a pious mother who imposed a strict regime of religious and moral rectitude on her nine children, Wesley, by age six, had become, in his own words, "serious in religion."[2] He was a curious, questioning child, always looking for the deeper reasons for the way things are or should be. Because of his intellectual gifts, his parents sent him at age ten to Charterhouse School in London, and then at age sixteen he enrolled at Christ Church in Oxford. After graduating in 1724, he stayed on to work for a master's degree. At the same time, with his mother's encouragement, he began to examine the state of his soul and prepare for ordination. Two books proved to be decisive for him. The first, Jeremy Taylor's *The Rules of Holy Living and Dying*, had already influenced him in college. In 1725, he picked up the second, Thomas à Kempis's *The Imitation of Christ*. As one biographer has explained, "It was *Holy Living and Dying* which inspired Wesley to become a 'whole Christian,' becoming like Christ in body and spirit rather than merely obeying his laws. *The Imitation of Christ*

---

[1]Entry of June 11, 1739, in *The Journal of John Wesley*, ed. Percy Livingston Parker (Chicago: Moody, 1951), www.ccel.org/ccel/wesley/journal.vi.iii.v.html.

[2]Stephen Tomkins, *John Wesley: A Biography* (Grand Rapids: Eerdmans, 2003), 15. The following biographical information also draws on Tomkins.

pointed the way to achieving that goal."[3] In the same year, Wesley composed and committed himself to rules of personal conduct that "were almost identical to those which he later required members of his Methodist Connexion to follow," including disciplined prayer, study, and use of time.[4] He also began a rigorous process of daily self-examination.

In 1726, Wesley left Christ Church to become a fellow of Lincoln College in Oxford, where he continued his master's studies and assumed tutorial responsibilities. After several extended leaves of absence, he returned briefly to Oxford in 1728 to be ordained as a priest, and in 1729 he took up his tutorial responsibilities again and quickly became involved in a small religious society founded by his brother Charles. Known as the Holy Club, its members saw religion as "a constant ruling habit of the soul; a renewal of our minds in the image of God."[5] While Oxford had many such societies, the Holy Club became especially well known for its zealous piety. The young men committed themselves to holy living, mutual confession, weekly reception of Communion, fasting on Wednesdays and Fridays, evening meetings to discuss spiritual classics, and, eventually, social outreach in the city's debtors' jails and the charity hospital.[6] During these years, Wesley continued to read voraciously and encountered William Law's *Serious Call to a Devout and Holy Life*, which further fed his desire for Christian perfection.[7]

In 1735, at the invitation of the Society for the Promotion of Christian Knowledge, Wesley left England to serve as a parish priest in Georgia. During the four-month voyage, his ship encountered several storms so violent that Wesley, to his shame, feared for his life, while a group of Moravians on board calmly sang hymns and declared they were not afraid of dying.[8] In Georgia, the Moravians continued to impress him with their practices of prayer, study, and self-examination and their conviction that "a personal relation with God marked the true path to salvation," something for which he longed but could not find. His ministry in Georgia ended in failure, with charges that he had scandalized a woman to whom he was giving spiritual counsel and that he had

[3]Roy Hattersley, *The Life of John Wesley: A Brand from the Burning* (New York: Doubleday, 2003), 60.
[4]Hattersley, *Life of John Wesley,* 62.
[5]Hattersley, *Life of John Wesley,* 74.
[6]Hattersley, *Life of John Wesley,* 71-77.
[7]Hattersley, *Life of John Wesley,* 81.
[8]Hattersley, *Life of John Wesley,* 104.

distorted the Anglican liturgy by introducing hymns (a measure that the Moravians had inspired).[9]

In 1738, Wesley returned to England, exhausted and close to a nervous breakdown yet exhilarated by new possibilities. He took leadership of a London Society of Methodists founded by a former member of the Holy Club, and sought out Peter Böhler, a Moravian missionary, "who told Wesley that he had no saving faith; he believed intellectually, but still hoped to become righteous by virtue of his own deeds, lacking the true faith that comes in an instant, bringing rebirth and an utter certainty of salvation."[10] Wesley and Böhler moved the London Society to Fetter Lane and began running it according to Moravian principles, dividing it into small groups that practiced prayer and mutual confession and came together once a month for a love feast (i.e., a fellowship meal). On the evening of May 24, Wesley attended another Moravian meeting near Aldersgate in London. As a member of the society read from Luther's *Preface to Romans*, Wesley finally experienced an emotional conversion. In words that would later become famous, he reported: "I felt my heart strangely warmed. I felt I did trust in Christ, Christ alone for my salvation, and an assurance was given me that He had taken away my sins, even mine."[11]

Biographers today dispute that the Aldersgate experience was *the* decisive turning point of Wesley's life. On the one hand, Wesley had experienced earlier turning points, as with his reading of Taylor and à Kempis. On the other, even after Aldersgate he would experience moments of doubt and uncertainty.[12] But with Aldersgate he did come to embrace more fully than before the Reformation doctrine of justification by grace and by faith, even as he continued to insist, more strongly than his Calvinist friends, that salvation also depended on good works; indeed, without them, one could fall from grace.[13]

In 1739, under the influence of the great revivalist George Whitefield, Wesley began preaching out of doors. While many regarded Whitefield as the more accomplished orator, Wesley too attracted large crowds. Soon he was demonstrating remarkable skills not only as a preacher but also as an organizer who could unite people under his leadership. Methodism would no longer be just a random, local collection of newly enthused Christians; it would become a national revival

---

[9]Hattersley, *Life of John Wesley*, 114.
[10]Tomkins, *John Wesley*, 58.
[11]Tomkins, *John Wesley*, 61; Hattersley, *Life of John Wesley*, 136.
[12]Tomkins, *John Wesley*, 61-62; Hattersley, *Life of John Wesley*, 137-39.
[13]Strict Calvinists insisted on the "perseverance of the saints."

movement, the "Connexion." Wesley worked to the end of his life to keep the Connexion within the Church of England, but he also gave his followers a distinctive identity that would in time lead to their establishment of an independent church.

RULES FOR REVIVAL

Wesley believed that the revival sweeping through England and the American colonies had convicted people to repent, to be justified by God's grace, to "taste of the heaven to which we are going," and to "sit in heavenly places with Christ Jesus."[14] Now they wanted to know how to sustain their revival, and he had an answer ready: "Strengthen you one another. Talk together as often as you can. And pray earnestly with and for one another."[15] Wesley therefore composed rules of conduct and organized structures of accountability for his followers. He wanted the Methodists—like the Moravian small groups, like the Holy Club in Oxford, and like the Fetter Lane Society—to gather on a regular basis to assist each other in deepening their assurance in God's saving work and in becoming as perfectly holy as possible.

In 1743, Wesley formulated three "General Rules" for his movement as a whole: (1) do no harm, (2) do good, and (3) attend all the ordinances of God. The General Rules included examples of each. A person does no harm by avoiding profanation of the Sabbath, drunkenness, quarreling, cheating, and self-indulgence. A person does good "by giving food to the poor, by clothing the naked, by visiting or helping them that are sick, or in prison," and especially by helping those of the household of faith. Under the ordinances of God, the General Rules list "the public worship of God; the ministry of the word, either read or expounded; the supper of the Lord; family and private prayer; searching the Scriptures; and fasting, or abstinence."[16]

To help people remain true to these rules, Wesley organized them into small groups. The most basic structure of accountability became the "class meeting." Each class had about twelve members as well as a leader assigned by Wesley. At first, he wanted class leaders to visit members one-on-one in their homes. But, as Wesley later wrote, "Little misunderstandings and quarrels of various kinds

---

[14]*The Works of John Wesley*, ed. Albert C. Outler et al. (Nashville: Abingdon, 1984–2005), 9:255.
[15]Outler, *Works of John Wesley*, 9:256.
[16]John Wesley, "The Nature, Design, and General Rules of the United Societies," in *The Works of John Wesley*, ed. Thomas Jackson, 14 vols. (Grand Rapids: Baker, 1978), 8:270-71.

frequently arose among relations or neighbours [i.e., members of the classes], effectually to remove which it was needful to see them all face to face."[17] Thus, the class members began meeting together once a week. Typically, the leader would open the meeting by relating where he had experienced joys, sorrows, hopes, fears, conflicts, and longings in the course of the week. His intent was not so much to make a confession of specific sins but rather to give an account of his struggle, yet determination, to live the Christian life, and in this way to instruct the entire group. The leader would then proceed to ask each member of the class about the state of his or her soul and "to advice, reprove, comfort, or exhort," as the occasion required.[18] Until the movement grew too large, Wesley would meet weekly with the class leaders, through whom he extended his authority and oversight to the membership as a whole.[19]

Many class members were still at the beginning of their journey into spiritual renewal. When a class member experienced justifying grace and felt ready for a more rigorous discipline, he or she could join a second kind of small group, the band, for which Wesley composed additional rules.[20] Like the classes, the bands met weekly with a leader. But they were smaller than the classes, and men and women, single and married, met separately, thus providing for more intimate exchange and fellowship than was possible in the class meeting. According to Wesley, band members were often dealing with temptations "of such a kind, as they knew not how to speak in a class, in which persons of every sort, young and old, men and women, met together. These, therefore, wanted some means of closer union; they wanted to pour out their hearts without reserve, particularly with regard to the sin which did still easily beset them."[21] Their desire was to confess specific sins and receive a "renewed outpouring of sanctifying grace."[22] In addition, members of the different bands met together quarterly to celebrate a love feast. While the food was simple—"a little plain cake and water"—the mood was joyful as participants shared in prayer and testimony.[23]

---

[17]Outler, *Works of John Wesley*, 9:261-62.

[18]Outler, *Works of John Wesley*, 9:261.

[19]David Lowe Watson, *The Early Methodist Class Meeting: Its Origins and Significance* (Eugene, OR: Wipf and Stock, 1985), 98.

[20]John Wesley, "Rules of the Band-Societies," in Jackson, *Works of John Wesley*, 8:272.

[21]Jackson, *Works of John Wesley*, 8:258.

[22]Kevin Watson, *Pursuing Social Holiness: The Band Meeting in Wesley's Thought and Popular Methodist Practice* (New York: Oxford University Press, 2014), 67.

[23]Jackson, *Works of John Wesley*, 8:259.

Wesley organized "select societies" for those who had progressed in holy living even beyond the level of the band. Wesley believed that their members "had no need of being encumbered with many rules; having the best rule of all in their hearts."[24] Nor was there need for a leader; everyone "has an equal liberty of speaking, there being none greater or less than another."[25] Even Wesley felt free to "unbosom" himself in their company. Together, they "rose higher than before; being more watchful than ever; and more meek and lowly, as well as stronger in the faith that worketh by love."[26]

HOLY CONVERSATION

As we have noted, Wesley saw these different groups as opening up space for conversations in which Christians could encourage each other to grow in holiness. To be sure, especially in the classes and bands, these conversations were guided by a leader; they were never freewheeling. But Wesley, despite the authoritarian tendencies in his own personality, valued conversation. When a Moravian faction in the Fetter Lane Society began insisting that justifying faith excluded any doubts or fears, Wesley asserted the importance of "Christian openness and plain speaking."[27] He believed that if people were free to speak from the heart, they would grow in holiness and help others do the same. He had a profound confidence in the power of well-chosen words to exercise spiritual discipline as well as to provide spiritual nourishment. As scholar Kevin Watson has written, "As [people] learned to speak candidly to one another in class, Wesley found that they also grew in relationship with Christ."[28] For Wesley, conversation could bring them to break through to a level of Christian fellowship that they had never experienced before.[29]

Wesley offers striking examples of the power of open conversation that he experienced at Methodist love feasts. In a journal entry of February 18, 1750, he records that "the honest simplicity with which several people spoke, in declaring the manner of God's dealings with them, set the hearts of others on fire."[30]

---

[24]Jackson, *Works of John Wesley*, 8:261.
[25]Jackson, *Works of John Wesley*, 8:216.
[26]Jackson, *Works of John Wesley*, 8:260.
[27]As quoted in Hattersley, *Life of John Wesley*, 159.
[28]Watson, *Pursuing Social Holiness*, 62.
[29]Outler, *Works of John Wesley*, 9:259.
[30]Outler, *Works of John Wesley*, 20:321.

An entry from July 19, 1761, declares that "the very design of a love-feast is a free and familiar conversation, in which every man, yea, and woman, has liberty to speak whatever may be to the glory of God." Wesley then proceeds to tell of a love feast in which several "did speak, and not in vain: the flames ran from heart to heart. . . . We then joyously poured out our souls before God and praised him for his marvelous works."[31]

In the class and band meetings, open conversation had a different but no less important dynamic. Scholar Henry Knight argues that in the classes, interpersonal conversation helped members to resolve differences and be reconciled, while in the bands "each member was both the recipient of the advice and prayers of the others and a spiritual director for the others."[32] In his rules for the bands, Wesley proposed that each member be asked whether he or she desired that "we should cut to the quick, and search your heart to the bottom," and whether he or she intended "to speak everything that is on your heart without exception, without disguise, and without reserve."[33] In both the classes and the bands, adds scholar Russell Richey, members engaged in deep, probing, and sustained "conversation about one another's spiritual state."[34] Loving and considerate conversation provided for fellowship and accountability.[35] People learned to speak Christian truth in Christian love (Eph 4:15).[36]

Wesley was aware, however, that humans are constantly tempted to misuse words. Under his general rule to "do no harm," he asks people to avoid "taking the name of God in vain," "using many words in buying or selling," "uncharitable or unprofitable conversation," and "singing those songs, or reading those books, which do not tend to the knowledge or love of God." Under the second rule, to "do good," he includes "instructing, reproving, or exhorting all [you] have any intercourse with" as well as "submitting to bear the reproach of Christ."[37] And while Wesley does not elaborate on the third rule, it is clear that the ordinances of God—worship, prayer, and attending to the Scriptures and preaching—also depend on the right use of words.

---

[31]Outler, *Works of John Wesley*, 21:336.

[32]Henry H. Knight III, *The Presence of God in the Christian Life: John Wesley and the Means of Grace* (Mutuchen, NJ: Scarecrow Press, 1992), 99, 101.

[33]Jackson, *Works of John Wesley*, 8:273.

[34]Russell E. Richey, *Marks of Methodism: Theology in Ecclesial Practice* (Nashville: Abingdon, 2005), 34.

[35]Knight, *Presence of God*, 109.

[36]Watson, *Pursuing Social Holiness*, 62; Knight, *Presence of God*, 110.

[37]Jackson, *Works of John Wesley*, 8:270.

Wesley further elaborated on the right use of his words in a 1767 sermon, "The Repentance of Believers." Wesley warns his listeners against all conversation "which does not spring from brotherly love . . . [and the] golden rule." He calls believers to examine their words and to determine whether they are speaking to please God or to assert their own willful selves. We should always be asking ourselves, he says, whether all our words are "pure, free from unholy mixtures."[38]

The right use of words was an especially critical matter in the class and band meetings. Wesley's rules for those who handled the societies' financial affairs (the stewards) suggest the spirit in which he hoped all members would speak to each other: "Utter no trifling word; speak as in [God's] presence. . . . In all debates . . . watch over your spirits, avoiding, as fire, all clamour and contention, being 'swift to hear, slow to speak'; in honour every man preferring another before himself."[39] Wesley was especially concerned about what would happen after people had bared their souls to one another. As scholar Kenneth Kinghorn notes:

> Many of Wesley's converts had come from the poorer and less educated segments of society. . . . [They] were both grateful and humbled by their new life. However, they faced the temptation to gossip about those who had formerly regarded them as inferior people. . . . Furthermore, Methodism's system of class meetings provided opportunities for class members to learn about the personal and intimate details of one another's lives. The possibility of careless gossip was constant.[40]

Wesley met this problem head-on in a 1760 sermon titled "The Cure of Evil-Speaking," which he later ordered "to be read aloud in each society every year."[41] The sermon is especially concerned with the problem of "backbiting"—that is, speaking ill of a person behind his or her back. Wesley does not deny that we may sometimes be concerned about another Christian's sinful behavior, but he asks that we follow Christ's command to go directly to the person first, then if necessary with one or two witnesses, and only if the offender still refuses to listen, to take the issue to the church as a whole (Mt 18:15-17). Of particular concern to Wesley is the way in which we speak to the offender: "Take great care that you have a right

---

[38]Outler, *Works of John Wesley*, 1:341, 342.

[39]"Rule for Stewards" (1747), in *The Journal of the Rev. John Wesley*, A.M., ed. Nehemiah Curnock (London: Charles H. Culley, n.d.), 300-301, https://archive.org/stream/a613690401wesluoft#page /n9/mode/2up.

[40]Kenneth Cain Kinghorn, ed., *The Standard Sermons in Modern English* (Nashville: Abingdon, 2003), 3:301.

[41]Hattersley, *Life of John Wesley*, 297.

spirit. . . . See that you speak in a gentle and humble spirit. . . . Always speak in a spirit of tender love."[42] Quoting a stanza of a hymn by his brother Charles, he adds:

> Love can bow down the stubborn neck.
> The stone to flesh convert;
> Soften and melt and pierce, and break
> An adamantine heart.[43]

Wesley notes that it is sometimes wise to approach the offender indirectly, as when he or she "has an excitable and impulsive disposition that does not easily bear correction, especially coming from an equal or subordinate."[44] In such a case, we may decide to send a common friend on our behalf or to write a letter, although "whenever you can speak personally, it is far better."[45] If the offender does not change his or her ways after being approached personally, the concerned Christian may take along one or two others who are "meek and gentle, patient and longsuffering . . . endowed with wisdom from above . . . fair, unbiased, and free from any kind of intolerance. . . . Choose, above all others, people who are acceptable to the one to whom you seek to minister."[46] The responsibility of these witnesses is to confirm that the offended party has spoken appropriately and to add authority to his or her words.

If even this measure makes no difference to the offender, the offended party may turn to the elders or overseers of the flock but must not air complaints before the congregation as a whole or to others beyond the congregation.[47] Indeed, from this point on we will let go of the matter. If the offending parties persist in sin, we will refrain from further fellowship with them, but we will nevertheless demonstrate goodwill toward them and refrain from further action against them.[48]

After asking his followers to practice self-denial in their use of words, Wesley concludes his sermon with an appeal: "Let the absence of evil-speaking be the characteristic mark of you as Methodists. By this trait you can know the Methodists: They censure no others behind their backs."[49] Nor will Methodists listen

---

[42]John Wesley, "Sermon 49: The Cure of Evil-Speaking," in Kinghorn, *Standard Sermons*, 307.
[43]Wesley, "Sermon 49," 308.
[44]Wesley, "Sermon 49," 309.
[45]Wesley, "Sermon 49," 308.
[46]Wesley, "Sermon 49," 311.
[47]Wesley, "Sermon 49," 312-13.
[48]Wesley, "Sermon 49," 314.
[49]Wesley, "Sermon 49," 315.

to gossip that comes from others. In this way, brotherly love and care will abound within the church and so impress a "wild, unthinking world" that it will cry out, as did Julian the Apostate in the fourth century, "'See how these Christians love one another!'"[50]

Wesley was so concerned about backbiting that he included a rule against it in his directions to the band societies of 1744: "You are supposed to have the faith that 'overcometh the world' . . . . [Therefore, do not] mention the fault of any behind his back, and . . . stop those short that do."[51] Further, he expelled class or band members who persisted in sins such as backbiting. Wesley or one of his helpers would visit each class quarterly, examine its members, and issue "tickets" to those who were living rightly.[52] As David Watson notes, "Those who were keeping the society rules were thereby provided with a visible means of encouragement, and at the same time those who were 'disorderly' could be removed in a 'quiet and inoffensive' manner simply by withholding their new ticket."[53]

WORDS OF GRACE

Wesley so valued conversation that eventually he came to regard it as a "means of grace." In the document that came to be known as the "Large Minutes," Wesley added "Christian conference" to the other "instituted" means of grace that he had earlier identified in the General Rules, such as prayer, the Eucharist, and searching the Scriptures. According to scholar Ted Campbell, Wesley was referring to practices instituted in Scripture and thus "binding on the church at all times and in all places."[54]

One of Wesley's first and most important statements of his understanding of the means of grace occurs in a sermon by that title from the late 1730s. According to Wesley, "By the 'means of grace' I mean *the outward symbols, words, and actions that God ordained to be the ordinary channels through which he might convey to us his prevenient, justifying, and sanctifying grace.*"[55] Here Wesley focuses on three "chief" means of grace: "*prayer* (whether in secret or with the large congregation),

---

[50]Wesley, "Sermon 49," 316.

[51]Jackson, *Works of John Wesley*, 8:273.

[52]Outler, *Works of John Wesley*, 9:265.

[53]Watson, *Early Methodist Class Meeting*, 105.

[54]Ted A. Campbell, "Means of Grace and Forms of Piety," in *The Oxford Handbook of Methodist Studies*, ed. William J. Abraham and James E. Kirby (New York: Oxford University Press, 2009), 282.

[55]John Wesley, "Sermon 16: The Means of Grace," in Kinghorn, *Standard Sermons*, 270, emphasis original.

searching the Scriptures (which implies reading, hearing, and meditating on the Bible), and *receiving the Lord's supper.*"[56]

Wesley directs his sermon especially to those "who have been completely awakened out of the deep sleep of spiritual death and have begun to feel the weight of their sins as a burden too heavy to bear. . . . They most likely try nearly all of the outward means of grace, only to find no comfort in them."[57] Wesley agrees that the means of grace cannot by themselves effect salvation; only Christ can. But we need not wait passively on him to act. Christ invites us—indeed, commands us—to use the means of grace as we wait to receive a saving faith. Christ asks us to trust the promises of Scripture that he will strengthen us through the means of grace. "Do not use them," says Wesley, "for their own sake, but in order to renew your soul in true righteousness and holiness."[58] He declares: "By the means of prayer and by persistently asking, we may receive from God what otherwise we would not receive";[59] "Scripture is also a means by which God reveals, confirms, and enlarges true wisdom";[60] and "Holy Communion is a standard, stated means of receiving the grace of God."[61]

Wesley acknowledges that prayer, Scripture, and the Eucharist are "the certain and ordinary rule for all who yearn for the salvation of God."[62] But God is always free to work in other ways as well. In later adding "Christian conference" to the means of grace, Wesley was perhaps drawing from his own experience of the healing power of open conversation in the Methodist societies, noting that God's "free Spirit is most pleased to work in our hearts" as we go through life.[63] Under Christian conference, he included "both the fellowship of believers and rightly ordered conversation which ministers grace to hearers."[64]

Wesley valued grace-filled conversation not only at the class and band meetings but also in his interactions with their leaders, some of whom began to function as "lay preachers."[65] Because the majority of them lacked formal

---

[56]Wesley, "Sermon 16," 270.
[57]Wesley, "Sermon 16," 269.
[58]Wesley, "Sermon 16," 282-83.
[59]Wesley, "Sermon 16," 273.
[60]Wesley, "Sermon 16," 275.
[61]Wesley, "Sermon 16," 276.
[62]Wesley, "Sermon 16," 281.
[63]Wesley, "Sermon 16," 281.
[64]Knight, *Presence of God*, 5.
[65]Richard P. Heitzenrater, *Wesley and the Methodists*, 2nd ed. (Nashville: Abingdon, 2013), 158.

education, Wesley worked tirelessly to guide their preaching. Scholar Ryan Danker has noted that Wesley never composed a systematic theology but preferred more conversational and spiritually "formative" genres for his educational efforts.[66] Wesley tried to meet with his helpers weekly, and by 1748 he was examining them annually to ensure their theological and moral integrity.[67] When he could not interact with them in person, he extended his conversation with them through the written word. As scholar Richard Heitzenrater observes, Wesley "wrote every preacher at least annually to prod, encourage, chastise, and exhort them to exercise their calling in more exacting way."[68]

Further, Wesley expected his preachers to keep a rigorous schedule: arise at 4 a.m.; pray and meditate on Scripture and a book of practical divinity until 5 a.m. (and again from 5 to 6 p.m.); and from 6 a.m. to noon (or beginning at 7 a.m., if they had preaching responsibilities at 6 a.m.) to read slowly and prayerfully theological literature carefully selected by him.[69] From 1746 to 1760, he published forty-four of his own sermons, in four volumes, as a pedagogical tool, which along with his *Explanatory Notes upon the New Testament* of 1754 would become Methodism's doctrinal standards. In 1755, Wesley completed preparation of a fifty-volume Christian Library of Church Fathers and Divines. In his "Address to the Clergy" of 1756, he vigorously argued for a broad education in the arts and sciences so that a minister develops "a good understanding, a clear apprehension, a sound judgment, and a capacity of reasoning" and is able to steer people "through a thousand difficulties and dangers, to [a] haven."[70] This kind of education meant a continuing conversation with the past.

"Conference" was such an important principle to Wesley that it became the name of the annual gathering of his preachers as well as of their quarterly regional gatherings.[71] At the annual conference of 1744, the six Anglican priests, not yet knowing how many other members of the clergy might eventually join the

---

[66]Ryan A. Danker, "The Sermons of John Wesley (1872 Edition)—An Introduction," http://wesley.nnu.edu/john-wesley/the-sermons-of-john-wesley-1872-edition/an-introduction/. See also Thomas Edward Frank, "Methodism's Polity: History and Contemporary Questions," in *T&T Clark Companion to Methodism*, ed. Charles Yrigoyen (New York: T&T Clark International, 2010), 314.

[67]Heitzenrater, *Wesley and the Methodists*, 196, 207.

[68]Heitzenrater, *Wesley and the Methodists*, 265.

[69]Outler, *Works of John Wesley*, 9:272.

[70]Jackson, *Works of John Wesley*, 10:481.

[71]Heitzenrater, *Wesley and the Methodists*, 124-25, 161.

movement, approved including lay preachers in their discussions with Wesley.[72] Scholar Thomas Edward Frank has noted that the annual conference, just "like the class meetings for laity, [encouraged all to] grow in their vocation through searching questions of how they were conducting their preaching and teaching and how to make it more effective."[73] The preachers' conversations with Wesley about the relationship between faith and works, and between assurance and doubt, were later published as minutes in question/answer form, "a method of communicating complicated ideas which," as one biographer has noted, "was to become a standard Methodist technique."[74] While Wesley was the theological authority in these exchanges, his answers allowed for doctrinal flexibility and therefore for further conversation and clarification.[75] Frank argues that Wesley

> sought to make the conversations in conference like a class meeting writ large, that is, as searching as possible. He pushed the preachers to think more constructively about the most effective means of preaching, the most responsible way to handle funds, the most appropriate way to address conflicts with other theological views. Conference was not for the faint of heart.[76]

Nevertheless, Wesley believed that conversation at conference, like that in the classes and bands, would deepen Christian fellowship, as at the conference in 1751, where Wesley declared, "The more we conversed, the more brotherly love increased."[77] For many preachers, the annual conference became the high point of their year.[78]

In explicating "conference" as a means of grace, Wesley took up again the theme of speaking rightly. He asked, "Are you convinced how important and how difficult it is to 'order your conversation right?' Is it 'always in grace? seasoned with salt? meet to minister grace to the hearers?'"[79] While these questions applied to every Methodist, they were particularly important for those entrusted to preach the gospel. In his "Twelve Rules of a Helper" (1744),

---

[72]Heitzenrater, *Wesley and the Methodists*, 158.

[73]Frank, "Methodism's Polity," 319.

[74]Hattersley, *Life of John Wesley*, 210. For the Minutes of 1744 and 1745, see Jackson, *Works of John Wesley*, 8:275-338.

[75]Hattersley, *Life of John Wesley*, 210.

[76]Thomas Edward Frank, "Discipline," in Abraham and Kirby, *Oxford Handbook of Methodist Studies*, 248-49.

[77]As quoted in John Telford, *The Life of John Wesley* (New York: Hunt and Eaton, n.d.), 230.

[78]Telford, *Life of Wesley*, 227.

[79]As quoted in Frank, "Discipline," 248.

Wesley asks his preachers to "avoid all lightness as you would avoid hell-fire, and laughing as you would cursing and swearing."[80] In his examination of preachers in 1746, he inquires whether they are "holy in all manner of conversation," whether they "speak justly, readily, clearly," and whether their words bear fruit: "Do they not only speak as generally either to convince or affect the hearers? But have any received remission of sins under their preaching?"[81] In his "Address to the Clergy" of 1756, he poses similar questions: "Am I 'a pattern' to my 'flock' in word [?] . . . Is my 'word,' my daily conversation, 'always in grace'? . . . Does the love of God and man . . . shine through my whole conversation?"[82]

As in his sermon "The Cure of Evil-Speaking," Wesley especially warned his preachers against backbiting: "Keep your thoughts within our own breast, till you come to the person concerned. . . . [But then] tell everyone what you think wrong in him, and that plainly, and as soon as may be, else it will fester in your heart."[83] In 1752, he asked the preachers to enter into covenant not to speak evil behind each other's backs, and if they heard anything ill of another, to communicate it to that person—and to him alone—as soon as possible.[84]

Wesley eventually composed a number of practical rules for choosing words carefully and relating them to a congregation. In his "Directions Concerning Pronunciation and Gesture" of 1749 (also known as "Rules of Action and Utterance"), Wesley notes that "the first business of a speaker is . . . that he may be heard and understood with ease." A preacher will therefore speak neither too loudly nor too softly and will avoid an affected tone of voice: "Endeavor to speak in public just as you do in common conversation." Moreover, a preacher will "labor to avoid the odious custom of coughing and spitting while . . . speaking" and will vary his voice, for "nothing more grates the ear, than a voice in the same key. . . . Let the thing you are to speak be deeply imprinted on your own heart; and when you are sensibly touched yourself you will easily touch others, by adjusting your voice to every passion which you feel."[85]

---

[80]As quoted in Heitzenrater, *Wesley and the Methodists*, 160.

[81]Heitzenrater, *Wesley and the Methodists*, 180.

[82]Jackson, *Works of John Wesley*, 10:499.

[83]Heitzenrater, *Wesley and the Methodists*, 160.

[84]John Wesley, "To the Methodist Preachers," in Outler, *Works of John Wesley*, 26:490-91.

[85]"Wesley's 'Directions Concerning Pronunciation and Gesture,'" Seedbed, July 17, 2016, www.seedbed .com/pronunciation-and-gesture/.

Wesley also considers how gestures can strengthen or weaken one's words. The body "ought not to change its place or posture every moment; neither on the other hand, to stand like a rock, in one fixed and immovable posture; but to move in a natural and graceful manner. . . . [Look upon your auditors] decently in the face, one after another, as we do in familiar conversation. . . . The mouth must never be turned awry; neither must you bite or lick your lips, or shrug up your shoulders, or lean upon your elbow; all of which give just offense to the spectators. . . . Never clap your hands nor thump the pulpit. . . . Your hands are not to be in perpetual motion."[86]

Wesley's "Advice to Preachers" of 1786 offers similar advice:

1. Always . . . conclude the service in about an hour.
2. Never scream.
3. Never lean upon or beat the Bible.
4. Wherever you preach, meet the Society.[87]

Wesley was convinced that the Methodist call to holiness would be persuasive only if both preachers and church members chose their words carefully. These words needed to be consonant with Scripture but also to have the quality of a conversation that welcomed others into fellowship. Authoritative guidance yet open conversation would characterize the Methodist movement.

CHOOSING WORDS CAREFULLY TODAY

Wesley never composed a pastoral rule as such. But the General Rules set forth a basic way of life for every Methodist, including the preachers. Additional rules, as well as Wesley's own example and writings, elaborated on the specific significance of the General Rules for those entrusted with preaching. Wesley's movement came to have the features that characterize other pastoral rules over the centuries: a commitment to practices and disciplines that open people to God's Spirit, structures of accountability whereby Christians help each other grow in faith and love, and a missionary impetus to share the gospel.

At the same time, Wesley deserves special attention. His concern for conversation and conference, while not unique, is an especially striking dimension of his implicit pastoral rule. Thomas Edward Frank laments that "little scholarship has

---

[86]"Wesley's 'Directions Concerning Pronunciation and Gesture.'"
[87]Heitzenrater, *Wesley and the Methodists*, 330.

pursued the implications of the conversational format for Methodism's character, or the consequences of replacing it in recent generations with more formal discursive statements of church law."[88] Conference has come to be more a matter of church business and parliamentary meeting than a matter of open, searching conversation.[89] Frank nevertheless argues that Wesley's impulses have not been entirely lost: "His appeal for conversation, rightly ordered and ministering grace to participants, has transformed many conferences into gatherings of intense encounter, prayer, personal engagement of decisions, and consensus forms of decision-making."[90] Today, more than ever, the principle of Christian conference can shape how church meetings are structured. But, adds Frank, the future of conference will depend on people's "courage to make hard decisions or to speak difficult words" in an age of "mass media, constant distraction, competing ideologies, individualistic identities, and voices from multiple cultures."[91]

Pastors, in particular, face the challenge of speaking the comforting yet demanding words of the gospel amid the many competing voices of a pluralistic, consumer-driven society. We live in an era in which truth has become elusive. "Fake news" is all too loud, and advertisers and politicians constantly exaggerate and spin their claims to "truth." The relative anonymity of social media tempts people to level sharp, even vicious accusations against those with whom they disagree. We have learned, to our dismay, that bullying can happen online and that a person's intimate photos posted on Facebook not only may prove personally embarrassing later on but may also harm his or her prospects with an employer conducting an online background check. Tweets, too, can perpetuate lies and destroy another's reputation. When words become instruments of power and control, they undermine rather than enhance fellowship and mutual understanding between people.

In such a time, preachers need more than ever to choose their words carefully. Through sustained and deep study of Scripture and theological classics, pastors can find—and communicate—precious, enduring words that inspire us to embrace faith and service and that convict us of our sinful neglect of what is right and good. When officiating a wedding, pastors may find that 1 Corinthians 13,

---

[88]Frank, "Discipline," 249.
[89]Campbell, "Means of Grace," 287-88.
[90]Frank, "Methodism's Polity," 315.
[91]Frank, "Methodism's Polity," 321-22.

Paul's great ode to love, says more than any secular hit song about what is true and of abiding worth in human relationships. At a funeral, Psalm 23 or Romans 8 can evoke a sense of God's merciful presence and care in a way that no eulogy can. "In the beginning was the Word," John 1 tells us, and the Word "dwelt among us . . . full of grace and truth." Wesley challenges pastors to seek words that flow from the church's communion with the One who is the very Word of God.

Regular gatherings in which pastors ask each other searching questions about the faith and how to express it can also discipline their use of words, as we have seen in relation to Calvin's Company of Pastors and Wesley's conferences with pastors. In such settings, ministers can practice being open and transparent. We can work at speaking words that inspire trust. Wesley further asks us to become more aware of how others perceive us and our words. How do we sound as preachers? Do our voices challenge or grate, comfort or annoy? What about our gestures? Do they distract our listeners from or help them focus on what truly matters about life before God? How do we interact with our audience? Do we win people's trust or raise their suspicions as we speak? Wesley asks pastors to open up spaces in which they, together with others, learn to wait on God's Spirit to become our teacher.

Finally, Wesley reminds us that preaching and pastoral care are never just a one-way street from minister to people. In setting forth the gospel, we will also seek to come into conversation with others about the "state of our souls," individually and communally. Pastors need spaces in which they can speak openly and candidly with each other and with the people they serve about the Christian struggle to grow in holiness. In today's word-weary, word-manipulated world—a world in which little seems sacred and even common human decency is too often absent—we have all the more reason to work to recover Christian conferencing as a means of Christ's life-giving grace. May people know pastors to be those who speak reliable, trustworthy words about what God has done and continues to do to renew the church and the world. And may pastors be known as people who rely on God's Holy Spirit to teach us what to say in our hour of need (Mk 13:11)— indeed, on the One who "intercedes for us with groanings too deep for words" when our language falls short (Rom 8:26).

QUESTIONS FOR DISCUSSION

♦ In social settings, do you tend to speak too much or too little? Why?

♦ What are some of your favorite words of Scripture? Why do they speak so powerfully to you?

♦ How would you sum up the gospel in two or three sentences? What would make it hard for a non-Christian to understand you?

♦ Discuss a time that your words hurt another person. Were you able to find a way to reconcile? What did you do or say to try to restore trust?

FOR FURTHER READING

Gravely, William B. *Gilbert Haven, Methodist Abolitionist: A Study in Race, Religion, and Reform, 1850–1880*. Nashville: Abingdon, 1973.

Heath, Elaine. *Longing for Spring: A New Vision for Wesleyan Community*. Eugene, OR: Cascade Books, 2010.

Knotts, Alice. *Fellowship of Love: Methodist Women Changing American Racial Attitudes, 1920–1968*. Nashville: Abingdon, 1996.

Peterson, Eugene H. *Under the Unpredictable Plant: An Exploration in Vocational Holiness*. Grand Rapids: Eerdmans, 1994.

Richey, Russell E., with Dennis M. Campbell and William B. Lawrence. *Marks of Methodism: Theology in Ecclesial Practice*. Nashville: Abingdon, 2005.

6

The 𝔓𝔞𝔰𝔱𝔬𝔯'𝔰 𝔖𝔱𝔲𝔡𝔶

JOHN HENRY NEWMAN

𝔄 STUDY LINED WITH SHELVES of weighty old books. A comfortable armchair for reading. A large oaken desk at which to write, perhaps even by pen in longhand. Subdued lighting, except for a table lamp. No computer, no telephone. Dark paneling. An oil painting on the wall, or pictures of great theologians. A comfortable, inviting atmosphere. A quiet retreat. Can we still find such places in churches, rooms in which pastors do nothing else than read and reflect? Or do pastors today no longer have studies—only offices in which they organize activities and conduct business?

We need not romanticize the past in order to say that pastors need to study—long and hard. But study is rarely a priority for pastors amid the endless demands of ministry. Many pastors study just enough not to embarrass themselves when they preach a sermon or deliver a Sunday school lesson. Otherwise, reading books, reflecting on faith and life, and writing something down on paper to crystallize one's thinking—these seem to be luxuries that pastors remember enjoying in seminary but perhaps even then did not fully take advantage of. Regardless, pastors need to study because understanding and communicating the truths of the Christian faith require sustained, disciplined attention to the Scriptures, church tradition and teaching, and the contemporary world in which pastors minister. Pastors need to study if they are to serve God and God's people faithfully.

If many pastors do not study, it is not necessarily due to a lack of desire. Instead, they are missing patterns and rhythms of everyday life that sustain serious engagement of ideas. For most of us, study will become a priority not by sheer willpower but rather by having it integrated into our daily activities. Study takes time and space—uninterrupted hours and protected places. To be sure, intellectual concentration is difficult under the best of circumstances, and its fruits can be hard to measure. When we study, are we really working—or just daydreaming? Do we accomplish anything—or are we frittering time away? Just getting started is half the battle. Do we have a "home" for our studies: a definite location and regular schedule that invite us into an inner mental world for the sake of our more faithfully serving the larger world around us? Does the pastor have a study? Does the pastor take time to study?

In this chapter, we examine one great Christian pastor and thinker who put study at the center of his life and ministry. Today, John Henry Newman is perhaps better known in Catholic than Protestant circles. He was made a cardinal in 1879. Beatified by Pope Benedict XVI in 2010, his canonization is being actively promoted by others today. Nevertheless, Newman began his life as an Anglican and did not convert to Catholicism until he was forty-five years old. Today he can teach Protestants and Catholics, pastors and priests alike, the importance of making a home for reading, thinking, and writing. Although the way in which he went about making that home will not necessarily be ours, we will see that Newman drew deeply from a rule of life that can be suggestive for us as we strive to live in more disciplined ways.

NEWMAN'S SETTING

John Henry Newman lived at a time of great social and intellectual upheaval in Europe. A rapidly industrializing England had crowded more and more people into its cities. Many of these people were workers subject to twelve-hour shifts and six-day weeks, their children often began working by age seven, and living conditions were squalid: slums, polluted air, constant threat of disease, and inadequate health care. At the same time, a small but growing middle class was emerging and upending the nation's traditional class hierarchy. Money could now be made, not just inherited. Pressure grew to allow wider access to education, including the great universities at Oxford and Cambridge.

These forces were also reshaping England's religious landscape. The dominant Anglican Church no longer had a firm hold on the new working classes. Renewal movements such as Methodism drew some people away, promising them a more personal, emotional faith, while many in the educated classes were attracted to new rationalistic philosophies. Historical critical study of the Bible was undermining faith in revelation. Scientific inquiry was calling into question belief in miracles. For many educated Englishmen, religion offered little more than a humanistic morality.

Newman—first as an Anglican and then as a Catholic—saw clearly that the church desperately needed reform if it were to speak to people under these new circumstances. One of his central concerns was worship. As an Anglican priest in Oxford, Newman won acclaim for his thoughtful, eloquent preaching. But he also worked hard to renew daily prayer and weekly Eucharist. Newman had a related concern for religious education. He believed that laypeople needed to know the Scriptures and the church's great historic teachings. Religious education should aim at communicating the Christian gospel not as abstract ideas but rather as truths that reorient our lives.

Through his study of church history, Newman became increasingly persuaded that the Catholic Church, more faithfully than any other Christian body, had preserved and developed the truth. His efforts to reform the Anglican Church eventually led him to Rome. But Newman saw clearly that the Catholic Church too needed reform. Like Anglicanism, it suffered from complacency of spirituality, formalism in worship, and neglect of lay education. Newman was not interested in effecting reform by entering into church politics. Rather, he would take a quieter path: he wanted to study, think, and write on behalf of the church while serving as a priest in a mission to the city.

NEWMAN'S LIFE

Newman was born in London on February 21, 1801, as the son of a banker. Raised as an ordinary churchgoer, Newman was converted to a more evangelical, Calvinistic expression of Anglicanism after a serious illness at age fifteen in which he had a profound sense of God's personal presence. The next year he entered Trinity College at Oxford. He barely received his degree in 1820, in part because of overwork and mental exhaustion. Abandoning his plans to study law, he was nevertheless successful in becoming a fellow of Oriel College, where he developed his remarkable gifts for logic and philosophy. In 1824 he was ordained as an Anglican deacon, assumed a pastoral post at St. Clement's Church in Oxford, and a year later became its priest.

Newman relished his years at Oriel and would always remember with special fondness the Senior Common Room in which he enjoyed many stimulating intellectual conversations. In 1826, he resigned his post at St. Clement's to become a tutor at the college. But a serious illness in 1827 and his youngest sister's death in 1828 brought about a second turning point in his religious life. While continuing his tutorship at Oriel, he became vicar at St. Mary's, the university church, and became close with the Oxford professors Edward Pusey and John Keble, with whom he shared a concern to recover the Catholic strands of the Anglican Church.

During these years, Newman developed a distinctive sense of vocation. He wanted to educate people in a way that would draw them more deeply into the truth of their existence before God. At Oriel, as one biographer has written, Newman did not simply transmit knowledge to his students: "Rather, he envisioned himself as a teacher with moral and religious sensibilities, who had a responsibility for the souls in his charge as well."[1] But the way ahead would not be easy. The provost of the college disagreed with Newman's approach and refused to send him students. In 1832, Newman's tutorship lapsed.

Newman had a similar sense of vocation—and similar challenges—at St. Mary's. Because university professors typically led the Sunday morning services by rotation, Newman was left to preach at the evening service (evensong), which was typically attended by only "a few shopkeepers, charwomen, and college servants," who were not always sure what to make of his forty-five-minute, deeply intellectual sermons.[2]

With the lapse of his tutorship, Newman took a six-month trip to Rome and the Mediterranean. In Sicily, he fell seriously ill. As he recovered, he experienced a third turning point in his life, marked by a profound sense that God had given him a mission to which he must now sacrifice everything else. On the way back to England, he wrote a poem expressing his new sense of resolve:

> Lead, kindly light, amid the encircling gloom,
> Lead Thou me on!
> The night is dark, and I am far from home—
> Lead Thou me on!

---

[1] Jean Honoré, *The Spiritual Journey of Newman*, trans. St. Mary Christopher Ludden (New York: Alba House, 1992), 31.

[2] Louis Bouyer, *Newman: His Life and Spirituality*, trans. J. Lewis May (New York: P. J. Kennedy & Sons, 1958), 176.

> Keep Thou my feet; I do not ask to see
> The distant scene,—one step enough for me.

Within days of his arrival, Newman joined Pusey, Keble, and others in what would come to be called the Oxford Movement (or Tractarian Movement because of the many tracts they would publish calling the Church of England back to its apostolic roots). For Newman, the next years would be intellectually fertile yet politically turbulent. As he immersed himself in the history of the church's first centuries—and especially as he studied the Monophysite and Arian heresies—he came to believe that the via media between Protestantism and Catholicism that he had so often vigorously defended in Anglicanism was no longer tenable.

Meanwhile, Newman found growing success as a preacher at St. Mary's. Every week, newcomers appeared, at first students and then Oxford's most brilliant professors. They were drawn not only by Newman's deep familiarity with Scripture and the early church fathers, who for him "lived in familiar contact with all that the Bible speaks of," but also by his knowledge of the human heart.[3] As a biographer writes, Newman's hearers "were overwhelmed by the feeling that he was talking to *them*. . . . Masks are dropped, make-believe, pretence are thrown aside . . . [Newman] opened the way to hidden depths in the Word of God beyond the range of ordinary vision."[4]

In 1841 Newman made one last effort to reconcile his Anglicanism with the Catholic Church. In his *Tract 90*, he argued that the Thirty-Nine Articles of the Church of England were compatible with the Decrees of the Council of Trent, the Catholic Church's response in the late sixteenth century to the Protestant Reformation. Newman's intent was to restrain some of the youngest and most enthusiastic Tractarians from bolting to Rome. But the Anglican Church's reaction was fiercely negative. Twenty-four of its bishops eventually condemned the tract. Newman became further alienated from his church when he caught wind of its plan to establish a bishopric in Jerusalem in cooperation with Prussian Protestants. Anglicanism, it seemed to him, was allying itself with Protestantism against Rome.

Newman moved from Oxford to the nearby village of Littlemore, where several years earlier he had established a small parish church attached to

---

[3]Bouyer, *Newman*, 179.
[4]Bouyer, *Newman*, 180.

St. Mary's. While continuing his pastoral duties in both places, he began working on what would become his *Essay on the Development of Christian Doctrine*, in which he concludes that Catholicism best represents the truths of the gospel. In 1843 he resigned from St. Mary's, and in 1845 he gave up his Oriel fellowship and was received into the Catholic Church. The break was finally complete.

In the following years, Newman would receive priestly ordination in the Catholic Church and emerge as one of its most brilliant and controversial thinkers. Nevertheless, Newman regarded his conversion to Catholicism less as a rejection of Anglicanism than as a deepening of convictions and spiritual practices that had long accompanied him.[5] In Catholicism he found a way of life that most fully supported the vocation he had already claimed in Anglicanism as a priest, thinker, writer, and educator.

NEWMAN'S SPIRITUAL DISCIPLINES

From a young age, Newman had a deep sense of God's personal reality. As a priest, he wished for other people to know God intimately, and he believed that to care for their souls was, above all, to care for their minds. For Newman, Christian sanctity depends on knowing the truth about God as Creator and Redeemer. This truth asks of people what Newman would later call a "real" rather than simply a "notional" assent.[6] Christian truth is the kind of truth on which a person is willing to stake his or her life.

According to Newman, practicing the Christian religion disposes a person "to exercise his thinking along lines that will effectually lead him to the truth."[7] Preaching is one means of reorienting people's thinking, and in his sermons at St. Mary's Newman understood himself to be inviting his listeners "to see the invisible in and beyond the visible."[8] Newman also believed that participation in personal and corporate prayer, the Eucharist, and acts of mercy draw one more fully into the truth that is God. At St. Mary's, he instituted daily matins, evening services during the week, and a weekly Communion service on Sunday mornings, practices prescribed by the Anglican Book of Common Prayer but long neglected

---

[5]Hal M. Helms, *Lead, Kindly Light* (Orleans, MA: Paraclete Press, 1987), 192.
[6]See Newman's *An Essay in Aid of a Grammar of Assent* (London: Longmans, Green, and Co., 1898).
[7]Bouyer, *Newman*, 186.
[8]Bouyer, *Newman*, 181. See, for example, Newman's sermon "The Invisible World," in John Henry Newman, *Plain and Parochial Sermons*, vol. 4 (London: Longmans, Green, and Co., 1909), 200-213.

in most parishes.[9] For Newman, a person shaped by this way of life becomes a living testimony to God. And it is his or her new character—what Newman calls "personal influence"—more than prescribed rules of conduct that helps others discover the truth of their lives before God.[10]

If the church's pastors and priests are to minister faithfully, they too must be shaped by these practices. Of course, a pastor or priest participates in the prayer, worship, and education of a congregation. But Newman believed that a priest also needed a personal spiritual regime. In 1837, Newman began reciting on his own the daily offices of prayer as contained in the Roman Breviary, a practice that takes three to four hours a day.[11] He would arise at midnight to recite matins and lauds.[12] By 1839 he was annually observing a strict Lenten fast, taking a several-day Lenten retreat, and keeping careful notes about his sinful conscience.[13] And throughout these years, he typically spent several hours each day in his study, doing the reading and writing that fed his sermons, tracts, and parish ministry.

At the same time, Newman was forming a community of spiritual friends. He knew that a person is grounded in Christian truth not only through personal study and reflection but also through discussion and debate with other believers and common prayer and worship. After establishing the Littlemore parish, he began turning several nearby farm buildings into cottages to which he and others could retreat. Rumors spread that he was starting a "popish monastery."[14] In April 1842 he stayed overnight in his new quarters for the first time. Soon he was joined by a friend (J. D. Dalgairns), and "they started to say the daily office from the Roman breviary; they observed silence for the greater part of the day; [and] they tried to live in a very simple way."[15] In the next days, several other enthusiasts joined them. According to Newman's dairies, they rose around 5 a.m., spent an hour in private meditation, and then gathered for Matins and Lauds at 6 a.m. At 9 a.m. they recited Terce, after which they ate breakfast while standing in silence.

---

[9]Ian Ker, *John Henry Newman* (1988; repr., New York: Oxford University Press, 2009), 103, 145; Bouyer, *Newman*, 188.

[10]See John Henry Newman, "Personal Influence, the Means of Propagating the Truth," *Fifteen Sermons Preached before the University of Oxford*, 3rd ed. (London: Longmans, Green, and Co., 1918), 75-98.

[11]Ker, *John Henry Newman*, 145.

[12]Dr. Capuchin Zeno, *John Henry Newman: His Inner Life* (San Francisco: Ignatius, 1987), 99.

[13]John Henry Newman, *Autobiographical Writings*, ed. Henry Tristram (New York: Sheed and Ward, 1957), 215-45.

[14]Zeno, *John Henry Newman*, 98.

[15]Zeno, *John Henry Newman*, 98.

They dispensed with servants and made their own beds. During Advent and Lent, they fasted from meat at least three times a week.[16]

In 1843 their Lenten fast was especially severe—the first meal was not until 5 p.m.—and they abstained from all meat. Newman tried reducing his sleep to four or five hours a night. He noted that "besides the Breviary Offices, we have had Meditations of an hour or an hour & a half every morning—& this last week [i.e., Holy Week], when we have been . . . in retreat, as much as three hours."[17] In the first weeks of Lent, those who had gathered (Newman and four others) meditated on their own prior to Matins, guided by the dialogues in the *Paradisus Animae*, a popular devotional work of the early seventeenth century. During Passion Week (with a fifth companion now present), they observed three periods of meditation—early morning, midmorning, and evening—using a sixteenth-century work, Francis de Salazar's *A Sinner's Conversion*.[18]

After Newman's conversion in 1845, Bishop Nicholas Wiseman offered him and his companions the buildings of Old Oscott College (which Newman renamed Maryvale) near Birmingham, where they continued the rhythms of life of Littlemore while adding several monastic customs, such as mutual confession of faults, adoration of the Blessed Sacrament, and set prayers before their time of study. A priest came regularly to celebrate the Mass.[19] But Newman's diaries from this period are much sparser. We no longer find anguished reflections on his spiritual failures. Something was changing. And the spiritual rhythms of his life would also change as he traveled to Rome in the fall of 1846 to prepare for receiving priestly orders in the Catholic Church.

INTELLECTUAL STUDY AS A SPIRITUAL DISCIPLINE

Newman would spend more than a year in Rome, where he heard lectures in Catholic theology and philosophy at the College of Propaganda, continued his own reading, visited the city's holy sites, and had several opportunities to meet with the pope. Throughout this time, Newman was searching for a niche in his new church. After carefully considering the church's various religious orders,

---

[16]Newman, *Autobiographical Writings*, 242-45. One author asserts that they rose as early as 3 a.m. See Zeno, *John Henry Newman*, 99.

[17]Newman, *Autobiographical Writings*, 222.

[18]Newman, *Autobiographical Writings*, 222. The references are to Jacob Merlo Horstius's (1597–1644) *The Paradise of the Soul* and Francisco Cervantes Salazar's (1537–1599) *A Sinner's Conversion*.

[19]Zeno, *John Henry Newman*, 122.

especially the Dominicans and the Jesuits, he decided to join the Congregation of the Oratory, a spiritual society founded by St. Philip Neri in the sixteenth century. After a four-month novitiate, Newman returned to England with a brief from the pope to found an English Oratory in Birmingham, although for the first year (1848–1849) it would be located at Maryvale.

St. Philip Neri lived in Italy at the time of the sixteenth-century Catholic Reformation in Europe.[20] According to Newman, Philip had found the Catholic Church of his time to be in deep peril.[21] Its leaders were implicated in sin and lawlessness, avarice, and impurity. The moral degeneracy of the age—life as "one long revel"—had also infected the church.[22] Educated by Dominicans, Philip later visited Monte Cassino, the monastery that Benedict had founded in the sixth century, where he breathed the spirit of early Christianity and experienced a model of Christian community in which small group of disciples "were settled in one place, and had no duties beyond it. . . . [T]hey had no large plan of action for religious ends; they let each day do its work as it came; they lived in obscurity, and laid a special stress on prayer and meditation; they were simple in their forms of worship; and they freely admitted laymen into their fellowship."[23]

When Philip returned to Rome, he walked along the city streets and struck up conversations with people of all social classes—high and low, rich and poor—about spiritual matters. Many of his new acquaintances began coming to him for confession. Philip did not organize them into a holy community apart from this world but rather brought the church to them in the city so that they could pursue sanctity in their everyday lives—in Philip's words, so that they could be "saints in their own homes."[24] Soon a small group of disciples regularly gathered in his room to pray; to read and comment on spiritual books, discourses on the saints, and church history; and to sing hymns. After his death, some who had been inspired by his example founded "congregations" in which small groups of secular priests (i.e., not members of a religious order) lived and prayed together to sustain each other's faith and ministries.

---

[20]Sometimes also called the "Counter-Reformation."

[21]John Henry Newman, "The Mission of St. Philip Neri," in *Sermons Preached on Various Occasions* (London: Longmans, Green, and Co., 1904), 201.

[22]Newman, "Mission," 207.

[23]Newman, "Mission," 225.

[24]Charles Stephen Dessain, *Cardinal Newman: The Oratory and the Laity* (Birmingham, AL: The Oratory, n.d.), 5. See also Newman, "Mission," 239.

Newman was deeply attracted to Philip's vision of Christian community. Philip had combined prayer, intellectual learning, and service. Several scholars have noted that the Oratory, as Newman imagined it, harks back to Oriel College and Oxford more than to Littlemore. It was a way of life that, he believed, would support his vocation to think on behalf of the church. As one scholar has written, Newman understood himself to have "an apostolate to the intellect."[25] Four elements of the Oratorian way of life cultivated especially favorable conditions for the studying and writing that lay at the heart of his ministry.

1. Life in community. For one thing, Newman believed that he needed life in Christian community to keep him focused on central gospel truths such as humility, sacrifice, and service to others. In contrast to the religious orders, the Oratorians understood asceticism not so much in terms of physical deprivation as in terms of the give and take of everyday life together. Newman liked to cite St. Philip's saying, *vita communis, mortificatio maxima* ("life in community [is] the greatest mortification"). What held a congregation together was less a set of rules than a certain spirit—or, in Newman's terms, the members' personal influence—characterized by self-giving love.[26] At the same time, the aim of the Oratory was "not so much to sanctify its members by means of the practices of their common life, as to dedicate them to a work for the sanctification of their neighbor, which would at the same time ensure their own."[27] The members' mutual care within the Oratory would guide and strengthen their individual missions to the world—in Newman's case, his studying and writing.

Philip had no formal rule for his community, and while constitutions eventually emerged as the Oratorian movement grew, Newman emphasized that the absence of formal vows was key to the Oratorian way of life. Newman knew that community life depends on mutual submission—"mutual concession," in his words.[28] He worried that monastic vows of obedience could touch only external behavior whereas true community develops on the basis of natural affection. A congregation should therefore never be so large "that the faces of all are not known to each other" (Newman preferred a maximum of twelve priests), and its members should genuinely like each other.[29]

---

[25]Placid Murray, *Newman the Oratorian* (1968; repr., Leominster: Gracewing, 2004), 121.
[26]Murray, *Newman the Oratorian*, 122.
[27]Dessain, *Cardinal Newman*, 13.
[28]Dessain, *Cardinal Newman*, 9.
[29]Raleigh Addington, *The Idea of the Oratory* (London: Burns and Oates, 1966), 121.

Moreover, those who live together should have common interests. Part of what first drew Newman to the Oratorians—and what he hoped to cultivate in his English Oratory—was their conviction that shared intellectual interests could help create and sustain Christian community. He believed that "in a community where there is not the bond of vows, charity must be the bond. This charity needs the 'virtue of humanity'. . . . This virtue in turn is normally produced by a refined education."[30] Newman hoped that his Oratorians would be well educated in the liberal arts and sciences. He wanted them to pursue interests not only in theology but also in a wide range of secular subjects such as history, antiquities, and topography.[31] He believed, moreover, that those who had been liberally educated would have a greater capacity to bear with each other in community life. A liberal education enlarges and disciplines the mind "to make it patient of differences, and to give it self-command amid differences of opinion and conduct."[32] While these virtues are not specifically Christian, "when a Christian mind takes them up into itself they cease to be secular, they are sanctified by their possessor."[33]

2. Stability and attachment to a particular place. For Newman, the intellectual dimension of the congregation was closely connected to a second emphasis: stability and attachment to a place. Study and intellectual reflection require protected times and spaces. Learning occurs slowly as one reads, ponders ideas, and formulates his or her understanding of an issue, often by writing something down. As with obedience, Newman refused to make stability a vow; rather, he hoped that those who joined a congregation would desire to remain there for the rest of their lives. They should want to make a home together, a place where each person would feel comfortable and welcome to develop his interests. Newman again seemed to be remembering his days at Oriel. Even the library of the Birmingham Oratory looked like that of an Oxford college: oval in shape with dark paneling, a balcony, and shelves full of books on both levels.

One of the original attractions of the Oratorian movement to Newman was precisely its attention to material comfort. While in Rome and shortly before his ordination, Newman had written, "I do not desire riches, power or fame, but on the other hand I do not like poverty, troubles, restrictions, inconveniences."[34]

---

[30]Murray, *Newman the Oratorian*, 117.
[31]Addington, *Idea of the Oratory*, 123.
[32]Dessain, *Cardinal Newman*, 12.
[33]Murray, *Newman the Oratorian*, 214.
[34]Newman, *Autobiographical Writings*, 245.

With the Oratorians, he discovered that "one has his own rooms, and his own furniture; and . . . without being luxurious, they should be such as to attach him to them. . . . He is to have his things about him, his books and little possessions. In a word, he is to have what an Englishman expresses by the distinctive word *comfort*."[35] Following the lead of the Italian Oratorian Fathers, Newman referred to the congregation as a *nido*—a nest—hence, a place of security and well-being.

The importance of attachment to a particular place and the material things that make it a home was already evident in Newman's relationship to Littlemore. When he left it for good after his conversion to Catholicism, he wrote, "I . . . could not help kissing my bed, and mantelpiece, and other parts of the house."[36] Newman's attention to a sense of place appears again when he opens the first Birmingham Oratory in 1849 in "a gloomy gin distillery" that he had leased in Alcester Street amid the city's slums. It was hardly his idea of an Oxford college, but he nevertheless hoped that "he was 'where I may live and die, having been for 10 years without what promised to be a home.'"[37] Soon, however, Newman was raising money to construct a new building in Edgbaston, on the outskirts of the city, in the hope that it would more adequately serve the congregation's desire for peace, quiet, and beauty. When the new house opened in 1852, Newman again paid close attention to material details. He noted that "while we were in our first dwelling, in many respects we did not fulfil the idea of St. Philip's Institution. . . . [Now] we are in a condition for aiming at it . . . [and] we may begin by making the House itself, in which we dwell, a subject matter for the exercise of our devotion to St. Philip."[38] He asked the Oratorians to set the rooms in order and do their best to provide the house with "visible attractiveness."[39] The new chapel, library, and refectory would all be central spaces for their life together.[40] And just as the Oratory should be a comfortable home, it should make itself at home in the surrounding community.[41]

---

[35]Murray, *Newman the Oratorian*, 192.

[36]Ker, *John Henry Newman*, 320.

[37]Ker, *John Henry Newman*, 344.

[38]Murray, *Newman the Oratorian*, 287.

[39]Murray, *Newman the Oratorian*, 288.

[40]Newman also had definite ideas about the architecture of the church that would adjoin the Oratory and welcome people from the wider community: it should be in "a Roman style" with "a smack of moorish and gothic." See Ker, *John Henry Newman*, 364.

[41]Murray, *Newman the Oratorian*, 193.

3. Daily rhythms of prayer, worship, and Christian service. Intellectual bonds and good material conditions as well as daily communal spiritual disciplines were essential to the congregation's life. Newman knew that the Oratorians' natural affection for one another would not be enough; human sociability had to be perfected by supernatural grace. "Hence it is," says Newman, "that, in the evening exercise of the Brothers, we pray so earnestly for perseverance."[42] What they sought to create in the congregation would truly be home only if it were sanctified by the spiritual home that God offers his people in worship and the Eucharist.

Interestingly, Newman, in contrast to his detailed descriptions of life at Littlemore, says little about the daily patterns of the Birmingham Oratory, but his addresses at chapter meetings and what we know of other congregations make an approximate reconstruction possible of the usual weekday schedule (Sundays were different). The members probably rose at about 6 a.m.[43] Each privately spent half an hour in mental—that is, silent—prayer. Depending on the individual, it could take the form of simple contemplation or involve meditation on the Lord's Prayer or a short biblical text.[44] While Newman did not keep a spiritual journal of thoughts that came to him, some biographers have suggested that, just as at Littlemore, he jotted notes that he later developed into the pieces published posthumously as *Meditations and Devotions*.[45]

Confession, Mass, and recitation of the office in the Oratory church followed.[46] Breakfast was taken individually, in silence. The members then attended to their own work responsibilities—for Newman, time in personal study. He also used this time for his extensive correspondence, which included spiritual direction to a wide range of friends and acquaintances.[47] At midday, dinner was served in the refectory, which Newman called a "domestic chapel."[48] He believed that the food should be hearty and plentiful—not to provide for the concupiscence of the flesh but rather to strengthen the members for their service in the

---

[42]Murray, *Newman the Oratorian*, 336.

[43]See "Rules to Be Observed in the Probation of Our Tyrones, or Youth, Commonly Called Novices" (Dec. 1856), unpublished archives of the Birmingham Oratory.

[44]Dessain, *Cardinal Newman*, 22; Jerome Bertram, *Traditions of the Oratory: The Constitutions of 1612 with Commentary* (Oxford: Oxford Oratory, 2012), 21.

[45]Honoré, *Spiritual Journey*, 215-16. See also William Neville's prefatory note to John Henry Newman, *Meditations and Devotions* (New York: Longmans, Green, and Co., 1893), xiii.

[46]Murray, *Newman the Oratorian*, 161.

[47]Honoré, *Spiritual Journey*, 204. For further development of this point, see Peter C. Wilcox, *John Henry Newman: Spiritual Director, 1845–1890* (Eugene, OR: Pickwick, 2013).

[48]Murray, *Newman the Oratorian*, 289.

world.[49] In most modern English Oratories, this meal, in contrast to the evening meal, is informal, and the Oratorians may speak with each other, but in Newman's time, formality and silence were observed at both meals. From 1853 on, the midday oral reading was from Newman's adaptation of Pietro Giacomo Bacci's seventeenth-century *Life of St. Philip of Neri*; Newman regarded St. Philip's life and spirit as formative patterns for the members of the English Oratory.[50]

In the afternoon, the members again scattered to their separate tasks. They also had time for rest, such as taking an early afternoon walk or working at a hobby.[51] At about 5 p.m. they gathered in the Oratory chapel for evening prayer, which consisted of half an hour of individual mental prayer followed by spoken prayers.[52] At about 6 p.m. they walked silently to the refectory, entered according to seniority, stood at their places, bowed to the cross on the wall, and seated themselves. Once the provost gave his permission, they began eating, in silence, while one member read aloud selections from Scripture and a spiritual book; Newman suggests use of the church's Martyrology.[53] Each member of the Oratory took his turn in reading and serving tables.[54]

In accord with Oratorian tradition, the members of the community afterward discussed a point of dogmatic or moral controversy; Newman often took the lead in proposing a resolution. A brief time of community relaxation and recreation followed, at which coffee was served. Newman liked to share memories and catch up on current events.[55] Throughout the day, the Oratorians, like other secular priests, said the daily offices privately and as best they could, given their individual schedules, rather than communally or with the strictness that Newman and his group at Littlemore had practiced.[56] Every two weeks a "chapter of faults" took place, in which the Oratorians would publicly acknowledge any breaches of the rule.[57] Chapter meetings took place once a month, and Newman as superior would address the community.

---

[49]Murray, *Newman the Oratorian*, 290.
[50]Bertram, *Traditions*, 206; Michael Eades, "Newman's Adaptation of Bacci's *The Life of St. Philip Neri*," *Newman Studies Journal* 4, no. 1 (Spring 2007): 42.
[51]Bertram, *Traditions*, 143; Honoré, *Spiritual Journey*, 207.
[52]Murray, *Newman the Oratorian*, 161; Dessain, *Cardinal Newman*, 22.
[53]Murray, *Newman the Oratorian*, 192; Bertram, *Traditions*, 206-8; Eades, "Newman's Adaptation," 42.
[54]Bertram, *Traditions*, 200.
[55]Honoré, *Spiritual Journey*, 207.
[56]Meriol Trevor, *Newman: The Pillar of the Cloud* (Garden City, NY: Doubleday, 1962), 454.
[57]Murray, *Newman the Oratorian*, 431.

4. Faithfulness in daily duties. This spirituality of prayer, study, and worship profoundly shaped the way in which each member of the Oratory did his ministry. In Newman's understanding, an Oratorian did not need to accomplish heroic deeds. Rather, it was enough to perform daily tasks quietly, well, and for God alone, "without the distractions of human applause."[58] For Newman, "perfection . . . is the power or faculty of doing our duty exactly, naturally and completely, whatever it is."[59] Those duties could change according to external circumstances. Newman therefore declared that "our time, our trouble, our abilities, are not our own. Thus it is a rule of the congregation that no father can refuse an office put upon him."[60]

When the Oratory first settled in Alcester Street, Newman wrote,

> We have deliberately set ourselves down in a populous district, unknown to the great world, and have commenced, as St. Philip did, by ministering chiefly to the poor and lowly. We have gone where we could get no reward from society for our deeds, nor admiration from the acute or learned for our words. We have determined, through God's mercy, not to have the praise or the popularity that the world can give, but, according to our Father's [i.e., St. Philip's] own precept, "to love to be unknown."[61]

Newman participated wholeheartedly in this ministry. Even though it did not fit his picture of an Oxford-like Oratory, here, too, disciplined reading and thinking could bear good fruit. The Oratorians developed catechism classes for children working in the factories; soon more than one hundred were in regular attendance. The Oratorians gave lectures in the parish twice a week, preached to a congregation of six hundred on Sunday evenings, and won a growing number of converts.[62]

In 1851 the Irish bishops asked Newman to help establish a Catholic university in Dublin. Newman agreed, even though it would mean prolonged absences from the Birmingham Oratory, where he served as superior. We know

---

[58]Newman, "Mission," 242.

[59]Murray, *Newman the Oratorian*, 316. For a study of this spirituality of everyday tasks, see Kevin Mongrain, "Newman and the Spirituality of the Oratory," in *Newman and Life in the Spirit*, ed. John R. Connolly and Brian W. Hughes (Minneapolis: Fortress Press, 2014), 187-200.

[60]Murray, *Newman the Oratorian*, 224.

[61]Newman, "Mission," 241.

[62]Ker, *John Henry Newman*, 344. For some of Newman's sermons from Birmingham, see his *Discourses to Mixed Congregations* (London: Longmans, Green, and Co., 1897).

little about the spiritual rhythms of Newman's life during this period, but his chapter addresses demonstrate that his commitment to the Oratorian way of life had not wavered. Study and writing remained at the heart of his vocation as he worked on the essays that would later become *The Idea of a University*. We have every reason to think that this intellectual work was nourished by, even as it fed into, regular practices of praying, attending the Mass, and receiving the sacrament. These practices, as well as his deep sense that he had a home in Birmingham, gave him the strength to try to win over the Irish bishops to his educational vision, an effort that was ultimately unsuccessful.

When he resigned his university rectorship in 1858, Newman returned to Birmingham, where his daily "unknown" tasks shifted again. He faced new leadership challenges after neglecting the Oratory during the years of travelling to and from Dublin. As noted earlier, he and the Oratorians still had work to do to settle into their new house in Edgbaston. About the same time, the English bishops asked Newman and the Oratorians to work on a new translation of the Bible. Soon, Newman proposed that the Oratory also establish a school for boys. In addition to their confessional and parochial duties, the members of the house were already ministering to inmates of a jail and a workhouse. As one biographer has noted, there were "too few Fathers for too many tasks. . . . So very often Newman was forced to take over other Fathers' work."[63] For a number of years, he published little. But he could nevertheless say that "the daily business of the community—'the trifles of the day'—has at least the advantage that 'those trifles are wholes, and have their value, such as it is—whereas one does but waste time, if one makes preparations for a future which is never to be one's own.'"[64] And he eventually completed significant intellectual works, including his autobiography, *Apologia pro Vita Sua*, and *An Essay in Aid of a Grammar of Assent*.

In Newman's last years, the Oratory and its rhythms of life became all the more important to him. He was usually the first to arrive for the community's spiritual exercises. Moreover, "devotion to the Eucharist was at the center of his prayer life. . . . He used to pass entire hours before the tabernacle in fervent colloquies."[65] Study and correspondence continued to occupy much of his day. He was so completely at home in the Oratory that at first he hesitated when Pope

---

[63]Zeno, *John Henry Newman*, 179.
[64]Ker, *John Henry Newman*, 492.
[65]Honoré, *Spiritual Journey*, 212.

Leo XIII proposed making him a cardinal; Newman was afraid that he would have to move to Rome. To his relief, the pope assured him that he could remain in Birmingham. Later, as Newman's strength declined and his eyesight weakened, he gave up saying the Mass and the Breviary, replacing the latter with the Rosary.[66]

Newman's concern for perfection in small, everyday tasks extended to the community's observance of prayer and worship. He once told the Oratorians that "to rise at the exact time, to give the due time to prayer, to meditate with devotion, to assist at mass with attention, to be recollected in conversation, these and similar observances carried duly through the day, make a man . . . half a saint, or almost a saint."[67] Similar care was to be taken in the refectory, where "the punctuality of attending, the bowing to the Cross, the grace, the reading, the waiting, the theological questions proposed, bring before us emphatically that our meal is . . . one of the chief religious acts of the day."[68]

THE PASTOR'S STUDY TODAY

In practice, this Oratorian spirituality—with its four elements of life in community; stability and attachment to place; daily rhythms of prayer, worship, and service; and faithfulness in daily tasks—was full of tension. Oratorians did not always get along with Newman or each other; some of them sharply criticized Newman for failures in leadership, and to his great distress, some eventually left the community, even as he struggled to attract new members. Newman also experienced numerous disappointments in his daily work responsibilities. During the first years of the Birmingham Oratory, he was so impoverished that he could not afford new shoes and socks.[69] He was sued for libel. He did not get his way with the bishops in Ireland. The project to translate Scripture had to be abandoned. The English bishops failed to support him at critical moments, as when he became editor of *The Rambler*, a leading Catholic intellectual periodical. And long stretches of time passed in which Newman was unable to write productively and felt spiritually dry. He survived these trials and tribulations because his life of study and reflection remained firmly embedded in the Oratory's patterns of prayer, worship, devotion, and priestly service, alone and with others.

---

[66]Honoré, *Spiritual Journey*, 213.
[67]Murray, *Newman the Oratorian*, 235.
[68]Murray, *Newman the Oratorian*, 289.
[69]Zeno, *John Henry Newman*, 136.

Newman was an extraordinary intellect whose thinking has lasting value. But he was also very much a person of his time and place—an Oxford-educated English gentleman of the nineteenth century who enjoyed material comfort and cultural privilege. In both his theological timelessness and historical limitations, Newman seems distant from the realities of pastoral ministry in twenty-first-century America. Nevertheless, his struggle to be true to his vocation as a priest and member of the Oratory clearly has lessons for us.

Few pastors will, like Newman, put academic study and reading at the center of ministry. But Newman reminds us that disciplined attention to the greatest thinkers of past and present helps pastors think more deeply about ministry today. Regular study of Scripture is essential not just for Sunday preaching but also for pondering the ways of God in our everyday lives and those of the people around us: think of Job and the problem of suffering, or Joseph and God's providential care. A study of early church history teaches us about ministry in societies in which Christians are in the minority, as is increasingly the case in North America. Reading a great classic theologian such as Thomas Aquinas, John Calvin, or Karl Barth reminds pastors that they too are called to communicate a comprehensive vision of life before God.

Further, Newman reminds pastors of the value of reading more than just theology. Contemporary studies of race and gender help us understand the troubled dynamics of Western societies. Historical studies give us insight into different cultures and why a people thinks as it does. Readings in literature or the natural sciences stretch us beyond what we take for granted. No matter what a pastor's major in college, his or her ministry will benefit from continuing attention to the liberal arts and sciences. As Newman said, this kind of education encourages us to be more patient and understanding of other points of view, even it asks us to plumb the truth of human existence before God.

While few pastors will compose learned academic tomes, Newman reminds us that writing is not just for the sake of communicating information about church beliefs, activities, or concerns. Taking notes and making summaries as we read difficult texts draws us into them more deeply and encourages us to formulate our reactions and reflections more carefully and systematically, whether by informal journaling or formal composition. The first aim of this writing is greater thoughtfulness rather than publication. It may become part of a sermon, presentation, or blog—or never see the light of day—but it will inform our everyday ministry. Writing, like reading, opens up space for us to ponder ideas that may change us and the people whom we serve.

Newman teaches that, for Christians, reading and writing are spiritual exercises. By itself, study can become self-indulgent and abstract. But when anchored by disciplines of prayer, worship, reception of the sacrament, and Christian service, study is sanctified. It attains a moral dimension that takes us beyond reason for reason's sake to knowing the living God personally. And just as our studying will be conditioned by other spiritual disciplines, disciplined study will condition our praying, preaching, leadership of worship, celebration of the sacraments, and service to others. A studious pastor will point in all that he or she does to the truth in Jesus Christ.

We can easily be dismissive of Newman's desire for comfort. But Newman saw clearly that disciplined reading and writing can be supported—or undermined—by material conditions and social relationships. Study is enhanced by *life in community*. Even though reading and writing are solitary activities, they are sustained by communities that value liberal education and give us intellectual friends. Thinkers can easily get too wrapped up in a world of ideas. They need people who bring them down to earth and remind them of the church and world for whose sake they study.

Our ability to study productively is strengthened by *stability and attachment to a place*. A pastor benefits by having a specific location and time for reading books and pondering ideas. No, the paneling does not have to be dark, and the desk does not have to be oaken, but the space should be inviting. Its books, mementos, and pictures should remind the pastor that he or she is called to divine realities, not just the workaday world. The pastor's study should be comfortable—a space into which he or she looks forward to retreating. And it should be protected because study does not easily take place if one is constantly interrupted by phone calls, emails, text messages, or knocks on the door.

Daily rhythms of prayer, worship, and service sustain pastoral study. Newman knew our thinking needs to be directed by God and to God. Study has its proper place alongside daily practices of prayer, worship, and Christian service. These disciplines need not compete with each other for time and attention; rather, they can enhance each other so that each strengthens ministry to the glory of God and the good of our neighbor. Newman calls us to prayerful study and studious prayer.

Finally, study is characterized by *faithfulness in daily duties.* Like prayer and worship, reading and thinking require dedication, energy, exactness, and persistence. New insight comes slowly, sometimes painfully so. A person who studies has to keep at it quietly, day by day. Reading a book about the ancient church or the sociology of religion draws little attention to ourselves. Writing a letter of spiritual counsel to a parishioner may—or may not—make a difference. Composing a thoughtful reflection that goes into a church newsletter or sermon probably will not change the world. And parishioners may not understand why a pastor takes time alone in a study. They may see no obvious payoff. If anything, they may be suspicious that the pastor could be doing something better, something more measureable. Reading and writing are mysterious, hidden processes that, we trust, will nevertheless bear good fruit. St. Philip Neri's and Newman's words—that an Oratorian will "love to be unknown"—apply to the life of study.

Newman challenges pastors today both to reclaim a space that they can call "the study"—with its shelves of books and pieces of comfortable furniture—and to spend disciplined time in that place. Study matters because intellectual work sustains pastoral ministry. Reading and reflection are not academic luxuries; rather, they are the church's lifeblood when they draw us into deeper fellowship with our Lord. When we retreat into our studies and make time to read and think, as we open books or jot down notes, may we also pray with Newman:

> Come, O my dear Lord, and teach me day by day, according to each day's opportunities and needs. Give me, O my Lord, that purity of conscience which alone can receive Thy inspirations. Teach me, like Mary, to sit at Thy feet, and to hear Thy word. Give me that true wisdom, which seeks Thy will by prayer and meditation, by direct intercourse with Thee, more than by reading and reasoning. Give me the discernment to know Thy voice and answer me through my own mind, if I worship and rely on Thee.[70]

QUESTIONS FOR DISCUSSION

♦ What books have you read in the past year? Which if any have you seriously studied?

♦ Do you have a space set aside for study? If so, where? How is it arranged? How often do you use it? How often do others disturb it?

---

[70]Newman, *Meditations and Devotions*, 380. I have lightly edited and abbreviated the selection.

♦ Do you do any writing beyond that which is necessary for your work (such as sermons)? Do you keep a journal? Have you ever considered writing for publication?

♦ Do you have anyone with whom you can discuss what you read or write? Where could you find such people?

FOR FURTHER READING

The Cambridge Companion to John Henry Newman. Edited by Ian Ker and Terrence Merrigan. New York: Cambridge University Press, 2009.

Currie, Thomas W. *Bread for the Journey: Notes to Those Preparing for Ministry.* Eugene, OR: Resource Publications, 2015.

Newman, John Henry. *Parochial and Plain Sermons.* New York: Longmans, Green, and Co., 1908–1911.

———. *Spiritual Writings.* Edited by John T. Ford. Maryknoll, NY: Orbis, 2012.

Peterson, Eugene H. *The Pastor: A Memoir.* New York: HarperOne, 2012.

7

The Gift of Physical Presence

DIETRICH BONHOEFFER

MINISTRY CAN BE LONELY. Pastors know things about the people they serve that must be kept in strict confidence. They must make decisions about what to preach or what position to take on a controversial matter in the church, and members of the congregation will not always understand or approve. Ministry can be lonely because pastors are not sure with whom they can entrust their doubts or talk about their shortcomings. That would be to expose vulnerability when one's parishioners—and perhaps one's colleagues in ministry—expect strength, confidence, and an invariably positive attitude about life. But then pastors just keep their loneliness inside themselves, where too often it festers and leads to anger and even burnout.

But ministry can also be filled with joy. Pastors have the incredible privilege of being with others in their most important life moments—as they come to faith, or marry, or have children, or face illness or even death. Pastors have the wondrous opportunity to point to God in Jesus Christ as they preach, teach, and offer pastoral care week after week. Pastoral work can free ministers from things that do not really matter so that they can devote themselves to the things of God for the sake of the people they serve. Ministry is a high and honorable calling.

These dynamics—of loneliness and joy, of doubt and confidence, of being set apart and yet being for others—are the stuff of ministry in every time and place.

But these dynamics have a particular poignancy for us today because old certainties about the place of the church and ministry in society are passing away. Ministers experience disorientation as they try to understand who they are supposed to be and what they are supposed to do in a world that is changing so rapidly around them. Christian churches are fragmented because of debates about sexuality and politics and pressures to succeed numerically and financially.

Nearly a century ago, Dietrich Bonhoeffer was already anticipating many of these new features of ministry. He experienced it in his own life in a Germany that was becoming something completely different from before, and he saw it in the young men that he was training for ministry. A new loneliness was casting its shadow over the church and its ministers. But Bonhoeffer also recognized the new sense of joy that ministers could experience just by being in the physical presence of other Christian brothers and sisters and especially by coming together to pray, to read the Scriptures, to reflect together on how to proclaim the gospel, to confess their sins to each other, to celebrate the Lord's Supper, and to reach out to one another in times of physical and spiritual need.

Each great Christian figure that we have explored in this book has, like Bonhoeffer, emphasized life in community: Augustine with his friends searching for truth, Benedict in the monastery, Gregory and his flock of believers, Calvin and the Company of Pastors, Wesley and the Methodist bands and groups, and Newman and the Oratory. Each of these church leaders emphasizes a particular dimension of Christian life together: theological debate and discussion (Augustine), obedience to a spiritual director (Benedict), pastoral oversight of other Christians (Gregory), pastors' responsibility for mutual formation and correction (Calvin), choosing words carefully (Wesley), and theological study (Newman). Bonhoeffer reiterates these themes while lifting up yet another dimension of life together: the incomparable value of Christians' physical presence to each other.

"Life together" in the sense of physical presence sustains pastoral ministry in every age and is so crucially important again in our time of social confusion and fear. Ultimately, ministry is about the experience of deep fellowship with the God who has entered history and with particular Christian brothers and sisters—with particular physical bodies and specific personalities and behaviors—who by God's grace become a part of our personal history. Ministers will endure much loneliness. But, says Bonhoeffer, God comes to us in every gesture of trusting relationship between Christians. In Christ, believers, even when scattered, can be near to each other, as present and real as the wine and bread that we receive in Communion.

SCATTERING AND SOWING

If Protestants had saints, Dietrich Bonhoeffer would rank high among them, as is evident at Westminster Abbey in London, where he is honored by a statue as a twentieth-century Christian martyr. His life story, culminating in his execution by the Nazis for his involvement in a conspiracy to assassinate Hitler, has inspired movies, plays, and television documentaries. Many North American and European Christians are drawn to Bonhoeffer because he lived as we think we should live. He was a well-educated, middle-class Christian who nevertheless was not afraid to confront injustice, even at the cost of his life.

Some Christians today, as in parts of the Middle East, face the threat of imprisonment or execution, as did Bonhoeffer. But many of us in the West do not. Whatever the injustices and inequalities of our societies, we live in democracies, not under dictatorships. We are able to protest against government policies that espouse racist ideologies or disregard the dignity of other peoples. We have no fear of martyrdom at the hands of state-sponsored persecutors. Our everyday lives are blessedly mundane, although we know that they too can quickly take unpredictable and threatening turns into illness, impoverishment, or fearfulness. Bonhoeffer inspires us, not because we face his same choices but rather because he recognized that the church was entering a dramatically new era. The world, in his words, was "coming of age."[1] People no longer needed God in the way they once had. Bonhoeffer foresaw what theologians in recent years have come to call the end of "Christendom." From now on, Christians would have to learn to live as a minority in a world that would be increasingly indifferent, even hostile, to their beliefs and values.

What would ministry look like in a world come of age? After years of visiting various intentional Christian communities and a two-year experiment of intentional community with several groups of seminarians, Bonhoeffer wrote *Life Together*, a book that remains immensely popular to this day and has inspired thousands of Christians to commit themselves to deeper forms of intentional community. In the book's opening pages, Bonhoeffer frames an arresting image:

---

[1]Bonhoeffer develops this theme in some of his last writings. See, for example, Dietrich Bonhoeffer, *Letters and Papers from Prison*, ed. John W. de Gruchy (Minneapolis: Fortress Press, 2010), 478-79.

"scattered like seed." He writes, "According to God's will, the Christian church is a scattered people, scattered like seed. . . . That is the curse and its promise. God's people must live in distant lands among the unbelievers, but they will be the seed of the kingdom of God in all the world."[2]

In developing this image, Bonhoeffer makes explicit reference to four biblical passages, two from each Testament. In Deuteronomy 28:64, God warns the people of Israel that if they do not obey him, he will "scatter [them] among all peoples." In Zechariah 10:9-10, God promises that he will nevertheless gather and redeem those whom he has "scattered . . . among the nations." John 11:52 reinforces this image of redemption when the high priest prophesies that Jesus must die "to gather into one the children of God who are scattered abroad," and in Matthew 24:31, Jesus declares that at the end of time God will send his angels to "gather his elect [scattered] . . . from one end of heaven to the other."

While deeply biblical, Bonhoeffer's understanding of "scattered like seed" relates to his distinctive situation as well, with a key difference from the four biblical passages being *why* Christians are scattered. In contrast to Deuteronomy and Zechariah, Bonhoeffer nowhere suggests that the church is scattered on account of its sins. The church is scattered "among the unbelievers" not as punishment for its failings but rather because it faces indifference and even resistance in a world in which God has not yet completed his redemptive work. Until God establishes his new heaven and earth, Christians will be scattered.

A second difference is that God's people are "scattered like *seed*," says Bonhoeffer, yet none of the four biblical passages he cites identifies Israel or the church explicitly as seed. Surely Bonhoeffer had other biblical passages in mind as he wrote, perhaps especially the parable of the sower. In an age in which Christians would increasingly feel like exiles and aliens, he must have wondered whether their ministry would be like sowing seed. They would wonder whether their words would take root. Would they sprout? Would there be any yield?

Or did Bonhoeffer have another allusion in mind? As he foresaw a new era of persecution, he surely remembered the famous dictum of the ancient church father Tertullian: "The blood of the martyrs is the seed of the church." From the very beginning of Hitler's rise to power, Bonhoeffer recognized the demonic character of fascism. By the time he wrote *Life Together* in September 1938,

---

[2]Dietrich Bonhoeffer, *Life Together / Prayerbook of the Bible,* trans. Daniel W. Bloesch and James H. Burtness (Minneapolis: Fortress Press, 1996), 28 (emphasis added).

Hitler had instituted harsh anti-Semitic laws and had effectively taken control of the official German Protestant church. Pastors and professors who refused to take an oath of personal allegiance to Hitler could expect harassment and even loss of livelihood; Karl Barth, one of Bonhoeffer's most important theological mentors, had already quit a prestigious teaching post and returned to his native Switzerland. Seeking to remove any opposition that remained, the Gestapo closed the seminary that Bonhoeffer had briefly directed, and his small community of seminarians quickly scattered in the turbulent winds of Nazi Germany that soon became the storms of war.

The image of scattered seed applies to Bonhoeffer's own life. Since childhood he had never lived long in one place. Born in 1906 in Breslau, Bonhoeffer came with his family to Berlin six years later, when his father, a renowned psychologist and neurologist, received an appointment at the city's famous university. Bonhoeffer's parents were not close to the church, and he surprised them when in his early teens he declared that he wanted to become a theologian. University studies took him to Tubingen and Rome before he returned to Berlin, where he completed a doctoral dissertation on the communion of saints, foreshadowing his interest in the nature of Christian community.[3]

In 1928 Bonhoeffer took up an internship in a German congregation in Barcelona, Spain. A year later, he returned to Berlin but could not be ordained because he was not yet twenty-five, the minimum age set by the German church. In 1930 he completed a second doctoral dissertation (Habilitation) and traveled to America for a year of study at Union Theological Seminary in New York City. His encounters with Union's great theologians but especially with African American churches in Harlem and in the American South left a deep impression on him. They taught him that Christian discipleship could put one in conflict with the prevailing social and political powers.

In 1931 Bonhoeffer returned to Germany, was ordained, gave lectures, and served as a chaplain to students at the Technical University. But soon after Hitler became German chancellor in January 1933, Bonhoeffer left Berlin again to pastor two German congregations in London, England. He wondered whether he fit anywhere in a Germany that had turned to fascism. Although he was now away from developments on the ground in Germany, he nevertheless joined the

---

[3]See Dietrich Bonhoeffer, *Sanctorum Communio*, trans. Reinhard Krauss and Nancy Lukens (Minneapolis: Fortress Press, 1998).

Confessing Church, that part of the German church that would promulgate the Theological Declaration of Barmen in 1934 in an effort to defend the church's freedom and theological integrity.

Despite doubts and uncertainties about his future, Bonhoeffer returned to Germany in 1935, when leaders of the Confessing Church asked him to organize and direct one of its preachers' seminaries. But he had to move again only two years later, when the seminary was shut down. Indeed, as his biographer notes, "From this time on, Bonhoeffer's way of life was unsettled. Up to his death he never again had a permanent residence."[4] His very life was being scattered like seed.

In 1939 Bonhoeffer made a second trip to the United States. His American friends, including renowned theologian Reinhold Niebuhr, pleaded with him to remain. They recognized his extraordinary theological gifts and feared for his life. Bonhoeffer was deeply conflicted but later wrote to Niebuhr, "I have made a mistake in coming to America. I must live through this difficult period of our national history with the Christian people of Germany."[5] Upon returning to Berlin, he began a double life. While continuing to serve as a leader of the Confessing Church, he began secretly associating with a group of people, many of them German military officers, who were conspiring to assassinate Hitler. The plot of Bonhoeffer's life thickened further in 1941. In order to avoid military draft and provide a cover for his work on behalf of the Confessing Church and the German resistance movement, he adopted the persona of a secret informant for Germany's Military Intelligence Office, where his brother-in-law and fellow anti-Hitler conspirator, Hans von Dohnanyi, served on staff.

In 1943 Bonhoeffer was arrested on suspicion of helping Jews escape Germany. What he originally assumed would be only a few weeks' imprisonment on minor charges turned into months and then years of uncertainty, as the Gestapo, not yet knowing of his association with the conspirators, pondered what to do with him. Bonhoeffer was deeply lonely but found solace in reading the Bible and theological literature, praying, ministering to other prisoners, and conducting correspondence in which he could reflect with his trusted friend, Eberhard Bethge, about what was happening in Germany and how God was at work.[6]

---

[4]Eberhard Bethge, *Dietrich Bonhoeffer*, rev. ed., trans. Erich Mosbacher (Minneapolis: Fortress Press, 2000), 594.

[5]Bethge, *Dietrich Bonhoeffer*, 655.

[6]See Bonhoeffer, *Letters and Papers*.

When the conspirators finally acted on July 20, 1944, things went tragically awry. One of the conspirators, Claus von Stauffenberg, a military officer, brought a briefcase packed with a bomb on a timer into a meeting at which Hitler was present, placed the briefcase under the table next to Hitler, and left the room. Waiting nearby until he heard the explosion, he hurried off to Berlin to join in the planned coup. But by the time the bomb went off, Hitler had moved to a different part of the room. Four people died, but Hitler himself escaped with only a few minor injuries.

The plot quickly unraveled, and firm evidence of Bonhoeffer's connections to the conspirators finally emerged. The authorities transferred him from Tegel Prison in Berlin to the infamous concentration camp in Buchenwald and then on to the concentration camp in Flossenbürg, Germany, where on April 9, 1945, he was hanged. Germany would capitulate to the Allies less than a month later.

THE PREACHERS' SEMINARY

A high point of Bonhoeffer's life had been his two years in Finkenwalde, a village in Pomerania in northeastern Germany that would be annexed to Poland at the end of World War II. In an old abandoned schoolhouse, Bonhoeffer had gathered a group of young candidates for ministry entering their final stage of preparation. There, scattered seeds of the Confessing Church briefly came together.

Preachers' seminaries were a distinctive part of theological training in the German Evangelical Church.[7] Candidates for ministry had normally completed thirteen years of school before attending a theological faculty at a state university. The first two years of university were devoted largely to language study: Old Testament Hebrew, New Testament Greek, and Latin. During the last three years, students took courses in the classic theological disciplines, including Old Testament, New Testament, church history, and systematic theology.

The next step was a church internship, typically for a year, after which students entered a second kind of theological school: a so-called preachers' seminary, where for six months they would reflect on their pastoral experience, receive instruction in practical theological disciplines (homiletics, liturgics, church law, and pastoral care), and integrate their academic knowledge of theology with the practice of ministry. In contrast to the universities, the preachers' seminaries were directly under control of the church.

---

[7]The Evangelical Church is Germany's historic Protestant church, primarily Lutheran and Lutheran-Reformed in identity.

Once the Nazis seized control of the universities and co-opted much of the Evangelical Church, the Confessing Church established several preachers' seminaries of its own. Although these seminaries had no legal status, the government did not immediately shut them down, thereby briefly giving the Confessing Church a precious opportunity to shape a new generation of pastors. But candidates for ministry who had chosen to associate themselves with the Confessing Church knew that once they left the preachers' seminary, their future was uncertain. They could not count on a position in the official Evangelical Church or on its legal or financial assistance if the state took action against them. Informants might lurk in their congregations. The threat of arrest or the possibility of being drafted into the German army would never be far away.

Bonhoeffer's students (about twenty-five at a time) lived together at the seminary. All were young, single men (the Evangelical Church did not yet ordain women). Bonhoeffer continued the traditional academic program. But he was convinced that if the young men were to survive spiritually and as pastors, they would need something more. Only deep grounding in prayer, Scripture, and Christian community would sustain them for the challenges ahead. Bonhoeffer therefore took a step unprecedented for German theological education; he established an intentional Christian community. Informed by great Christian spiritual writers of the past as well as by his visits to Anglican monasteries when he lived in England, Bonhoeffer asked the seminarians to commit themselves to key practices and disciplines that would root their lives in Christ and his body, the church. The experiences and lessons of this time formed the basis for the reflections that became *Life Together*.

THE RHYTHMS OF THE DAY

Living conditions in the seminary were not easy. As a student later noted, "Most of the seminarians slept in halls. There were far too few bathing facilities."[8] The community depended on friendly congregations to donate food and supplies. Eberhard Bethge, Bonhoeffer's former student and his biographer, writes that despite the seminarians' great uncertainties, "The gifts continued over the years. When the harvest thanksgiving was celebrated, boxes of fruits [arrived]. . . . One March day in 1937 the telephone rang: 'This is the freight

---

[8]Gerhard Ludwig Müller and Albrecht Schönherr, "Editors' Afterword to the German Edition," in Bonhoeffer, *Life Together*, 123.

yard. A live pig has just arrived for Pastor Bonhoeffer.'"[9] The seminary even received a grand piano, which Bonhoeffer, an accomplished musician, loved to play.

The day began in silence. The seminarians arose at 6 a.m., washed, and gathered around tables in the dining room. The first words that they heard were those of the morning devotions. Bonhoeffer would later write that morning belongs to the community. At dawn, Christians gather to give thanks for the new day, for light after the dark night, and for fellowship after separating to sleep. In accord with the practice of the early church and monastic traditions, Bonhoeffer structured the morning devotions around the Psalms, Old and New Testament readings, hymns, and petitionary prayer. He believed that each of these elements of worship would help the community open itself to the living Word, the risen Jesus Christ, to whom Scripture testifies. Bonhoeffer's later reflections in *Life Together* demonstrate how concerned he was to find concrete and practical strategies for immersing every Christian community—whether seminarians, members of a family, or the members of a congregation—in Scripture. He was convinced that Christ truly speaks a living Word to his people through the words of the Bible.

For Bonhoeffer, the Psalter "is the vicarious prayer of Christ for his congregation."[10] The Psalms express the full range of human emotions and needs, but now as transformed by the One who was fully human, fully divine. Only in Christ can the community pray the Psalms of vengeance or lament. The One who was despised by humans and nailed to the cross has taken all human vengeance on himself and forgiven his persecutors. He who cries out from the cross, "My God, my God, why have you forsaken me?" experiences the depths of human suffering and abandonment yet trusts completely that God will redeem him.

Further, like many Christians before him, Bonhoeffer was convinced that the Psalms teach a Christian community how to pray, so he provided for morning and evening devotions to use all 150 Psalms in the course of a week, as was traditional for Benedictine monasteries. He hoped that over time a community would be so steeped in the words of Scripture that they would become the community's own words and would flow from the very heart of its being into all its words and deeds in the surrounding world.

---

[9]Bethge, *Dietrich Bonhoeffer*, 427.
[10]Bonhoeffer, *Life Together*, 55.

Bonhoeffer prescribed at least one chapter of the Old Testament and half a chapter of the New Testament for each devotional time. He acknowledged the difficulty of absorbing all the details and nuances but said that long readings remind us of Scripture's inexhaustibility, that it is always more than we can take in. The readings should be continuous from one day to the next, so that a community works through entire books of the Bible rather than jumping around from one part of Scripture to another. In this way, Christians begin to grasp how the different parts of Scripture fit together and invite us into God's history of salvation with humanity:

> Forgetting and losing ourselves, we too pass through the Red Sea, through the desert, across the Jordan into the promised land. With Israel we fall into doubt and unbelief and through punishment and repentance experience again God's help and faithfulness. . . . We are uprooted from our own existence and are taken back to the holy history of God on earth. . . . I find salvation not in my life story, but only in the story of Jesus Christ.[11]

Bonhoeffer declares that those who read Scripture aloud on behalf of the community need not add dramatic flair to the text but rather should speak the words as though reading a letter. In this way, the reader demonstrates interest and attentiveness to the words but allows them to speak for themselves. Bonhoeffer was confident that Scripture addresses a community clearly and directly, and at Finkenwalde he offered exegetical comments only on Saturdays.

Bonhoeffer believed that the biblical world also comes to us through the church's hymns. For him, the point of the music is not to delight our senses but rather to draw many separate individuals into one common voice. When the community sings, it practices its unity in Christ. Bonhoeffer therefore discouraged singing in parts. He warned of the soaring soprano or booming bass that draws attention to itself. Moreover, the music is for the sake of lifting up the words based on Scripture, so that we might hear them more clearly and mediate on them as God's living Word to us.

Bonhoeffer was similarly concrete in his recommendations about prayer. One person should be assigned to gather the concerns of the community and pray them aloud on its behalf. Bonhoeffer himself assumed this role at Finkenwalde. The one praying must intimately know "the cares and needs, the joys and

---

[11]Bonhoeffer, *Life Together*, 62.

thanksgivings, the requests and hopes" of each member.[12] The diverse concerns of the community should not become a cacophony of conflicting voices but rather, as with the singing, should come together as one. Bonhoeffer felt that this kind of intercessory prayer would be disciplined yet extemporaneous and from the heart.

After morning prayers, the community in Finkenwalde ate a small breakfast; money was tight and there was rarely enough food to fill the young men's stomachs. Nevertheless, Bonhoeffer regarded even the simplest meal as a time of fellowship not only among the members of a Christian community but also with the risen Lord. For Bonhoeffer, every meal has overtones of the Eucharist and therefore of the promise of the heavenly eschatological banquet as well.

Breakfast was followed by half an hour in which each member of the community quietly meditated on a verse or two of Scripture. Bonhoeffer developed this practice out of his familiarity with the Moravian Church and its annual publication of a book with short, daily Scripture verses from the Old and New Testaments.[13] In Moravian practice, people are invited to meditate on a different passage each day, but Bonhoeffer selected one biblical text for his seminarians to use over the course of a week. He believed that they would find new meaning in it each day as they returned to it.

Bonhoeffer recognized that this kind of quiet listening to even a verse or two of Scripture is difficult. Our thoughts wander; we are easily distracted. He encouraged his seminarians not to demand too much of themselves. They should not expect extraordinary inspiration or revolutionary insight each day. It would be enough to dwell on the one word or phrase that might strike them. Bonhoeffer was convinced that this kind of reading opened a person to the living Word of God and guided him into and throughout the new day. If the purpose of the extended Scripture readings in the common devotions was to draw the community into the broad sweep of salvation history, the time for individual meditation invited each seminarian to hear God's specific word to him.

Bonhoeffer believed that Scripture should also discipline how we pray by ourselves. Just as the community in its prayers gathers diverse members into one body, the individual brings together in his prayers the many people—close or

---

[12]Bonhoeffer, *Life Together*, 69.
[13]The texts are called *Losungen* (drawings) because they are drawn randomly. The Moravian Church continues to publish them today.

distant, loving or hating—who are scattered yet touch his life: "Offering inter-cessory prayer means nothing other than Christians bringing one another into the presence of God, seeing each other under the cross of Jesus as poor human beings and sinners in need of grace. Then everything about other people that repels me falls away. Then I see them in all their need, hardship, and distress."[14]

When the time of individual meditation ended, the seminarians went to "work"—that is, to their classes. Bonhoeffer's lectures to them would become the basis for his book *The Cost of Discipleship*.[15] He knew that for most Christians, going to work means leaving the safety of intimate community and entering a world of objective demands. He nevertheless regarded work as a blessing because it helps us forget ourselves and give ourselves to others. He affirmed the Bene-dictine motto *ora et labora*, "pray and work," for work is also a form of service to God and therefore a continuation of prayer.

Half an hour before lunch, the seminarians gathered to sing the great hymns of the German Protestant tradition (again, in unison). The midday meal pro-vided brief rest and fellowship. The afternoons were devoted to more study and work, but after the evening meal, the seminarians relaxed. Bonhoeffer believed that it was as important to set limits to work as to throw oneself into it. He and the seminarians would often play games and instruments, go for walks, or perform skits.

The day ended with evening devotions structured much like morning prayers but, as in Benedictine monasticism, with added elements of confession, for-giveness, and petition for God's protection during the coming night. The com-munity's prayers could begin as late as 10 p.m. and last forty-five minutes. Then the seminarians retired in silence to their rooms, tired but confident that the coming night would not separate them from the Lord.

DISCIPLINES OF THE WORD, THE SACRAMENT, AND ORDERED LIFE IN COMMUNITY

These rhythms of the day flowed out of, around, and back into Scripture. For Bonhoeffer, the Bible witnesses to the God who comes to us in the life, death, and resurrection of Jesus. In Christ, we recognize ourselves to be lost sinners who nevertheless receive God's forgiveness and renewing grace. This God who

---

[14]Bonhoeffer, *Life Together*, 90.
[15]The original German title should be translated simply as *Discipleship*.

reaches into history calls us to give ourselves in love to others, making genuine community possible.

Bonhoeffer had come to this realization personally in a dramatic moment in 1932. Only after he had completed his doctoral work and been ordained did he discover his true calling. As he later said, "Then something happened, something that has changed and transformed my life to the present day. For the first time I discovered the Bible. . . . I had often preached, I had seen a great deal of the church, spoken and preached about it—but I had not yet become a Christian. . . . It became clear to me that the life of a servant of Jesus Christ must belong to the church."[16]

For Bonhoeffer, disciplines of encountering Scripture were closely related to celebration of the Eucharist and living an ordered life in community. The sacrament, like the Word, calls us into life together, and when we understand that we are members of one another in Christ Jesus, we wish to encourage members of his body to grow in faith and faithfulness, even as we hold them accountable to the Savior's teaching and example.

Bonhoeffer speaks of the monthly celebration of Communion as the high point of the Finkenwalde community's life. Bonhoeffer encouraged his seminarians to prepare for the sacrament by finding a member of the community to whom they could confess their sins and who could speak God's Word of forgiveness to them. At first, the young men resisted. Bonhoeffer's idea seemed too "Catholic" to them, until one evening Bonhoeffer himself took one of them aside and quietly made confession to him. Moved by his example, the other members of the community soon followed suit.

Bonhoeffer firmly believed that unless we confess our sins before a brother or sister in Christ, we will not experience a breakthrough to forgiveness. When we confess to God by ourselves, we are too quick to offer ourselves "cheap grace." Such confession costs nothing and changes nothing. But when we must tell another Christian concretely what we have done wrong, our sin weighs on us. We have to admit to another human being that we are not everything we appear to be from the outside.

Bonhoeffer recognized the dangers that come with making ourselves vulnerable. The one listening to our confession must remember that he or she is not

---

[16]Bethge, *Dietrich Bonhoeffer*, 205.

commissioned to judge but rather to represent the risen Christ. He or she is not asked to provide psychological counseling or impose conditions of penance but rather to proclaim that in Jesus Christ we are forgiven. Indeed, patterns of mutual encouragement and accountability should shape all personal relations within the community of faith. The Word that we have received from Scripture places us beneath the cross and is the Word that we owe each other.

Bonhoeffer knew that a community's ability to practice this kind of mutual encouragement and accountability would depend on each member adopting two basic postures before others: holding one's tongue and regarding others as better than oneself.[17] Bonhoeffer therefore asked his seminarians to practice the "Finkenwalde Rule": not to speak about a brother behind his back, and if one nevertheless did, to confess it directly to the brother afterward.[18]

Besides practicing self-restraint, members of a community should actively serve one another. Bonhoeffer identifies three key practices: listening to others, helping others, and bearing with others.[19] We will be able to speak God's word of mercy and judgment to others only if they first knows that we truly make space for them. When we listen to another, we put our own agenda aside. When we help another, we let our plans be interrupted. When we practice forbearance, we allow others to weigh us down, both by accepting their unique personalities and quirks and by taking seriously yet forgiving their sin.

Encouragement leads to admonishment. Because we care about our brothers and sisters, we warn them when they go astray. Bonhoeffer knew that we must be very careful in how we confront one another. There is no room for self-righteousness. Nevertheless, "words of admonition and reproach must be risked when a lapse from God's Word in doctrine or life endangers a community. . . . Nothing can be more cruel than that leniency which abandons others to their sin."[20]

Word, sacrament, and ordered life in community are intertwined.[21] Each undergirds the others. One of Bonhoeffer's deepest contributions to the church

---

[17]Bonhoeffer, *Life Together*, 94-97.
[18]Bethge, *Dietrich Bonhoeffer*, 428.
[19]Bonhoeffer, *Life Together*, 98-103.
[20]Bonhoeffer, *Life Together*, 105.
[21]Note their similarity to three traditional marks of the church according to Protestant ecclesiology: proclamation, sacraments, and discipline (understood not as church court proceedings but rather as ordered life in community).

today is his insight that God comes to us in the imperfect, fleshly, everyday activities of Christian life together. We do not meet God through special religious or spiritual experiences that seem to lift us above this world into a more perfect realm. Rather, it is here and now in our embodied physical existence that we learn to be a community whose members come together to pray, sing, eat, work, study, play, confess sin, celebrate Communion, and care one for one another. And it is precisely in this way that we receive Christ and indeed represent him to one another.

In one of his last letters from prison, Bonhoeffer wrote,

> There is hardly anything that can make one feel happier than to sense that one can be something for other people. . . . Indeed, the most important thing in life are human relationships; even the modern "high achiever" . . . cannot change that; but neither can the "demigods" or the lunatics who know nothing about human relationships. God allows himself to be served by us in all that is human.[22]

Nothing sustains Christians more than shared physical presence—and nothing is potentially more fraught with tension and misunderstanding.

PHYSICAL PRESENCE TODAY

Bonhoeffer emphasized that because we are sinners, it is Christ alone who holds us together. Our relationships to one another must be mediated through him. Any human principle of unity—common social or political interests, a charismatic leader, or human likes or dislikes—ultimately poses a threat to true community. Bonhoeffer was clearly thinking of how Hitler and fascism offered Germany a principle of national unity that was demonic. The church, says Bonhoeffer, must make an alternative witness to such false unity by the character of its life in community.

But the Christian experience of life together is always fragmentary and incomplete. It never lasts for long. The seeds that have been gathered will soon be scattered again. Threats to Christian community may come from a hostile state or society, but they may also arise from within the church itself. Bonhoeffer trenchantly observed that whenever Christians gather, they cannot resist the common human temptation to calculate who is stronger and weaker. Rivalries and resentments inevitably arise.

---

[22]Bonhoeffer, *Letters and Papers*, 509.

Community is also threatened when one group of Christians calls another to accountability, as events within the German church under fascism had so clearly demonstrated. Even though the Confessing Church had refused to separate itself from the Evangelical Church or to declare itself the true German church, a profound break in community had nevertheless occurred. In such circumstances, says Bonhoeffer, we can only trust that "God joins together in breaking . . . [and] confers grace in judgment."[23] Indeed, it is precisely in the world's and the church's brokenness that Christ is present, and he calls us to join him in being present to one another and the world.

As Bonhoeffer observes at the beginning of *Life Together*, "Jesus Christ lived in the midst of his enemies. In the end all his disciples abandoned him. On the cross he was all alone, surrounded by criminals and the jeering crowds. . . . So Christians, too, belong . . . in the midst of enemies. There they find their mission, their work."[24] Christian community is necessarily elusive and transitory until Christ returns. The basic Christian condition on earth is to be scattered like seed. But Bonhoeffer assures us that Christ waters these seeds until they sprout into love, fellowship, communion, and life together with all its human messiness yet divine profundity.

In recent decades, ministers in the West have increasingly sensed that Christians are "resident aliens" in society. Something in Europe and North America, once so powerfully shaped by Christian traditions, has changed. The problem is not just declining church membership or changing social norms. Fundamentally, the church has lost its commanding voice in society. Its pronouncements no longer garner attention from the media or political leaders. For better or worse, the church has become just another point of view competing in a free market.

Even in this supposedly free market, religious voices, especially Christian voices, easily become marginalized. Race, gender, ethnicity, and sexual orientation have increasingly, and with good reason, become protected social categories whose representatives have privileged voices, but Christianity is often dismissed as historically oppressive or as nothing more than a private consumer choice with no relevance for public life.[25]

---

[23]Bonhoeffer, *Life Together*, 106.
[24]Bonhoeffer, *Life Together*, 127.
[25]See the analysis in George Marsden, *The Twilight of the American Enlightenment* (New York: Basic Books, 2014).

Ministers feel these changes even more acutely than their parishioners. In a world in which the central acts of Christian community—proclamation, celebration of the sacraments, and patterns of mutual encouragement and accountability—no longer have obvious meaning, ministers worry about how to spice up church life and grab people's attention. But that just stokes a new kind of loneliness: the loneliness of one who fears that he or she may be nothing more than a huckster who is trying to get people to buy what they really do not want or need. To be sure, pastoral ministry has always had a measure of loneliness to it, but today ministers have the added loneliness of wondering whether they are really saying anything at all when they use words such as *God, salvation,* and *sanctification.*

In a time that one philosopher has called "a secular age," proclaiming the basic language of Christianity may seem like scattering seed on hard, resistant ground.[26] But Bonhoeffer believed that in such circumstances God calls the church to find a new language, "the language of a new righteousness and truth, a language proclaiming that God makes peace with humankind and that God's kingdom is drawing near."[27] Bonhoeffer further believed that this new language could grow only out of a renewed Christian commitment to prayer, responsible action, and life in community. Today, as much or more as in Bonhoeffer's time, ministers need deep, trusting theological and spiritual relationships to sustain them for the lonely yet wondrous work of scattering the seed of the gospel.

Bonhoeffer challenges pastors to find at least one person to whom they can confess their sins and from whom they can hear the liberating words, "In Jesus Christ, you are forgiven." They should meet regularly with other pastors to struggle together to find the "new language" that will set forth the gospel today. Pastors should seek out brothers or sisters of faith because they will represent Christ's presence to one another in good times and bad. And pastors should reach out to other pastors and church leaders, for, as Bonhoeffer notes, "the physical presence of other Christians is a source of incomparable joy and strength to the believer."[28]

It is, of course, a special privilege for Christians to share daily rhythms of worship and service. But Bonhoeffer knew that other kinds of physical acts and

---

[26]See Charles Taylor, *A Secular Age* (Cambridge, MA: Belknap, 2007).
[27]Bonhoeffer, *Letters and Papers*, 390.
[28]Bonhoeffer, *Life Together*, 29.

gestures—things as simple as praying for others or visiting them when they are isolated or feel alone—can bring them close to us, as can the material objects that we share with one another. Upon receiving a parcel of clothes from his parents, the prisoner Bonhoeffer exclaims, "You can't imagine how much joy and strength I derive even from this indirect connection."[29] But it was the letters he received in prison that assured Bonhoeffer, above all, "of the nearness of those from whom he was separated."[30]

God's people, says Bonhoeffer, will "remain scattered," yet they will also be graced with moments of genuine Christian community in "gracious anticipation of the end time." Christians will often be alone, but they will also be privileged to "recognize in each other the Christ who is present in the body." Signs of presence to each other provide us "inexhaustible riches" and "an inexpressible blessing" for our ministry. Indeed, declares Bonhoeffer,

> The believer need not feel any shame when yearning for the physical presence of other Christians. . . . The Son of God appeared on earth in the body for our sake. . . . In the sacrament the believer receives the Lord Christ in the body, and the resurrection of the dead will bring about the perfected community of God's spiritual-physical creatures. Therefore, the believer praises . . . God, the Father, Son, and Holy Spirit, for the bodily presence of the other Christian.[31]

QUESTIONS FOR DISCUSSION

+ Discuss a time in which your physical presence was the most important thing to someone else. What made it so important?

+ What material thing has someone given you that you like because it reminds you of that person and his or her love for you?

+ How do you see the internet and social media bringing people closer together or driving them apart? How can Christians use the internet and social media more responsibly?

+ Do you have someone who can hear your confession of sins and assure you of God's forgiveness? If so, who? If not, how could you find such a person?

---

[29]Bonhoeffer, *Letters and Papers*, 80.
[30]"Editor's Afterword to the German Edition," in Bonhoeffer, *Letters and Papers*, 570.
[31]All these quotations are from Bonhoeffer, *Life Together*, 28, 29.

FOR FURTHER READING

Hauerwas, Stanley. *Hannah's Child: A Theologian's Memoir*. Grand Rapids: Eerdmans, 2010.

Marty, Martin E. *Dietrich Bonhoeffer's Letters and Papers from Prison: A Biography*. Princeton, NJ: Princeton University Press, 2011.

Nouwen, Henry J. M. *The Return of the Prodigal Son: A Story of Homecoming*. New York: Doubleday, 1992.

Tietz, Christiane. *Theologian of Resistance: The Life and Thought of Dietrich Bonhoeffer*, trans. Victoria J. Barnett. Minneapolis: Fortress Press, 2016.

Williams, Reggie. *Bonhoeffer's Black Jesus*. Waco, TX: Baylor University Press, 2014.

8

A Contemporary Pastoral Rule

IN THE FIRST DECADE of the twenty-first century, we, the authors of this book, participated in an initiative to reform and renew ministry in the Presbyterian Church (USA). While other members of the initiative pursued different areas of concern, the three of us eventually committed ourselves to formulating a contemporary pastoral rule that could guide and sustain the ministers of our denomination. We knew that we did not have to start from scratch. Each of us has deeply historical interests, and we spent several years in reading and discussing the seven figures that we have explored in this book. We came to see that while each of them belongs to a specific historical context different from our own, they have insights for—and issue challenges to—pastors and churches today. In response, we drafted a pastoral rule, which we reproduce in lightly edited form below. While this rule has no official status within the Presbyterian Church (USA), it has stimulated creative thinking and spiritual discipline among our pastors and churches, and we hope that it will be suggestive to pastors and churches of other Christian traditions.

A PASTORAL RULE: RE-FORMING MINISTRY

The apostle Paul begs us to live a life worthy of our calling. This pastoral rule is offered to you not as a set of regulations but as a guide that leads away from burdensome demands toward authentic freedom in Christ. We encourage you to read the rule slowly and prayerfully, in the hope that God will speak to you through it and that you will discover renewed patterns of faithfulness. The grace of our Lord Jesus Christ be with you.

A LETTER TO THE CHURCH

Brothers and Sisters in Christ,

We write to all who serve in positions of church leadership, especially to pastors. We are members of the Re-Forming Ministry Initiative of the Office of Theology and Worship—pastors, seminary professors, and officials in church councils. We met for five years, seeking to understand where God is leading the Presbyterian Church (USA) and how we can strengthen its ministry in a difficult time of social and ecclesiastical change.

In our times together, we explored the challenges facing pastors and studied classic and contemporary reflections on the work of pastoral ministry. Encouraged by these explorations, we offer pastors and all other ministers of the church a brief pastoral rule, which invites us all to shape our lives around personal disciplines, holy conduct in ministry, and patterns of mutual encouragement and accountability. Written in the tradition of Dietrich Bonhoeffer's *Life Together*, this rule is offered to you as a resource for sustaining faithful, vibrant ministry.

We give thanks to God for your ministry. No one has a greater responsibility to provide the church with a faithful theological vision for the challenging time in which we live. Your preaching and teaching are critically important if people are to hear the gospel clearly and respond to it faithfully. We know the sacrifices of time and energy you make each day. We want nothing more than to encourage you and build you up.

But we are also concerned for your ministry. Demands on your time and energy include regular visitation and successful stewardship programs, membership growth and an efficient committee structure, presbytery service and good sermons, community outreach and an attractive church school program—the list is endless. People expect you to be available, personable, and wise, successfully negotiating the new challenges that each day of ministry brings. But that is not all.

You know better than anyone else that you live out your ministry amid competing understandings of ministry itself. You are expected to be preacher, teacher, therapist, administrator, personnel director, organizational manager, entrepreneur, and CEO—all at the same time. What is at the center of your ministry? What at the periphery? You worry that you cannot get everything done or satisfy every expectation. But beneath those worries is a question: Of all that I am expected to do and be, what is worth doing and what is at the core of my vocation?

Pastoral isolation intensifies uncertainty about what really matters. While most pastors are constantly in touch with people, opportunities for deep fellowship among pastors are rare. Isolation appears even more intense when we remember that pastors need theological friendships to sustain them and hold them accountable to the gospel. Too few pastors gather on a regular basis to encourage and build up one another in the gospel. Pastoral loneliness contributes to the personal and ecclesial disasters of sexual misconduct, alcohol abuse, and financial impropriety.

Ours is not the first time in history that pastoral ministry has been in crisis. Seventy years ago, new political realities in Germany forced pastors to take a stand. Would they allow their ministry to be co-opted by Nazi ideology, or would they remain grounded in the gospel? Too many lost their way, but a few came to new clarity about the church and its leadership. The one best known to us is Dietrich Bonhoeffer.

Bonhoeffer saw clearly the need to form pastors in basic practices and disciplines of faith that would sustain them in the trying days ahead. Following in the footsteps of St. Benedict, Gregory the Great, John Calvin, and many others, he developed a set of guidelines and practices—a pastoral rule. He organized a program for pastoral candidates who lived together for six months, immersed themselves in Scripture and prayer, and developed patterns of mutual encouragement and accountability. The program lasted only two years before the Gestapo closed it down, but Bonhoeffer's reflections in *Life Together* continue to speak to us today.

When we hear the word *rule*, we worry about legalism or about who exercises power over others. But the classic understanding of a rule is that it acts as a measuring stick, a "ruler" that helps us to measure out our faithfulness to our calling. A rule gives pastors a set of criteria by which to measure their ministry, so that they may remain focused on the gospel and the heart of their vocation.

We propose a brief pastoral rule for the twenty-first century. It has three key components: personal disciplines, conduct in ministry, and structures of mutual accountability. We anticipate that our proposal will meet resistance, for we also find much in ourselves that resists it. Our culture rewards personal choice and success; a rule asks us to submit to a way of life together. We prefer to make our own choices; a rule tells us what we should be doing.

Nevertheless, we write to you because we are convinced that a pastoral rule meets the needs of our time. A pastoral rule invites us once again to hear the voice of our living Lord, "Come, follow me." We write to you because we believe that a pastoral rule, by helping us to focus on the core of our calling, can free us from the avalanche of demands that oppress us. A pastoral rule challenges us to grow in holiness for the sake of the gospel.

The apostle Paul asks us to encourage and build up one another (1 Thess 5:11). A pastoral rule can help.

The Grace of the Lord Jesus be with you all.[1]

PERSONAL DISCIPLINES

Practice these things, immerse yourself in them,
so that all may see your progress. (1 Tim 4:15)

Fundamental rhythms and patterns of pastoral life—often called practices of faith, spiritual disciplines, or exercises in piety—are designed to reshape us. Sanctification, growth in holiness, is the work of the Holy Spirit. The experience of Christians over the centuries shows us that personal disciplines of faith become instruments of the Holy Spirit that open up a space in which we again become aware of God's great mercy, leading us to respond in gratitude and to recommit ourselves to lives of righteousness before God.

If we want to remain rooted in our baptismal identity, true to our ordination vows, and open to the Holy Spirit,

♦ we will commit ourselves to regular, daily devotional practices, alone or with others.

♦ we will commit ourselves to regular opportunities for growth in theological and spiritual health.

---

[1]The letter is signed by Jerry Andrews, Senior Pastor, First Presbyterian Church, San Diego, California; John Burgess, Teaching Elder, James Henry Snowden Professor of Systematic Theology, Pittsburgh Theology Seminary; Barry Ensign-George, Teaching Elder, Associate for Theology, Office of Theology and Worship; Darrell Guder, Teaching Elder, Henry Winters Luce Professor of Missional and Ecumenical Theology, Princeton Theological Seminary; Jill Hudson, Teaching Elder, Coordinator for Middle Governing Body Relations, PC(USA); Michael Lindvall, Pastor, The Brick Church, New York, New York; Kevin Park, Teaching Elder, Associate for Theology, Office of Theology and Worship; Neal Presa, Pastor, Middlesex Presbyterian Church, Middlesex, New Jersey; Melissa Ramos, Teaching Elder; Joseph D. Small, Teaching Elder, Honorably Retired; Rebecca Weaver, John Q. Dickinson Professor of Church History, Union Presbyterian Seminary; and Charles Wiley, Teaching Elder, Coordinator, Office of Theology and Worship.

Pastors' devotions are formed around reading and meditating on Scripture, praying, and reflecting on great Christian theological and spiritual literature. We all know this, but do we do it?

Read Scripture. *Presbyterian Panel* research indicates that few pastors read the Bible devotionally on a regular basis. While we do read Scripture as we prepare to preach and teach, we often neglect listening for God's word to us personally. Apart from preparation for preaching and teaching, we read Scripture sporadically and according to no particular plan. Little wonder that our efforts do not sustain themselves.

Examine your own Bible-reading habits. How much time do you make for God to speak to you through Scripture, nourishing your faith and life? Do you long to be more faithful? We all want to say yes and deepen our attentiveness to God's Word. Two principles can guide us:

1. Select daily Scripture passages according to a plan, reading from both the Old and New Testaments.

- Read from a lectionary that offers Old Testament, Gospel, and Epistle readings each day. These lectionaries ensure coverage of the Bible's breadth of narratives, promises, and exhortations. They also place us in the company of a larger community of faith with whom we read the Scriptures together, even when we are by ourselves.

- Read through books of the Old and New Testaments from beginning to end (*lectio continua*) in order to keep larger themes and patterns of those books before you.

- Use a devotional guide that selects readings for you and offers brief meditations on them.

2. Set aside a regular time and place to read and meditate on Scripture.

- Shape time and place by daily and weekly rhythms.

- Read and meditate by yourself or with your spouse, your family, a friend, or a small group.

- Gather regularly with a group of elders or members of a Bible study group in the congregation.

Whatever plan you use, it is important to make a regular time to listen to the text as God's living word and to discern what God is saying to you personally.

Pray. Pastors regularly pray in worship, in hospitals, at church luncheons, and other public settings. But we do not always have a disciplined approach to our personal prayers. Prayer easily becomes a professional duty rather than a way of life.

Examine your own practices of prayer. How often do you pray? What do you include in your prayers, and what do you neglect to mention? We all want to deepen our prayer life. Two principles can help:

1. Select good models of prayer that will help you grow in your prayer life.

- Learn to pray the Psalms, praying through the Psalter or using a lectionary's psalms for the day. The Psalter has been Israel's and the church's prayer book from the beginning. Reformed Christians in particular have been shaped by praying and singing the psalms, which shape all our praying by expanding the range of our adoration, confession, thanksgiving, and intercession. They also remind us that we pray with the whole church through time and space, even when we pray by ourselves.

- Pray for your congregation, elders, colleagues in ministry, your judicatory, your denomination, and sister churches across the globe.

- Use the appointed prayers for each day in a prayer book or worship book (such as the daily prayer portion of the Book of Common Worship, which offers prayers for each morning and evening of the week).[2] These prayers call us to concerns of the larger church that we easily forget, and repeating the same concerns week after week helps to internalize them.

2. Set aside a regular time and place to pray.

- It may be as you first wake up and are still lying in bed.

- It may be at the end of the day before you go to sleep.

- It may be at the beginning or end of a meal.

- It may include gestures that help you to make space for prayer, such as kneeling, making the sign of the cross, folding your hands and bowing your head, or lifting up your hands and head.

- It may be alone or with others.

Regardless of how you pray, what matters most is that you pray what the Holy Spirit prays through you for your own life, including its connection to those around you in the church and the world.

---

[2]See "Daily Prayer," in *Book of Common Worship* (Louisville, KY: Westminster John Knox, 2018).

Read theological and spiritual literature. Most pastors have a wealth of classic theological and spiritual literature on their bookshelves, but many of us have not opened them since seminary. Too often we treat the church's great confessions as museum pieces rather than words of wisdom that call us into prayerful meditation.

We know that we need help from the wider church if we are to grow spiritually, for we are not wise enough to make sense of Christian faith and life on our own. We need more than books on church management or new social trends, as important and helpful as they are. We need nourishment for our minds and souls.

Examine your own reading habits. Are you regularly drawing from the treasures of the church's greatest thinkers, teachers, and guides? Two principles can help:

1. Read the church's theological and spiritual classics regularly.

♦ Read the church's great creeds, confessions, and catechisms according to a schedule, reflecting on how these confessions guide our reading of Scripture and challenge us to give account of our faith today.

♦ Read several significant books on a particular topic such as Trinity, Christology, salvation and sin, science and theology, medical ethics, and ecclesiology.

♦ Work through classic Christian works such as Calvin's *Institutes* in a year, or even Barth's *Church Dogmatics* at a measured pace over several years. These and other theological giants wrote for the church and its pastors.

♦ Read volumes from a series such as The Classics of Western Spirituality, The Brazos Theological Commentary on the Bible, the Ancient Christian Commentary on Scripture, or the Reformation Commentary on Scripture.

♦ Read great novels, poetry, and essays that struggle with the deepest questions of human existence, and thus of our lives before God.

♦ Read significant books and articles on the natural and social sciences that examine life and the cosmos.

2. Read slowly and deeply, differently from the way you read a newspaper or a committee report. Immerse yourself in the words, reading not only for intellectual content but also for growth in your living of the faith in prayer and action, word and deed. Reflective reading requires us to be disciplined and to set aside time and space.

- Close your office door at a set time each day, turn off the phone and the computer, and read and think for an hour.

- Form or join a covenant group that reads in common and gathers for discussion that will broaden and deepen understanding.

- Share insights from your reading with members of your session or church council.

- Make use of an online reading program that includes a chat room.

- Keep a journal of your reflections.

Attend to theological and spiritual health. Daily rhythms of Scripture reading, prayer, and theological reading are strengthened and complemented by practices that take place on a weekly, seasonal, or annual basis. Weekly Sabbath-keeping is especially important. Other key disciplines include participating in a theological reflection group, making good use of study leave, caring for your body, honoring commitments to others, preparing to lead worship, examining your call to ministry, and confessing sin.

1. Keep Sabbath. Pastors understand Sabbath-keeping in two senses. We know that we need regular time to rest and refresh. We also know that we need regular time to focus on God. These two concerns sometimes intersect, but they are not identical, and we should be attentive to both.

The problem is that pastors are easily tempted to think that our work is so important and our presence so indispensable that we cannot make time either for ourselves or God. Do you work unreasonable hours? Do you take on too much? The Christian tradition includes practices that offer us guidance:

- *Make time for yourself.* Pastors need time to rest from all our labors so that we may see and enjoy God's work in us. Reserve time to rest from your pastoral labors, enjoy family and friends, and revel in the goodness of God's creation. You may protect time each day or take a whole day each week to rest from labors. Pastors' Sabbath will not always take place on Sunday, for it is filled with church responsibilities. You also benefit from the longer periods of vacation and rest that are provided in your terms of call.

- *Make time for God.* Pastors need regular times during which tasks and responsibilities are set aside so that God can speak and we can listen. Extended prayer, focused biblical and theological study, and intentional conversation are especially important ways to discipline our listening.

Attending to great literature, art, and the sciences can also direct us to the grace of the Lord Jesus Christ, the love of God, and the communion of the Holy Spirit.

The challenge before us is breaking the cycle of endless work. Several possibilities help to ensure times of rest:

♦ Set aside a twenty-four-hour period each month for prayer, reading, and reflection, in addition to your daily devotions.

♦ Make regular prayer retreats, listening for God's voice.

♦ Ponder how the Lord's Day can truly be the *Lord's* Day rather than the busiest day in your week. Let your preaching and leadership of worship be characterized by the special joy to which God calls you on this day. Live more spontaneously, open to the Spirit's guiding, whether you spend time with your family, pray and read, or run errands.

A commitment to the Lord's Day includes a commitment to participate in Lord's Day worship as regularly as possible, even when we are not leading it and even when we are on vacation or at conferences or meetings that take us away from our congregations or make going to church inconvenient.

2. Participate in a theological reflection group. Pastors know that we benefit from each other's insights into the faith and the practices of ministry. We know that we need people whom we can trust to encourage us and hold us accountable. Yet our experience of theological friendship is sporadic, too often restricted to occasional conferences or retreats. We then fall back into neglect of theological work and try to do ministry on our own.

♦ Find or organize a group of pastors with whom to meet regularly to discuss key issues of faith and faithfulness. Communities of theological friendship can be shaped in many ways, and possibilities for sharing are endless.

♦ Write about an important question of Christian life or doctrine, presenting what you have written to a group of colleagues as a basis for discussion.

♦ Listen together to a theological lecture—live or online—and then discuss it.

♦ Exchange and discuss the sermons that all of you preached on the previous Sunday, asking each other, "Did the congregation hear the gospel in this sermon?"

♦ Ask each other for guidance on admission to baptism or the Lord's Supper, pastoral care to those at the end of life, or other difficult pastoral questions.

♦ Explore what you are doing to make new disciples.

♦ Examine each other's efforts to teach the faith to elders and other church leaders.

3. *Take study leave.* Many pastors receive two weeks of study leave each year as part of their terms of call. Yet too many pastors fail to take study leave, or use it for vacation rather than for study, and too few congregations and judicatories hold pastors accountable.

♦ Pastors are challenged to take seriously the church's provision for disciplined reading and reflection. Do not squander it.

♦ Judicatories, church councils, and sessions are challenged to hold pastors accountable for their use of study leave by asking for proposals, reports of learning, and plans for further exploration during the year ahead.

♦ Pastors, judicatories, church councils, and sessions are challenged to plan and support sabbaticals that last for several months. Sabbaticals should center on prayer, engagement with Scripture, and disciplined reading and reflection.

4. *Care for your body.* Take the time and make the effort to be as physically healthy as possible so that you will be able to serve joyfully and energetically in your ministry. Pay attention to diet, sleep, and exercise.

5. *Honor commitments to others.* Honor your commitments to family— spouse and children, parents and grandparents. In your service to the church, do not neglect the "little church" to which you belong by virtue of your personal relationships.

6. *Prepare to lead worship.* Pastors make many practical arrangements for leading worship—consulting with musicians and other worship leaders, planning the order of worship, selecting hymns and prayers, writing and rehearsing sermons, and more. However, it is easy to neglect spiritual preparation for leading worship and for being a worshiper.

Preparation for every worship service should include both personal prayer and prayer with other worship leaders. Specific possibilities include arriving early for extended prayer at the baptismal font or Communion table and asking elders to pray for leaders and the congregation throughout the worship service. Disciplined preparation for celebrating baptism and the Lord's Supper is especially important. Pastors take hours to prepare sermons, yet too many simply read sacramental liturgies from a book rather than prepare to lead congregations into deeper communion with Christ.

7. Examine your call to ministry. Every pastor faces moments of boredom in ministry, and few pastors escape moments of conflict with a congregation. We sometimes imagine that boredom or conflict means that we are supposed to leave for another place of ministry. But boredom and conflict are inevitable parts of life, and when they appear, they may present an important, even if sometimes painful, opportunity to reflect again on whom God is calling us to be and what God is calling us to do.

If you do not reexamine your call regularly, you can become complacent or discouraged by doubts about the effectiveness of your ministry. Seek out people who can help you reflect on your call and assist you in focusing time and energy on the heart of the pastoral calling—proclaiming the gospel of Christ by interpreting it faithfully in your preaching, teaching, and pastoral care.

8. Confess sin. Make regular confession of sin. You join with others in general prayers of confession in Lord's Day worship. In addition, you may seek out a person whom you can trust to hear your personal confession of sin. This person may be a spouse, a spiritual director, another pastor, or a trusted friend. Their responsibility is simply to witness to your confession before God and to assure you of God's forgiveness.

The church calendar regularly calls us into seasons of self-examination and confession. Throughout the centuries, Advent and Lent have been distinct opportunities for Christians to draw back from "the way things are," pray, fast, and examine their spiritual lives. Pastors find it particularly difficult to observe Advent and live a good Lent in the midst of intensified church programming. We may be able to plan to accommodate for these seasons so that we, as well as our congregations, may receive blessings.

PERSONAL CONDUCT IN MINISTRY

> *As he who called you is holy,*
> *you also be holy in all your conduct. (1 Pet 1:15)*

Personal disciplines of faith focus us on Jesus Christ and the way of life that he makes possible. As pastors, we are to display the character of new creation in Christ so that our ministry may be credible. When we cultivate virtues of personal integrity, generosity, and hospitality, we fulfill our commitment to follow the Lord Jesus Christ in our own life, love our neighbors, and work for the reconciliation of the world.[3]

The shape of the holy life is no different for pastors than for all other baptized Christians. But pastors have an especially visible role in the life of the church. Our way of life can either display the shape of Christian living to our congregations or communicate that Christian faith makes no practical difference in the way life is lived. It can compel the world to listen to our gospel proclamation or bring discredit to the church and its message.

The holy life cannot be reduced to an abstract formula. On the contrary, the holy life is embedded in our communion with the one God who is Father, Son, and Holy Spirit and in our relationships with others. We are called to cultivate sensitivity to people both within and without the church.

Individuals. Pastors are to know and respect the individuals to whom we minister. You may ask the following about individuals in your church:

- What do they think about?

- What do they care about?

- What do they hope for?

- What are their idols?

- What are their gifts and callings?

- What pressures and stresses do they live under?

- What temptations do they struggle with?

Congregations. Pastors are to know and respect the character of the congregation in which we minister. You may ask,

- Can I see more clearly how God has been at work in this congregation throughout its history?

- Can I avoid the tendency to impose my own hopes and fantasies on the congregation?

- Do I equip the saints for the work of ministry, build up the body of Christ, and lead the congregation to the unity of faith and the measure of the full stature of Christ?

---

[3]This language echoes an ordination vow of the Presbyterian Church (USA).

♦ Will I regularly give thanks for the privilege of serving God and people in this place?

The world. Pastors are to understand the culture in which we live, the society in which we minister, and the world for which we pray. You may ask,

♦ Have I learned to take an active interest in the dynamics of the sociocultural context within which I minister?

♦ Am I actively interested in events beyond my congregation and denomination—locally, nationally, and internationally?

♦ Am I alert to the missional imperative and to particular challenges both nationally and internationally?

♦ Do I struggle with what it means to be "in but not of the world"?

My ministry. Ministry is not only a matter of intellectual content. The *way* in which we proclaim the gospel, administer the sacraments, and offer pastoral care also makes a powerful witness to the gospel. You may ask,

♦ Do I preach the gospel with conviction and clarity? Am I able to instruct and, if necessary, challenge church members who have embraced teachings contrary to the gospel?

♦ Does my worship leadership guide the congregation to a deeper experience of Jesus Christ, crucified and risen?

♦ Do I have the strength of character to make decisions that will be unpopular when I believe those decisions are faithful to the church's teaching and liturgical practice?

♦ Do I nurture an evangelistic spirit? Do I preach, administer the sacraments, and offer pastoral care in ways that invite nonbelievers to discover life in Christ? Do I invite believers to rediscover their life in Christ, remembering that the church itself is always in need of conversion?

♦ Am I committed to collegiality, helping every believer to discover and use his or her gifts for ministry?

♦ Do I exercise my ministry in hope—in God's power, despite my weakness; in the gospel, despite the world's resistance to it; in the church, despite its failures?

♦ Do I demonstrate that I stand beneath the gospel? Do I show others that I have been convicted by the gospel, that my life is being reformed in accordance with it, and that I trust God's power to establish the good news in my life and in the world?

My personal behavior. The way in which we speak and act in public also makes a witness to what is good and pleasing to God. Your manner of life and the impression it makes on others is more than a private matter. In every area of life, pastors are to demonstrate moral and loving relationships, trust within the community of faith, and care for God's creation. You may ask,

+ Do I demonstrate integrity in all my relationships?

+ Am I sexually moral?

+ Do I strive to understand and care for those with whom I disagree?

+ Am I honest?

+ Do I support the weak, the poor, the disenfranchised, and the ignored?

+ Am I financially responsible?

+ Do I seek peace, unity, and purity in my own life?

+ Am I aware of how I present myself to others and of how they perceive me?

MUTUAL ENCOURAGEMENT AND ACCOUNTABILITY

If anyone is caught in any transgression,
you who are spiritual should restore him in a spirit
of gentleness. . . . Bear one another's burdens. (Gal 6:1-2)

Whoever brings back a sinner from his wandering will save
his soul from death and will cover a multitude of sins. (James 5:20)

Pastoral concern to understand the dynamics of the congregations and societies in which we minister does not mean falsely accommodating or compromising the gospel. We are to recognize the scandal of the gospel as we live out our ministry. Proclamation of God's new way in the world always elicits counterpressure from the world, from the church, and even from ourselves. Expect conflict within yourself as you seek to be true to the gospel, for as Christ summons all to a new way of life, pastors also may resist, seeking comfort in the way things are.

The way of life shaped by this pastoral rule is too hard for any of us to sustain on our own. When we are honest with ourselves, we acknowledge that we need people who can encourage us and hold us accountable, just as they need us. But neither our society nor our church has taught us how to live in covenant relationships of mutual encouragement and accountability. On the contrary, we have learned to be suspicious of such relationships.

Power can be misused, and church leaders, seminary professors, and members of covenant groups have sometimes acted unfairly or even abusively toward those for whom they were responsible. But the absence of structures of encouragement and accountability is also disastrous, leaving pastors lonely and isolated.

Like all Christians, pastors are accountable to the Lord by virtue of our baptism. In addition, we have taken ordination vows that hold us accountable to Christ through the Scriptures and to the church's confessions and polity. Yet these commitments remain abstract and mechanical unless they are embodied in structured relationships within the church.

Both Scripture and the Christian tradition teach us that it is a blessing for us to have brothers and sisters who care enough to offer us guidance and warning. It would also be a blessing if the larger church asked us to submit to its wisdom. It would be a further blessing to have leaders who would call us back when we are going astray and encourage us when we walk in paths of righteousness.

Where can pastors find such blessings today? Church disciplinary rules and councils may hold us accountable for grievous behavior, but are pastors ever blessed with ordinary, everyday discipline? Where do we find leaders who care enough to ask, "Have you been saying your prayers?" Who will inquire if we are reading Scripture not only to prepare sermons or teach Bible study classes but also to place ourselves beneath God's Word of grace and judgment? Will anyone ask about the state of our theology or the condition of our soul?

Pastors are constantly pressed for time, so personal disciplines of faith easily slip away despite our best intentions. Congregations are constantly tempted to judge pastoral performance primarily in terms of programmatic, managerial, and entrepreneurial success. Short of illegal behavior, issues of personal conduct in ministry are too often ignored or excused.

Who, then, will encourage us and hold us accountable to the holy life, both for the sake of our own soul and the credibility of the gospel? Many congregations and judicatories are ill-equipped to deal with matters of ordinary, everyday discipline, and even where executive presbyters or bishops understand themselves as pastors, they frequently stand under the same time constraints and managerial demands as pastors in congregations.

The difficulty that the church faces in creating adequate structures for mutual affirmation and admonition reflects our ambiguity about accountability; we resist it even though we know we need it. We want to be free agents even though we know that our faith calls us to life together. At our best, we may be open to counsel and advice from like-minded brothers and sisters, but we cannot imagine a church that would ask us to obey it both for the sake of the gospel and our own well-being.

It is time for us to rediscover the evangelical truth that accountability to the gospel sets us free. It is time for us to submit to one another so that Christ may liberate us for faithful ministry. Christian churches can draw from a theology of covenant-making. We are responsible to each other, called to join together freely and joyfully in patterns of mutual encouragement and accountability. So, let each of us pledge the following:

I will seek out people who will covenant with me to encourage me in ministry, to hold me accountable to my practice of personal disciplines, and to help me maintain personal integrity in the conduct of my ministry.

♦ Ask your spouse to be your covenant partner.

♦ Covenant with a group of pastors to meet regularly and check up on one another's spiritual condition.

♦ Find a trusted colleague in ministry to guide you.

♦ Participate in a denominational program of daily prayer, Scripture reading, theological study, and pastoral gatherings for reflection on ministry.

♦ Meet regularly with a spiritual director.

The church's councils could also be of help.

♦ A judicatory could appoint one of its wise pastors to meet once a year with all other pastors to ask how they are doing with personal disciplines of faith and personal conduct in ministry.

♦ A judicatory could ask its pastors to commit themselves to a covenant group that meets for prayer, biblical and theological reflection, and discussion of issues relating to each member's personal disciplines of faith and personal conduct in ministry.

◆ An executive presbyter or bishop could meet regularly with pastors, one-on-one or in small groups, to discuss their spiritual well-being.

◆ A judicatory council on ministry could expand its responsibility for caring for pastors by regularly meeting with them to discuss their ministry and call.

◆ A seminary could ask its students to begin these patterns of mutual encouragement and accountability as part of their theological training.

THY KINGDOM COME

Let the peace of Christ rule in your hearts. . . .
teaching and admonishing one another in all wisdom. . . .
And whatever you do, in word or deed,
do everything in the name of the Lord Jesus,
giving thanks to God the Father through him. (Col 3:15-17)

Jesus sent disciples to proclaim that the arrival of God's kingdom. Jesus continues to send disciples today. Will we be worthy servants? Will we preach with power and authority? Will we call the world (and the church and ourselves) to repentance? Will we offer the world (and the church and ourselves) signs of the new life in Jesus Christ?

We believe that Jesus is calling the church and its ministers to renew commitment to personal disciplines of faith, holy conduct in pastoral ministry, and covenants of mutual encouragement and accountability. If our work speaks to you, and if you see the life-giving value of a pastoral rule, we ask you to join us in living it out.

But before you commit yourself, you must know that a pastoral rule cannot be layered on top of all that you do now. Perhaps you are persuaded of the value of the rule's practices and wish to begin them in your life. If so, you must stop before you start.

Stop your usual routine for a day—better yet, for a weekend or week. Be alone for some of the time, confessing your inattention to the invitation of God and seeking God's mercy. Seek God's grace to help you keep new promises. Spend some time with your spouse or with theological friends to pray, plan your practices of the rule, and commit all your hopes and plans to God.

Stop specific time- and energy-consuming practices that will compete with your new covenant. Know that changed patterns of ministry will not be welcomed by all. There is a cost to be paid for the renewal of your life.

Stop listening to all the voices that clamor for your attention. Listen instead to God's voice in Scripture, to your voice in prayerful reply, to the voices of those who have lived and died the faith before you, and to the voices of those with whom you hope to live in covenant. You are not alone.

Jesus encouraged his disciples and held them accountable. The risen Christ continues to offer us encouragement and accountability. Here we find blessing. Here we find our true pastoral vocation.

> *Jesus came . . . saying,*
> *"The time is fulfilled, and the kingdom of God is*
> *at hand. . . . Follow me." (Mk 1:15, 17)*

Conclusion

DEVELOPING *and* PRACTICING
a PASTORAL RULE

$\mathbf{I}$N THIS BOOK we have observed that many ministers today are burdened by competing and confusing demands. As a result, they too often lose a clear sense of what lies at the heart of their vocation. The figures we have considered in each of our chapters—from Augustine in the fifth century to Bonhoeffer in the twentieth—invite us to identify key practices and disciplines of the Christian life that can help sustain pastoral ministry and contribute to the formation of faithful and vibrant Christian communities.

Such practices and disciplines can be organized into a rule of life. As we have seen, such rules—implicit or explicit, personal or communal—have guided Christians and especially Christian leaders since the early centuries of the church. Bishops, priests, monks, nuns, reformers, leaders of church renewal movements, and pastors have established regular rhythms of praying, reflecting on Scripture and great theological writings, and serving others. Now we ask each of you: What would enable you to commit yourself to the disciplines that each of our historical figures has recommended? What would make it difficult? How could these disciplines strengthen your pastoral service, and where do you detect resistance to them in yourself or in your congregation? What kind of institutional structures do we need the church to develop in order to support you in exercising these disciplines?

In short, what would it take for us to commit ourselves to writing and practicing a pastoral rule today?

Here is a simple way to begin: try preparing a pastoral rule that is brief and doable within the constraints of your current schedule and obligations. It is better for you to do less and hold yourself to it than to take on too much and give it up because you do not have enough time or energy. If you are not a morning person, it may be unrealistic for you to commit to getting up an hour earlier each morning to pray. If you have limited time to read the Bible, find a plan that assigns you a few verses rather than commit yourself to all the daily lectionary readings. Above all, do not create a rule that just becomes another burden among the many you already have; rather, think of a rule as an opportunity to set priorities that will help you better sort out what needs attention in your life and ministry and what you can and perhaps should relinquish.

At the same time, see the rule as an opportunity to try something new. Could you try reading the entire Bible in a year, or could you take on a theological classic that you have always wanted to read but have never gotten around to? What about your physical well-being? Do you need to make time for a daily walk or some other form of exercise? Perhaps you are curious to learn about the Jesus Prayer or would like to set aside a brief time of silence each day. As you write your rule, feel free to take some risks. Be realistic, yes, but not overly cautious. Push yourself a little, knowing that growth in faith takes effort. After all, practices take practice (whether we are talking about piano playing, physical exercise, or attending to God), and disciplines require discipline.

Once you have written your rule, commit yourself to living it out for four weeks. You will need at least that much time to introduce a new set of rhythms into your life. But you will not want to go so long at your rule that you lose momentum and begin to feel that you are just going through the motions. Besides, you may be willing to take a bigger risk with your rule if you know that you can try something for just four weeks, without a commitment to continuing it if it does not work out.

After you have completed these four weeks, set aside a time for some honest self-evaluation. What worked or did not? What would you change or leave the same, and why? What did this exercise teach you about yourself and your vocation as minister? What could a rule mean for your leadership in the formation of Christian community? On the basis of your evaluation, try reformulating your rule and living it out again, but now for a longer period of time. After all, your goal is to make it a regular part of your life. At least every six months or once a year, step back again, ask yourself the same questions, and adjust your rule if necessary.

Here is what one pastor came up with for a "trial rule":

1. I will begin the day in silence with focused breathing. My rhythm will be to affirm God as I inhale and to release the cares of the day and stress of the pastorate as I exhale.

2. Following morning coffee, I will devote fifteen minutes to reading aloud the Scripture passage selected for preaching. The sequence of the reading will be as follows: first in English, then Greek, and again in English. In between each reading, I will take a healthy pause to digest the passage.

3. I will dedicate the first fifteen minutes in the office to prayer, using the morning Scripture to structure the themes and guide my words.

4. Twice per week I will perform manual labor around the church in the afternoon while listening to Benedictine chants or the Psalms being read.

5. I will be intentional about caring for my physical health. Thus, I will go to the gym twice a week and run three times a week.

6. Twice each week I will find time to enjoy the quiet of the nearby lake and allow my mind to wander.

7. Each night I will pray with my sons. I will ask my three-year-old what we should pray for, and I will hold my six-month-old on my lap as we pray together.

8. Each month I will read one theological text that challenges me. This month it will be Paul Tillich's *The Courage to Be.*

Four weeks later, this pastor reflected on what he had learned:

Finding balance in my ministry has always been elusive to me: balance of pastoral duties, personal devotion, family life, and physical health. As I began practicing my rule, I realized that in the past I have compartmentalized segments of my ministry. Yes, I have been praying and reading Scripture for my own edification, but I wasn't bringing my personal piety authentically into things such as church administration or dealing with difficult parishioners. By the second week of practicing my rule, things began to change. I began to experience integration of my life and my ministry. I can only describe this integration as a sense of being grounded, grounded in Christ and thus free to embrace my call to ministry.

As I awoke each morning, I would lie in bed with my eyes closed for a few minutes. As I inhaled, I thought, "God is in control" and as I exhaled, I thought, "I give my concerns to God." This practice of intentional breathing and focused thought set the tone for my day so that as I read Scripture out loud and prayed for guidance and the concerns of my heart, I was able to be present in the moment, not worrying about other ministerial demands. Later, when I counseled a couple whose marriage was in trouble or led a staff meeting with a challenging staff member, my prayer life guided me and added sensitivity, and the Scriptures that I had read gave me courage to engage conflict in a manner that sought reconciliation and wholeness.

To practice my rule with integrity meant that I had to achieve a balance between my personal spiritual/health practices, my responsibilities as pastor, and my family life. Prior to practicing my pastoral rule, I met all of the responsibilities of my office and the demands of the parish through self-destructive patterns. I would skip meals or eat fast food in the car on the way to a meeting or hospital visit. If something came up and my presence was requested, I would arrange for a family member to watch my boys on my day off, or I would leave before my wife and children were awake and return after they were in bed, thus we would go an entire day without seeing one another. Practicing my pastoral rule meant I could no longer cheat my family or myself. However, by establishing boundaries to create a healthier spiritual and personal life, I have irritated some parishioners who want me to be available 24/7.

Another pastor structured a trial rule around a daily practice of Scripture reading, prayer, and theological reflection and a weekly practice of making dinner for his spouse and children. He later wrote,

For me personally, this exercise has been transformational. However, sticking to the rule was far more challenging than I had originally thought. In some areas, I flourished, while in other areas I floundered and became frustrated. Nevertheless, the rule has helped me come to grips with a hard truth: I have been struggling in my own spiritual life. A calendar overflowing with commitments, meetings, and the general work of a parish minister . . . work and commitments at home with young children, . . . I have neglected my own life of faith to my own detriment. Now I want to balance and structure my life both at work and at home to allow me to grow in faith and faithfulness. I want to solidify my "holy living."

Because he had found a rule so helpful personally, he decided to ask members of his church council to join him in practicing a rule together. Their common rule included the four basic commitments of his personal rule:

1. Obedience to the Word: Being Guided by God's Holy Word in Lord's Day Worship

Once a month each council member will use a Worship Response Sheet to reflect on the following questions:

+ What did you hear God saying to you in the Scripture readings?

+ What did you hear God saying to you in the sermon?

+ What was your favorite hymn today, and why?

+ Was there a prayer that was especially meaningful or challenging for you today?

+ How might you apply what God has said to you today to your life this week?

2. Holy Living: Being in Prayer for One Another

Each Sunday one council member will arrive at worship five minutes early and pray for the worship leaders: the pastors, the liturgist, the choir, the music director, the organist, and the other worshipers.

3. Right Doctrine: Growing in Our Understanding of God

Together as a council we will read one of the church's historic confessions each month. We will then spend fifteen to twenty minutes at the beginning of our meetings discussing and sharing what we have read.

4. Mutual Service: Breaking Bread and Sharing a Meal Together.

We will divide council members into four groups. Once a quarter each group will make dinner to serve at the council meeting.

After several months, the pastor evaluated the results:

At our meetings, we talked about what was good and what was hard. The members of the council were honest in their responses. It was beautiful to witness these leaders take an interest not only in their personal spiritual lives, but also in the spiritual lives of their colleagues around the table. Together, we learned that each category brought its own successes and shortcomings.

"Obedience to the Word" has helped council members feel more connected to the worship service and how the flow and theme of the service work together. But it has been hard for them to remember to write their responses down. In the area of "Holy Living," several council members were so moved by praying for the worship leaders that they now do it every Sunday, even when it is not their assigned month. The reflection time on the historic confessions—"Right Doctrine"—has helped people open up and talk about their own faith, their questions, their struggles, and their understandings of what God is doing in the world. And "Mutual Service" meant that we could begin our meetings, which are scheduled for 6 p.m., feeling nourished and relaxed ahead of time. One council member remarked that this made for civil and respectful conversation. Along the way, we learned that it was a challenge to talk and work through the agenda while we ate. The council members preferred to eat, socialize, and simply be together. So we now share the meal at 5:30 and begin the agenda at 6:00. And no one complains about coming early to a council meeting!

The rule has helped shape and guide our meetings and the decisions that we make. Not only has it benefitted our personal spiritual lives, but, I believe, it has also made us better leaders as together we serve the people of God and grow and mature in our faith together.

One of the most difficult challenges of practicing a pastoral rule is building in an accountability structure. Each of us needs at least one other person with whom we can regularly check in about the state of our spiritual life. A number of years ago, a priest (we'll call him Max) told us of his bishop, who would visit each of the priests in the diocese at least once a year. After Max and his bishop had sat down and made themselves comfortable, the bishop's first question would always be, "Max, have you been saying your prayers?" If Max said no, the bishop would continue, "Then, tell me why you haven't been saying your prayers." And if Max said, "Yes, I've been saying my prayers," the bishop would say, "Then, tell me what you have been praying about." Each of us needs a "bishop"—a spiritual director, a small group, a mentor, a spouse, or a trusted friend—who cares enough about us to ask, "Have you been saying your prayers? Have you been reading the Scriptures? Have you been keeping Sabbath? Have you been making time for yourself and your family?"

So if you try out a pastoral rule, be sure to identify someone who can help keep you on track. The first pastor mentioned above was already meeting with a spiritual director when he began his four-week trial rule. The second pastor asked his spouse to keep him accountable, and when he introduced his church council to a rule that they would practice together, they set aside a few minutes at each meeting to discuss how they were doing.

OTHER CONTEMPORARY PASTORAL RULES

In recent years, a number of pastors committed to renewal of congregations have issued compelling calls for church leaders to recover spiritual practices and disciplines that sustain ministry for the long haul. Presbyterian pastor and author Eugene Peterson has been at the forefront of this movement. He argues that pastors too often neglect their spiritual lives. They succumb to career idolatry and focus on job efficiency and management. They accept "an offer by the devil for work that can be measured and manipulated at the convenience of the worker."[1]

In response, Peterson suggests that the search for holiness is central to a pastoral rule. Pastors need to set aside times and place for askesis, a confinement of the ego, such as monks have traditionally found within the walls of their monastery.[2] It is not enough for a pastor just to go on "retreat" to read books or write sermons. Rather, pastors need extended periods of reflection protected from interruption and disciplined by prayer. Working with a spiritual director is especially valuable.

Peterson further notes that if pastors are to offer themselves "in response to the living God, expressing [their] feelings is not enough—we need a long apprenticeship in prayer. And then we need graduate school. The Psalms are the school."[3] The Psalms shift our focus to God and what God is doing. They become the monastery walls that pull us away from self and free us to adore and seek God. Common worship on the Lord's Day and personal times of prayer randomly throughout the day provide additional protected space within which the spiritual life of a pastor can flourish.

Peterson urges pastors to see themselves not as program managers but rather as spiritual directors. That kind of ministry requires pastors to enter into the messiness of people's lives and to love them even when they seem difficult or dull. A pastor will grow disciples only by accepting people for who they are and creatively imagining how to point them to God's work in their lives. In the process, pastors will inevitably face moments of conflict or boredom that cause them to wonder whether it is time to leave a congregation. But, says Peterson, "Trouble,

---

[1]Eugene H. Peterson, *Under the Unpredictable Plant: An Exploration in Vocational Holiness* (Grand Rapids: Eerdmans, 1992), 5.

[2]Peterson, *Under the Unpredictable Plant*, 76.

[3]Peterson, *Under the Unpredictable Plant*, 102.

at least extreme trouble, storm level trouble, strips us to the essentials and reveals the basic reality of our lives. . . . The sea storms that call into question our vocations turn out to be the means of vocational recovery."[4]

Peter Scazzero is another influential pastor whose work and writings place spiritual practices and disciplines at the core of the pastoral calling.[5] In his course Emotionally Healthy Spirituality, Scazzero invites participants to prepare a personal rule of faith with four major categories and twelve areas of concern: prayer (Scripture, silence and solitude, daily office, study), rest (Sabbath, simplicity, play and recreation), work (service and mission, care for the physical body), and relationships (emotional health, family, and community/companions for the journey).[6] Scazzero has developed a pastoral rule along similar lines for the staff of the New Life Fellowship Church in Queens, New York, a large, multiracial church that he and his wife founded in 1987.[7]

Jason Goroncy, Senior Lecturer in Systematic Theology at Whitley College, University of Divinity, in New Zealand, offers additional orientation points for a pastoral rule. In his "Towards a Modest Manifesto for Pastors," he offers fifty-four provocative recommendations, including:

♦ Do not neglect the gift of prayer. Pray especially when you do not have time to pray, when prayer makes the least sense, and when God's aliveness seem the least likely version of reality.

♦ Read Scripture devotionally. Immerse your mind, your heart, your wallet, your time and your conscience in Scripture.

♦ Read Scripture in a scholarly way. Commit yourself to disciplined study of Scripture, preferably in the original languages. Pastoral ministry is about three things: exegesis, exegesis, exegesis.

♦ Immerse yourself in the thought and writings of two or three significant thinkers for the next twenty years or more. Let them teach you, pastor you, advise you in various pastoral situations. Argue with them heaps, and learn from them.

---

[4]Peterson, *Under the Unpredictable Plant*, 71-72.
[5]See *The Emotionally Healthy Church* (Grand Rapids: Eerdmans, 2003) and *Emotionally Healthy Spirituality* (Nashville: Thomas Nelson, 2006).
[6]"Emotionally Healthy Spirituality Course: Session 8; Go the Next Step to Develop a Rule of Life," www.emotionallyhealthy.org/wp-content/uploads/2015/10/Session-8-Go-the-Next-Step-to-Develop-a-Rule-of-Life.pdf.
[7]http://newlifefellowship.org/docs/Pastors_ROL.pdf.

♦ Cultivate the gifts of friendship. This is a biggie, and its neglect is the cause of much pain in the minister, of much scandal in the church, and of much lying in the world.[8]

Proposed criteria for the selection of bishops, developed by the US Conference of Catholic Bishops, suggest other key dimensions of a rule for priests and pastors:

♦ *Radical discipleship*: In his life and ministry, does this priest manifest a personal conversion to Jesus Christ and a deliberate decision to abandon everything to follow Christ?

♦ *Evangelical energy*: Does this priest preach the Gospel with conviction and clarity? Can he make the Church's proposal to non-believers? With charity, can he instruct and, if necessary, admonish Catholics who have embraced teachings contrary to the Gospel and the teaching authority of the Church?

♦ *Pastoral effectiveness*: Has this priest ever been a pastor? Did the parish grow under his leadership? If his primary work has been as a professor in a seminary, did his students flourish under his teaching?

♦ *Liturgical presence*: How does this priest celebrate Mass, in concrete and specific terms? Does his liturgical ministry lead his people into a deeper experience of the paschal mystery of Jesus Christ, crucified and risen?

♦ *Personal example*: How many men have entered the seminary because of this priest's influence? How many women have entered consecrated religious life under his influence? Does he encourage lay movements of Catholic renewal and the development of popular piety? In sum, is he a man who can call others to holiness of life because he manifests holiness in his own life?

♦ *The courage to be countercultural*: Does this priest have the strength of character and personality to make decisions that will be unpopular with other priests and religious, because those decisions are faithful to the church's teaching and liturgical practice?

♦ *Theological literacy*: Is this priest well-read theologically? Does he regard theology as an important part of his vocation? Can he "translate" the best

---

[8]Jason Goroncy, "Towards a Modest and Messy Manifesto for Pastors: A Draft," November 11, 2012, https://jasongoroncy.com/2012/11/11/towards-a-modest-manifesto-for-pastors-a-draft/.

of the Church's theology, ancient and contemporary, into an idiom accessible to his people?[9]

Whatever our contemporary reservations about "rules" and regulations, this renewed interest in rules of life demonstrates that many pastors—as well as the members of their congregations—are searching for a more disciplined way of living the Christian life.[10] We pray that the rules we have reviewed—ancient and contemporary, from classic theologians and from faithful pastors today—will support you in your efforts to order your ministries and root your vocations more fully in Jesus Christ. For in the end, no pastoral rule is simply a matter of how we will choose to serve God and others more faithfully; rather, we trust that Christ, the living Lord, will rule our lives.

"Now to him who is able to do far more abundantly than all that we ask or think, according to the power at work within us, to him be glory in the church and in Christ Jesus throughout all generations, forever and ever. Amen" (Eph 3:20-21).

---

[9] As quoted in George Weigel: *God's Choice: Pope Benedict XVI and the Future of the Catholic Church* (New York: Harper Perennial, 2005), 250.

[10] See also Stephen A. Macchia, *Crafting a Rule of Life* (Downers Grove, IL: InterVarsity Press, 2012); and *Practicing Our Faith*, ed. Dorothy Bass (San Francisco: Jossey-Bass, 1997).

Scripture Index

Finding the Textbook You Need

The IVP Academic Textbook Selector
is an online tool for instantly finding the IVP books
suitable for over 250 courses across 24 disciplines.

---

ivpacademic.com
